BEST OF **Dick Martin**

fun FOR eVeRyone

IN PLASTIC CANVAS

You don't need a special occasion to treat someone, yourself included, to a whimsical surprise! Showcasing more than 70 of Dick Martin's best-loved carefree designs, this collection contains irresistible creations for the whole family — babies, children, and Mom and Dad. The projects range from practical, everyday items to those that are designed simply to add a decorative touch to your home. So if you're looking for fun, you're sure to find it here!

LEISURE ARTS, INC.
Little Rock, Arkansas

BEST OF Dick Martin

fun FOR eVeRyoNe

EDITORIAL STAFF

Vice President and Editor-in-Chief:
Sandra Graham Case
Executive Director of Publications:
Cheryl Nodine Gunnells
Director of Designer Relations: Debra Nettles
Publications Director: Susan White Sullivan
Editorial Director: Susan Frantz Wiles
Photography Director: Lori Ringwood Dimond
Art Operations Director: Jeff Curtis

PRODUCTION
Managing Editor: Merrilee Gasaway
Production Assistants: Jo Ann Forrest and
Janie Marie Wright

EDITORIAL
Managing Editor: Suzie Puckett

ART
Senior Art Director: Rhonda Hodge Shelby
Senior Production Artist: Diana Sanders
Production Artists: Karen Allbright and Faith Lloyd
Color Technician: Mark Hawkins
Photography Stylist: Janna Laughlin
Staff Photographer: Russ Ganser
Publishing Systems Administrator: Becky Riddle
Publishing Systems Assistants: Myra S. Means
and Chris Wertenberger

BUSINESS STAFF

Publisher: Rick Barton
Vice President, Finance: Tom Siebenmorgen
Director of Corporate Planning and Development:
Laticia Mull Cornett
Vice President, Retail Marketing: Bob Humphrey
Vice President, Sales: Ray Shelgosh
Vice President, National Accounts: Pam Stebbins
Director of Sales and Services: Margaret Reinold
Vice President, Operations: Jim Dittrich
Comptroller, Operations: Rob Thieme
Retail Customer Service Manager: Wanda Price
Print Production Manager: Fred F. Pruss

Made in the United States of America.

Softcover ISBN 1-57486-255-3

10 9 8 7 6 5 4 3 2 1

TABLE OF CONTENTS

A TRIBUTE TO
DICK MARTIN

With his sparkling imagination and creative enthusiasm, Dick Martin amazed stitchers all over the world with his innovative plastic canvas designs. His passing leaves his many fans to carry on the unique and beautiful designs that have, for many years, brought joy to crafters everywhere.

For over 25 years, the freelance artist designed a multitude of plastic canvas favorites for Leisure Arts. He earned his reputation as the "father" of three-dimensional plastic canvas while creating designs for almost 100 leaflets. He once said, "I think I have a touch of engineer in my blood, because I love to figure out how things go together."

Dick began his artistic career as a commercial artist illustrating and authoring children's educational books, games, and toys while working for several major publishing and advertising agencies. He later moved on to become a freelance designer for Avon Cosmetics, where he spent nearly 20 years designing children's jewelry and cosmetic products.

With all of that experience behind him, it was natural curiosity that first led Dick to design with plastic canvas. At the time (1968), many artists were experimenting with three-dimensional designs. "What magic it is when it works!" he once said. "Since plastic canvas holds such fascination for me, I have discovered many ways of using it which to this point have not been done."

Dick's creative designs caught the attention of Leisure Arts after he began attending meetings of the Embroiderers' Guild of America. He once laughingly remembered, "The first time I went to a meeting, there were 90 women and me. I was so scared, I had my wife take me! I think most of the women were insulted, because they were accomplished cross stitchers and embroiderers, and no one was working with plastic canvas." He eventually started some of his fellow Guild members on plastic canvas projects. Soon after, he began designing projects for Leisure Arts.

Dick took much of his inspiration from nature, but he also enjoyed using images of toys and music boxes, along with Disney designs. Several trips to Disney World were great therapy for him. He once said,"I come home filled with new ideas and feeling like a kid again."

Subject matter for full-time designers quickly becomes seasonal, according to Dick. And although he liked creating projects for all the holidays, he admitted that Christmas was his favorite. "The entire season is so full of symbolism. The possibilities are endless."

It was the pursuit of these "possibilities" that kept Dick designing, and he acknowledged that what he liked most about his work was the challenge. He wished for everyone who works with their hands the same joy and satisfaction that he felt during the creative process. Looking back, Dick said he couldn't remember a time when he wasn't designing. He was once quoted as saying, "My first recollection [of designing] is coloring paper napkins and tablecloths in kindergarten. I was fortunate enough to have a teacher who encouraged my creativity."

Born February 19, 1931, in Hamburg, Iowa, a small town in the southwest corner of the state, Richard Allen Martin grew up surrounded by artistic influences. His mother and grandmother were both painters, and his brother won a scholarship to the American Academy of Art.

It was his love of design that led Dick to pursue an art degree from the University of Iowa, where his studies included silversmithing, fabric design, illustration, and layout. He said the four years of silversmithing offered a great experience in dimensional design. He explained, "It requires a great deal of patience, and so does needlepointing."

While in college, he met the woman who would become his wife of 48 years, Marjorie Kurtz, who was also an art major. "She's fabulous!" Dick once said enthusiastically. "She's my best critic and the reason I can do all I do. She makes it possible for me to concentrate my time on my creative work."

Dick resided in Tarrytown, New York, with Marjorie until his death on March 2, 2000. His three grown children carry on the tradition of creativity with various artistic interests, as does his wife, who continues to care for the extensive gardens that keep their yard colorful from early spring through late fall. Dick Martin took on the design world with his creativity and zest for life, and he leaves behind a following that lovingly takes his imaginative designs into the new millennium.

ESPECIALLY FOR BABIES

Welcome precious little ones into the world with adorable Baby's room accessories designed especially with them in mind! From wall décor and sweet picture frames to handy storage baskets and tissue box toppers, we've got your nursery needs covered! Proclaim the good news of Baby's arrival with a bear and duck birth announcement frame. Our friendly clown bear will share his wagon, so you'll have a convenient place to keep diapers and such.

Instructions on pages 16-18.

Instructions on pages 41-46.

NIGHTY-NIGHT SET

When the moon and stars come out, it's time to go nighty-night!
This celestial set includes a sleep-indicator door sign, a basket, a
storage box that's ideal for holding diapers, and a dreamy mobile.

Instructions on pages 19-27.

GIFT-BASKET BUNNY

Welcome a new arrival with this adorable bunny basket, complete with carrot handles! Filled with powder, lotion, and other newborn necessities, it's an ideal shower gift. Mom can use it later to store precious keepsakes as the baby grows.

Instructions on pages 28-30.

FRIENDLY BABY BEARS

These baby bears will soon become your little one's best friends when they're used to decorate the nursery. A wall hanging, a switch plate cover, and a handy storage box make up the set.

Instructions on pages 31-35.

PLAYFUL BEARS

Use this "beary" precious frame to show off a picture of Baby having a ball! The adorable accent is embellished with tiny flowers and French knots. The charming cubs can also be used to jazz up a container of baby wipes.

Instructions on pages 36-39.

FOR A LITTLE LAMB

"Ewe" will love having this handy basket to organize your nursery items! Adorned with a sweet, sleeping lamb, the handled container is ideal for holding bottles and more.

Instructions on pages 47-50.

PRECIOUS CARRIAGE

We've given a baby buggy a new purpose! This clever carriage is actually a tissue box cover that doubles as a novel decorative accent.

Instructions on pages 52-55.

LOVABLE LAMBS

You don't have to be Little Bo Beep to love these sweet sheep! The lively little lambs top a tissue box with a sense of innocent wonder.

Instructions on page 51.

"BEARY" CUTE PARADE

Balloon-toting bears parade around this tissue topper to add colorful fun to the nursery. Much of the design is worked using long stitch, so it's quick to finish.

Instructions on page 40.

BIRTH ANNOUNCEMENT FRAME

(Shown on page 6.)

Skill Level: Intermediate

Size: 9¹/₂"w x 13"h

Supplies: Worsted weight yarn (refer to color keys), two 10¹/₂" x 13¹/₂" sheets of clear 7 mesh plastic canvas, one 3" Uniek® plastic canvas circle, #16 tapestry needle, 4³/₄"w x 2³/₄"h paper insert, and craft glue.

Stitches Used: Backstitch, French Knot, Gobelin Stitch, Overcast Stitch, Reversed Tent, and Tent Stitch.

Instructions: Follow charts to cut and stitch Frame pieces, working backstitches and French knots last. Tack Nose to Bear Side. Matching ✖'s, use dk tan overcast stitches to join Right Arm to Bear Side. Matching ♥'s, join Right Ear to Bear Side. Matching ★'s, join Left Ear to Bear Side. Matching ▲'s, use aqua overcast stitches to join Bear Side to Duck Side between ▲'s. Matching ♠'s, place Left Arm on Bear Side.

Matching ■'s, place Left Leg on Bear Side. Matching ♦'s, place Frame on Duck Side. Using white overcast stitches, join Left Arm, Bear Side, Duck Side, and Left Leg, working through as many thicknesses of canvas as necessary. Using matching color overcast stitches, join remaining unworked edges of Frame to Duck Side. Glue photo to wrong side of Circle. Tack Circle to wrong side of Arms. Slip paper insert into Frame.

Bear Side (44 x 55 threads)

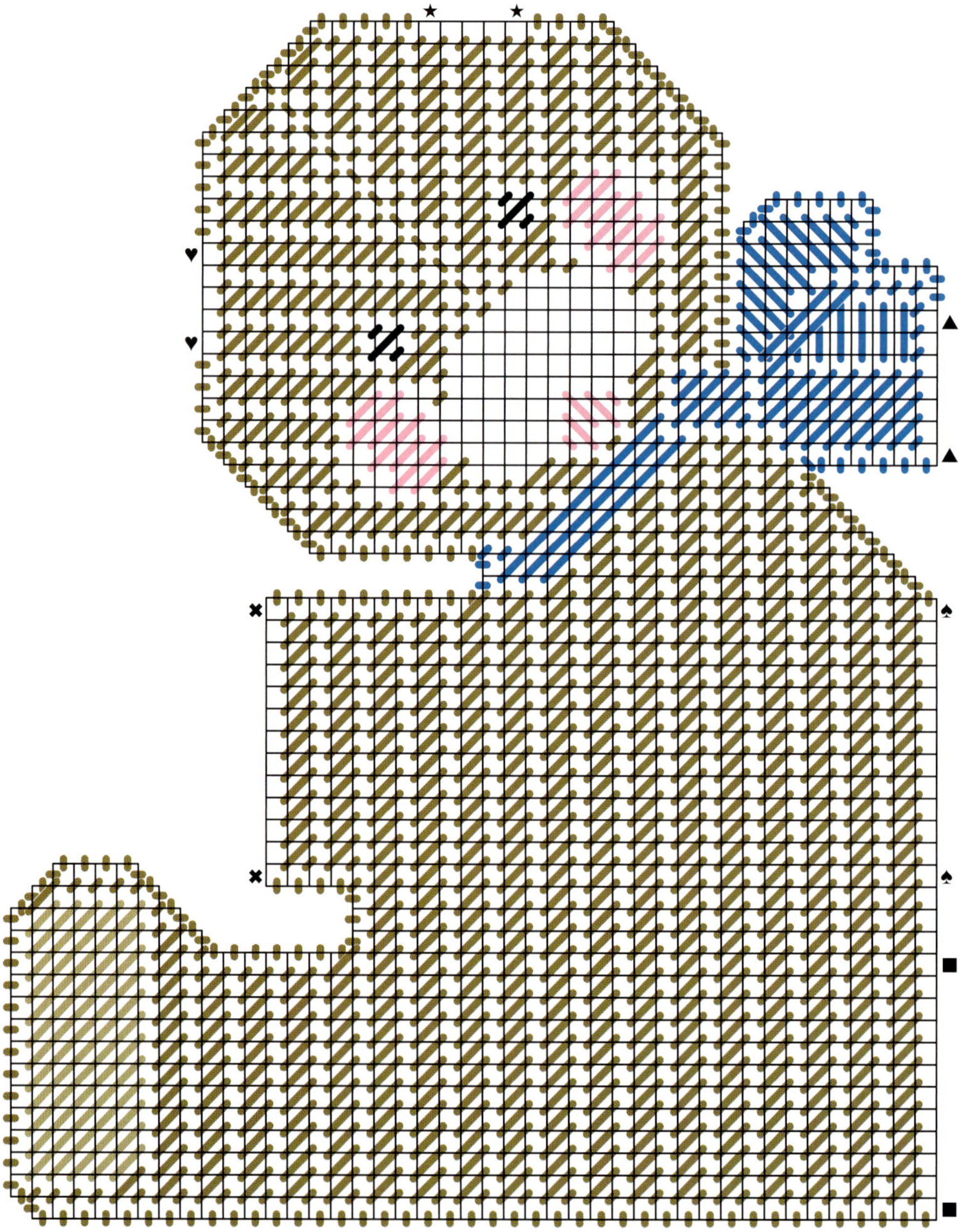

Nose Diagram
Work these stitches over existing stitches on Nose.

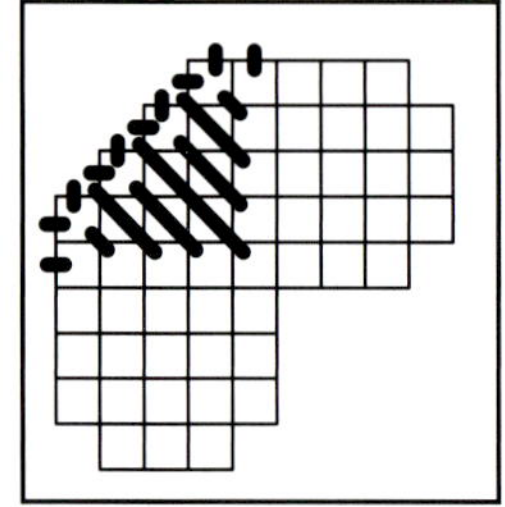

Nose (10 x 10 threads)

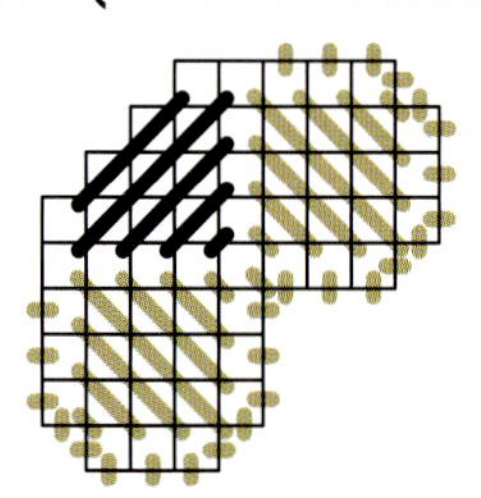

Circle
Cut from 3" circle.

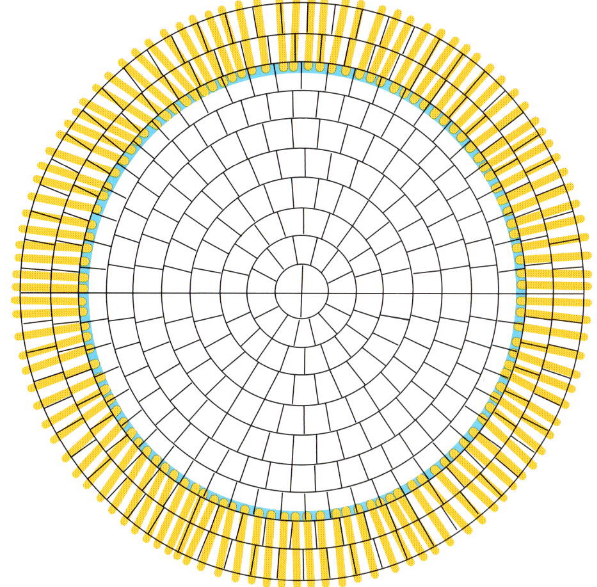

Left Ear (10 x 8 threads)

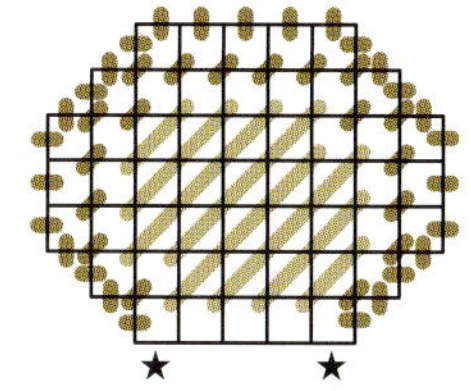

Right Ear (8 x 10 threads)

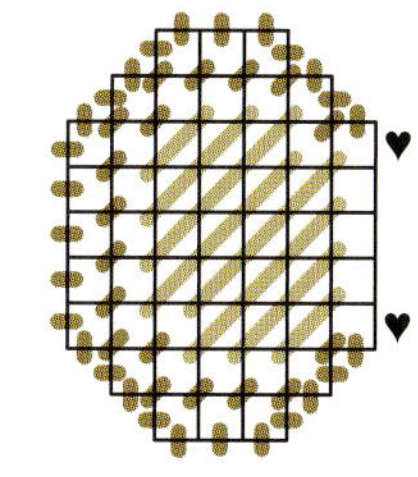

Left Arm (8 x 14 threads)

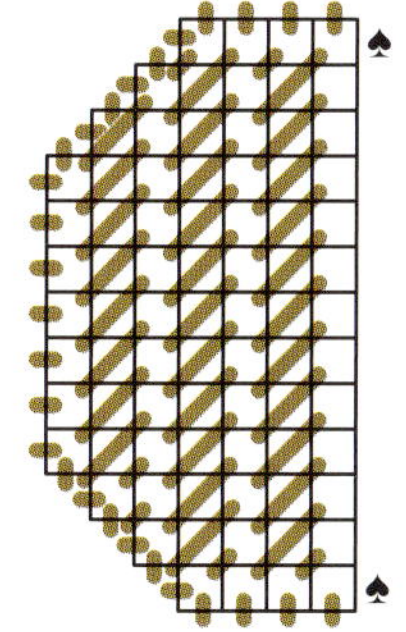

Right Arm (12 x 14 threads)

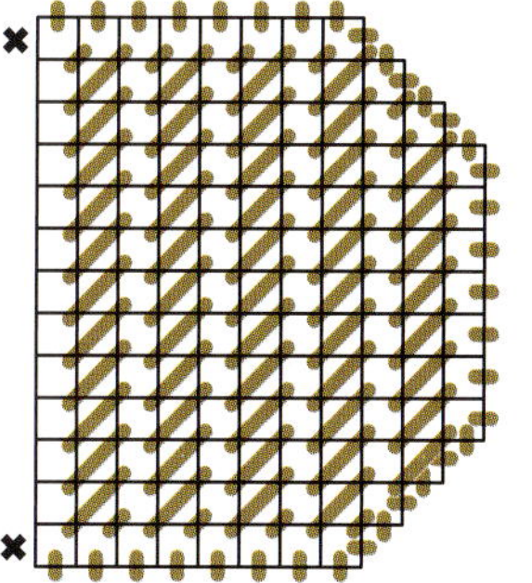

Eyes/Cheeks Diagram
Work these stitches over existing stitches on Bear Side.

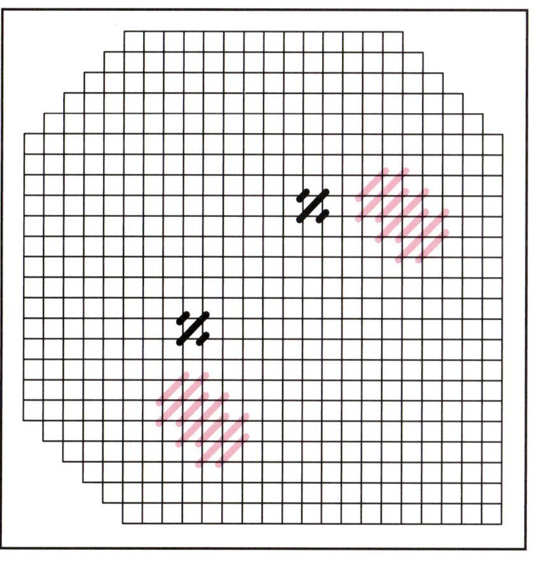

Left Leg (28 x 17 threads)

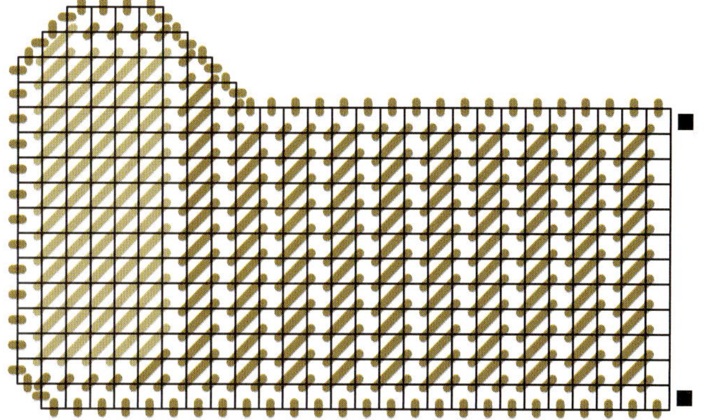

Frame (44 x 21 threads)

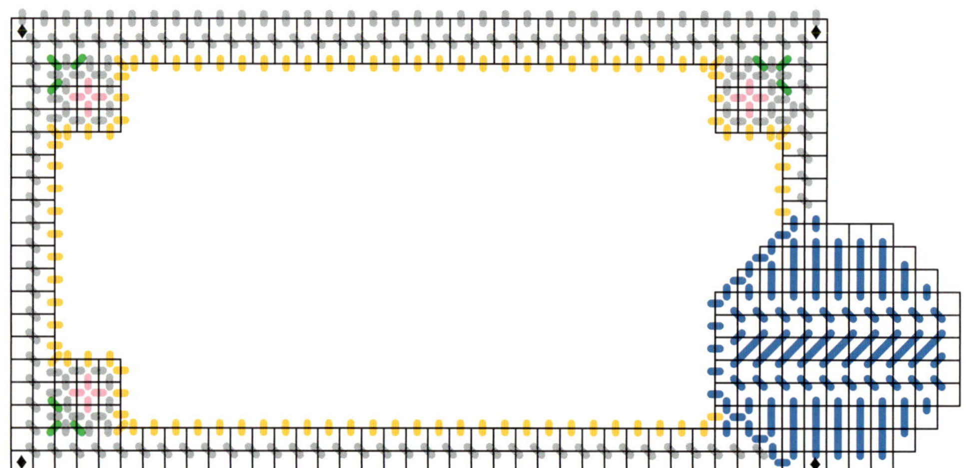

Duck Side (44 x 46 threads)

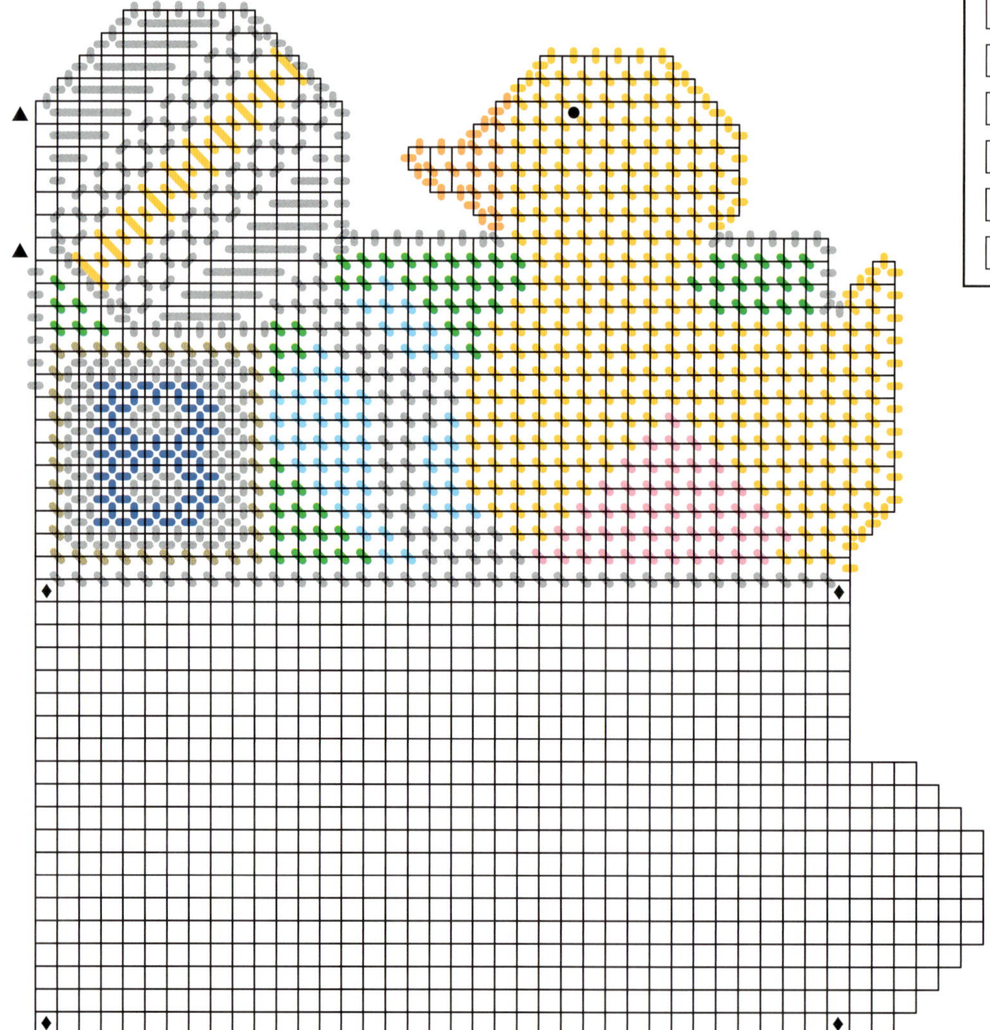

DOOR SIGN

(Shown on page 8.)
Skill Level: Beginner
Size: 7"w x 7¾"h
Supplies: Worsted weight yarn (refer to color key), one 10½" x 13½" sheet of clear 7 mesh plastic canvas, #16 tapestry needle, one ¾" pink pom-pom, 16" length of ¾"w blue satin ribbon, and craft glue.

Stitches Used: Backstitch, French Knot, Gobelin Stitch, Overcast Stitch, Scotch Stitch, and Tent Stitch.

Instructions: Follow charts to cut and stitch Door Sign piece, working backstitches and French knots last. Thread ribbon ends through Door Sign. Tie a knot in each ribbon end. Glue pom-pom to Door Sign.

COLOR	
╱	white - 16 yds
╱	yellow - 11 yds
╱	pink - 1 yd
╱	blue - 6 yds
╱	green - 3 yds
╱	black - 1 yd
●	white Fr. knot

Door Sign (46 x 52 threads)

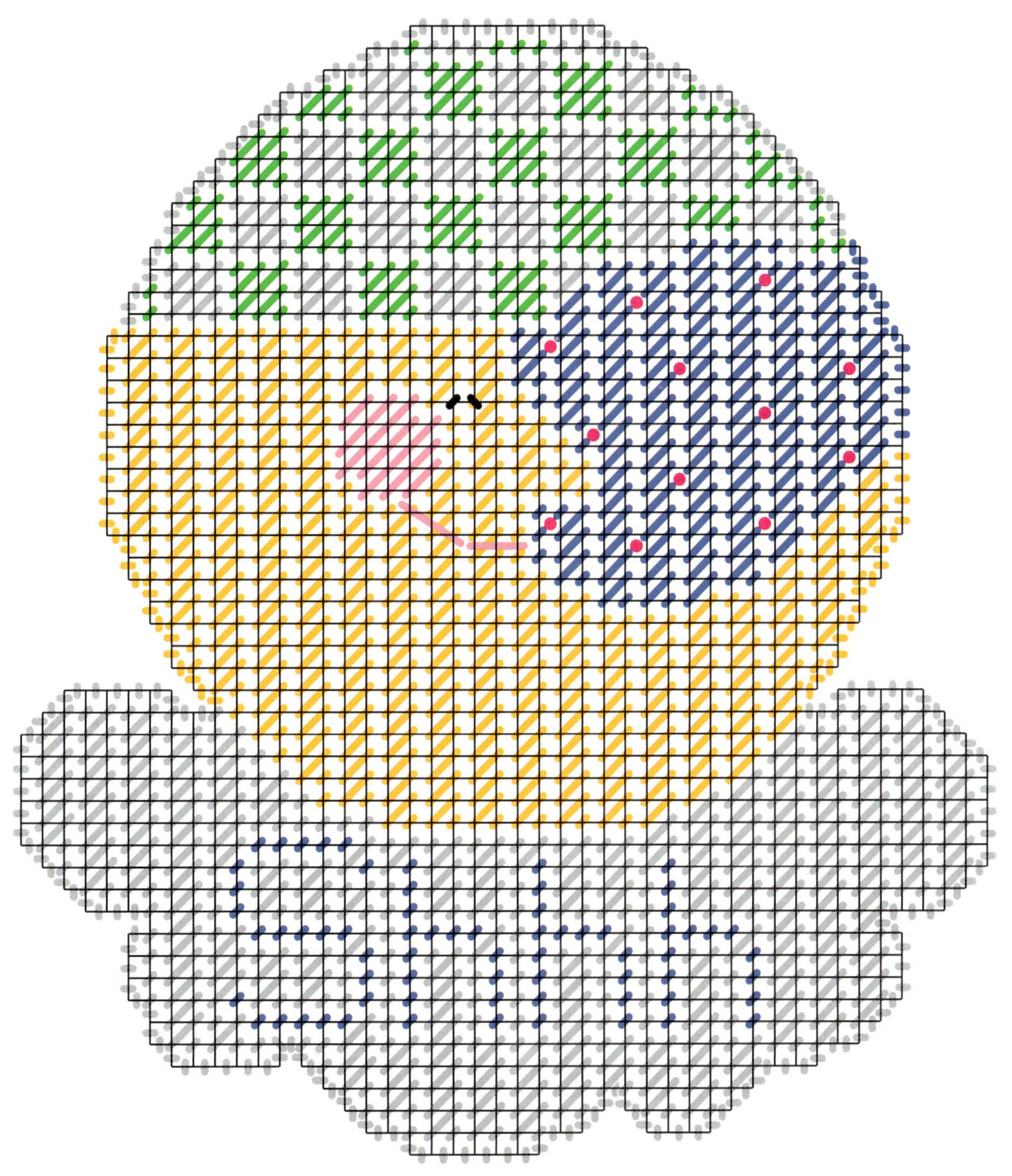

STORAGE BOX

(Shown on page 8.)

Skill Level: Intermediate

Size: 13³/₄"w x 4"h x 7¹/₄"d

Supplies: Worsted weight yarn (refer to color key), five 10¹/₂" x 13¹/₂" sheets of white 7 mesh plastic canvas, #16 tapestry needle, eight ¹/₂" pink pom-poms, eight ¹/₄" pink pom-poms, and craft glue.

Stitches Used: Backstitch, French Knot, Gobelin Stitch, Mosaic Stitch, Overcast Stitch, and Tent Stitch.

Instructions: Follow charts to cut and stitch Box pieces, working backstitches and French knots last. For Bottom, cut a piece of canvas 90 x 46 threads. For Insert Bottom, cut a piece of canvas 89 x 45 threads. Bottom and Insert Bottom are not worked. Using blue overcast stitches, join Long Sides to Short Sides along short edges. Join Long Sides and Short Sides to Bottom. Glue pom-poms to Long Sides and Short Sides. Using white overcast stitches, join Insert Long Sides to two Insert Short Sides along short edges. For Center, join the two remaining Insert Short Sides along one long edge. Referring to Diagram A, match ★'s to join one Divider to each side of Support through three thicknesses of canvas. Repeat for remaining two Dividers. Referring to Diagram B, match ♥'s to join Support to one Insert Short Side. Matching ♥'s, join Support to Center through three thicknesses of canvas. Join Center and Dividers to Insert Long Sides. Referring to Diagram C, place Insert inside Large Box. Join Insert to Large Box along top unworked edges.

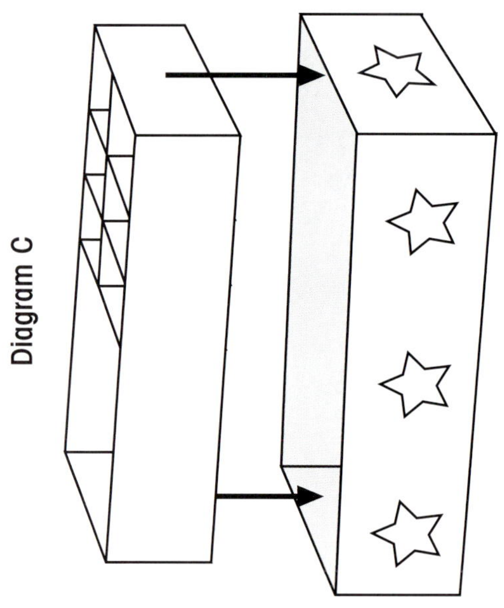

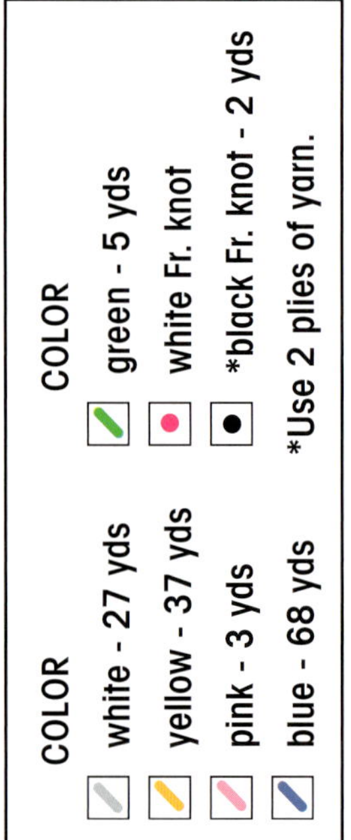

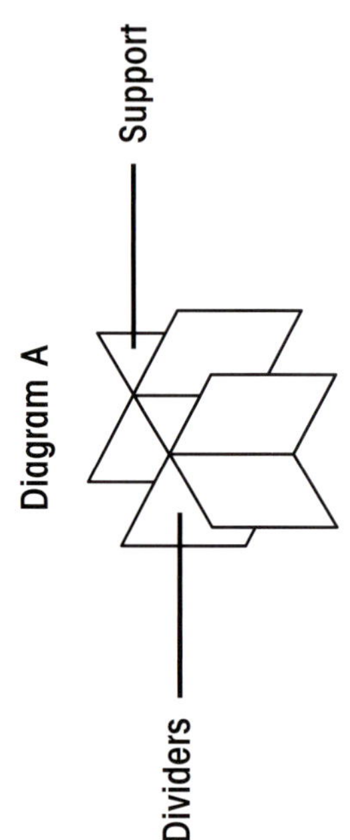

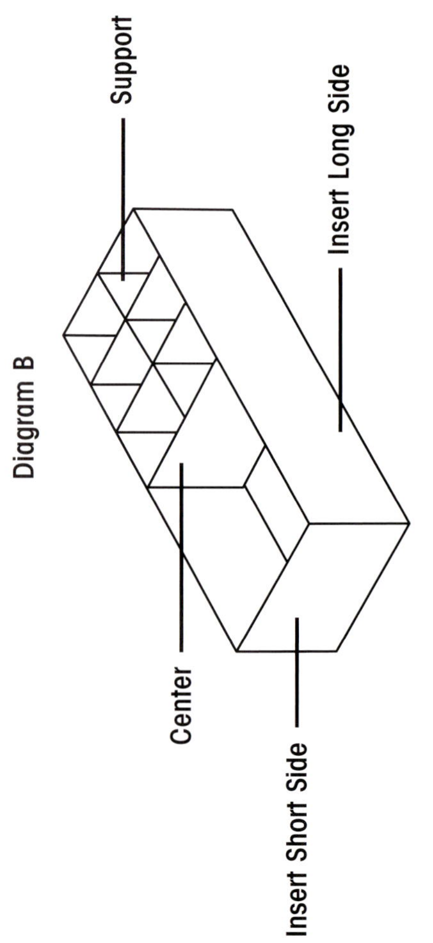

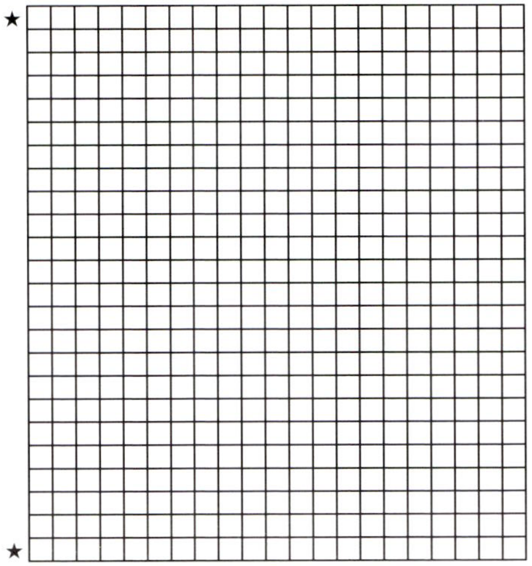

Short Side (46 x 26 threads) (stitch 2)

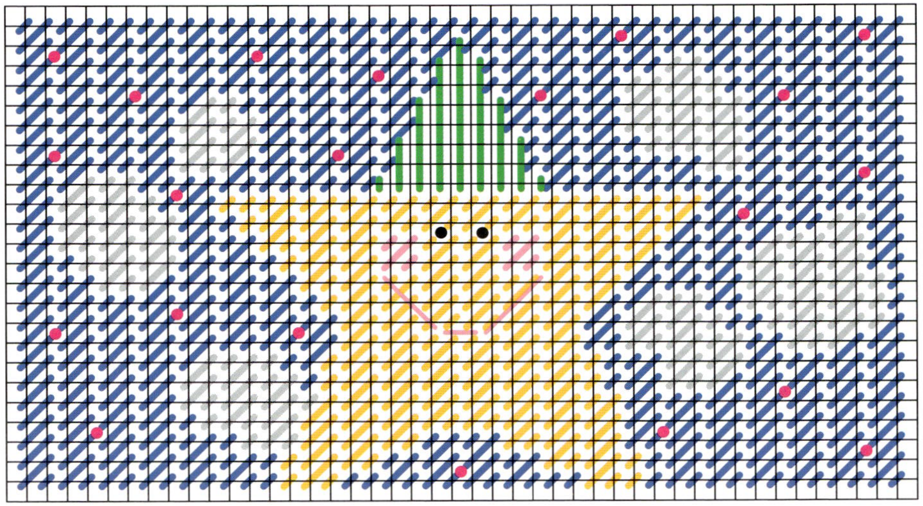

Divider (22 x 25 threads) (cut 4)

Long Side (90 x 26 threads) (stitch 2)

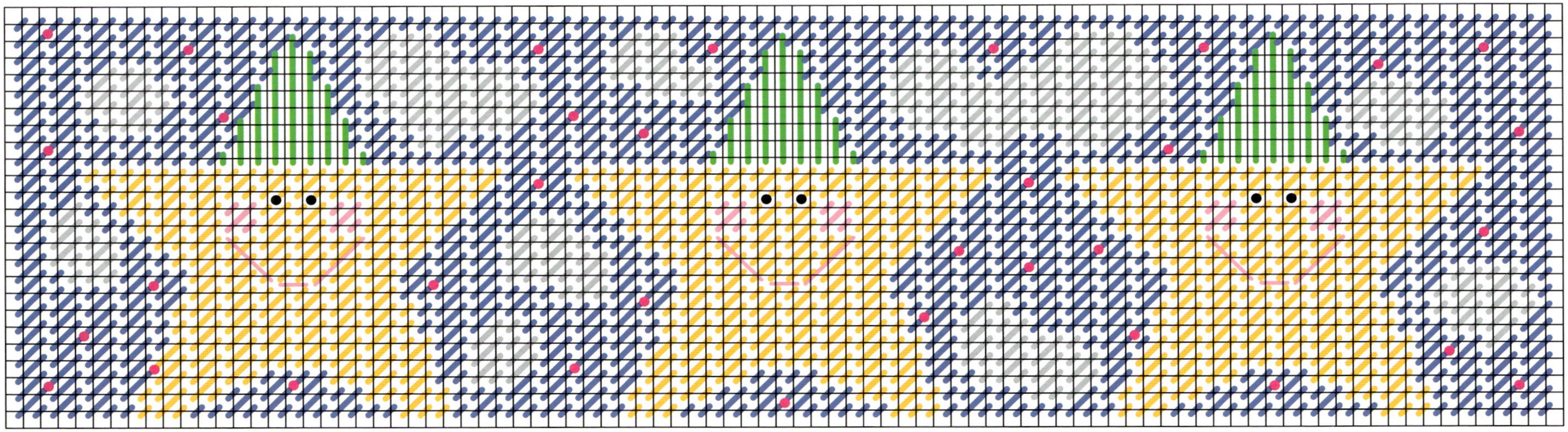

Insert Long Side (89 x 25 threads) (cut 2)

Insert Short Side/Center (45 x 25 threads) (cut 4)

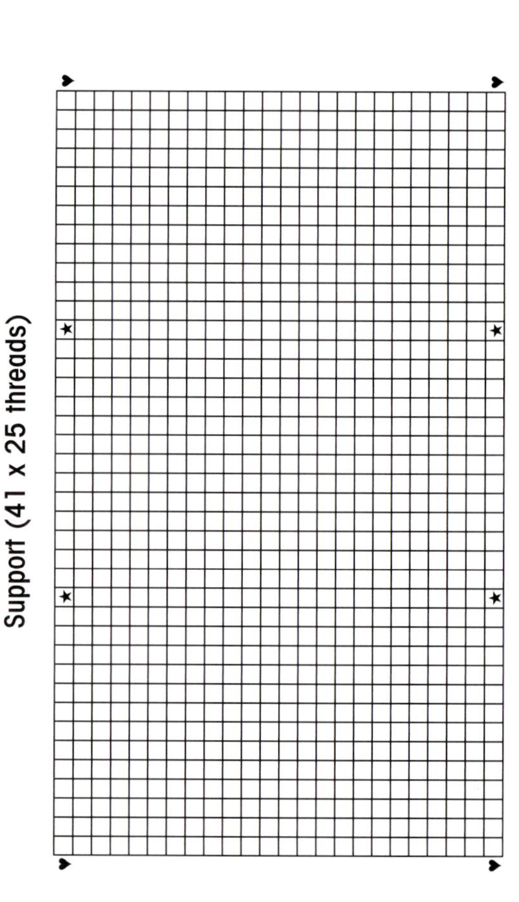

Support (41 x 25 threads)

BASKET

(Shown on page 9.)
Skill Level: Beginner
Size: 9½"h x 6¾" dia.
Supplies: Worsted weight yarn (refer to color key), three 10½" x 13½" sheets of clear 7 mesh plastic canvas, #16 tapestry needle, one 1" pink pom-pom, and craft glue.
Stitches Used: Backstitch, Diagonal Mosaic Stitch, French Knot, Fringe Stitch, Gobelin Stitch, Mosaic Stitch, Overcast Stitch, Scotch Stitch, and Tent Stitch.
Instructions: Follow charts to cut and stitch Basket pieces, working backstitches, French knots, and Fringe stitch last and leaving stitches in shaded areas unworked. For bangs on Baby, separate each strand of Fringe into plies. Matching ✖'s and ♥'s, work stitches in blue shaded areas to join Front to Back. Referring to Diagram, match ♦'s to place top side of Handle on right side of Back. Work stitches in pink shaded area of Handle to join Handle to Back through three thicknesses of canvas. Matching ★'s, place Handle on wrong side of Front. Work stitches in pink shaded area to join Front to Handle. Using white overcast stitches, join Bottom to Front and Back. Tack Baby to wrong side of Cloud; tack Cloud to Front. Glue pom-pom to Front. Tack Stars to Handle.

Diagram

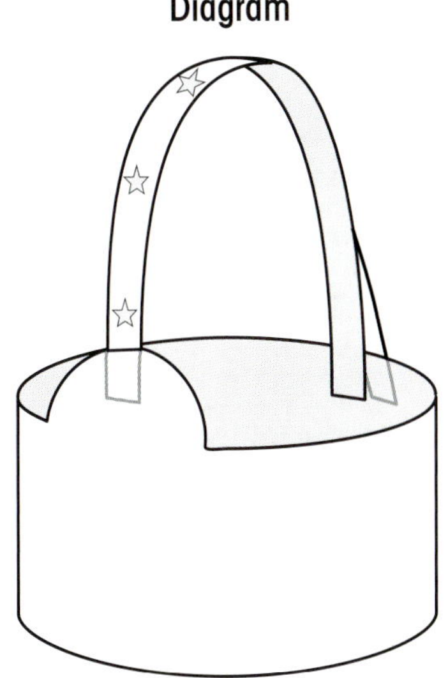

Bottom (44 x 44 threads)

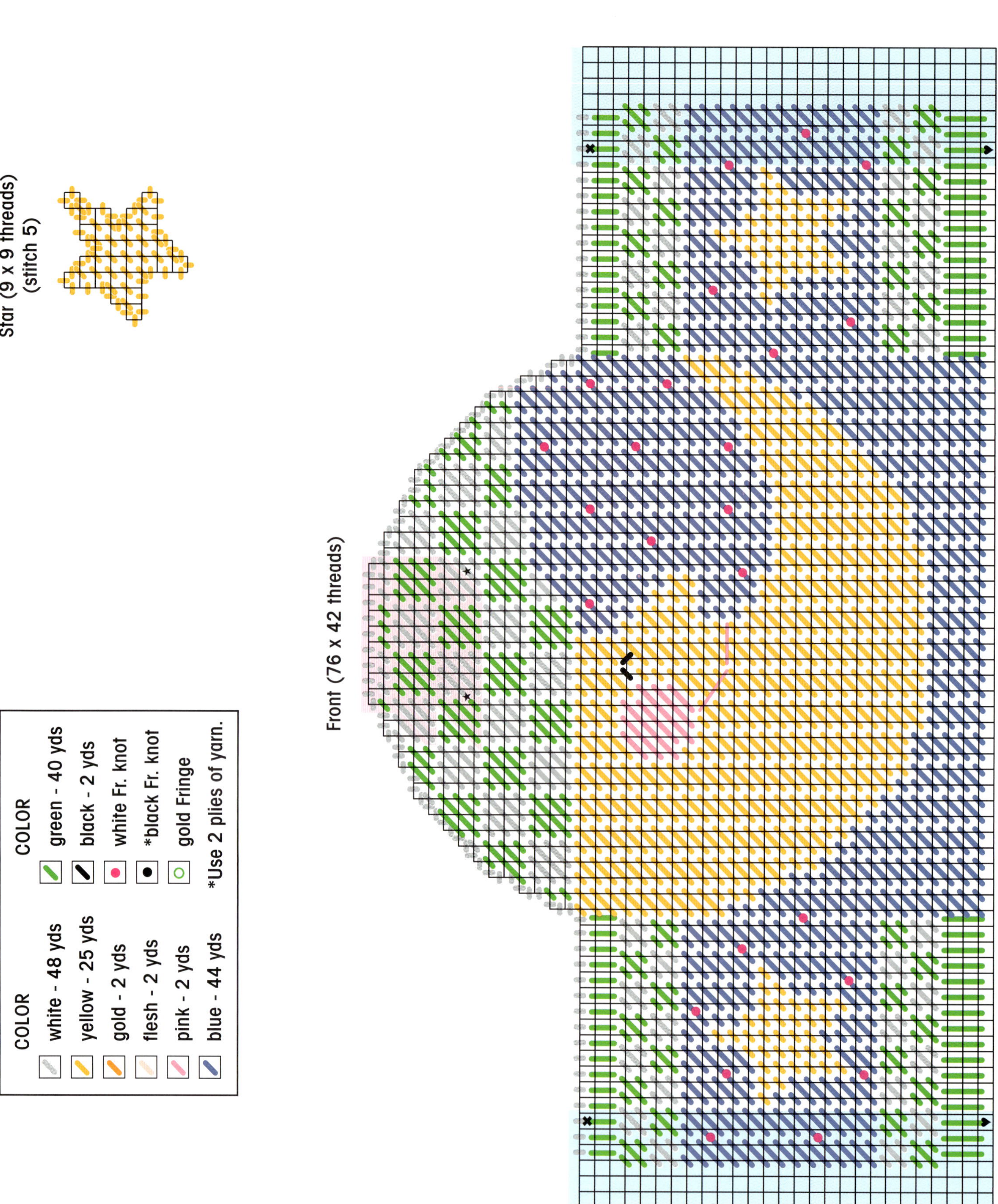

Star (9 x 9 threads)
(stitch 5)

Front (76 x 42 threads)

COLOR
white - 48 yds
yellow - 25 yds
gold - 2 yds
flesh - 2 yds
pink - 2 yds
blue - 44 yds

COLOR
green - 40 yds
black - 2 yds
white Fr. knot
*black Fr. knot
gold Fringe
*Use 2 plies of yarn.

Baby (17 x 17 threads)

Cloud (42 x 14 threads)

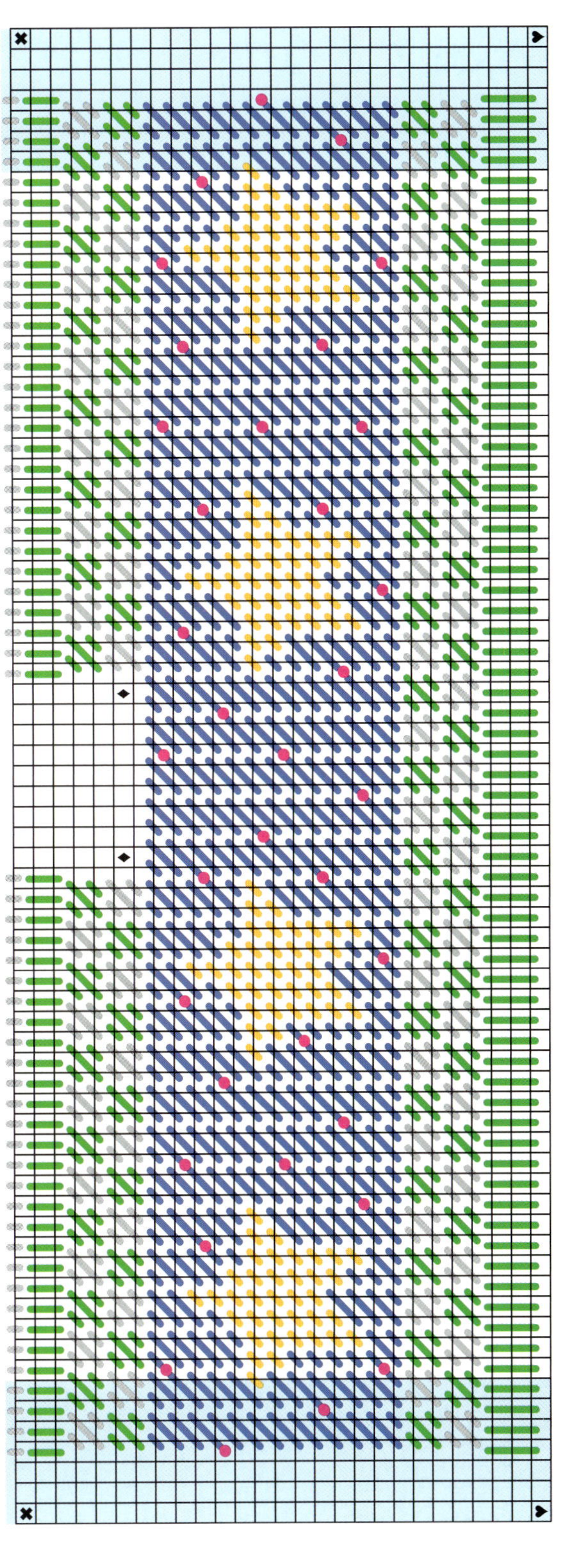

Back (74 x 28 threads)

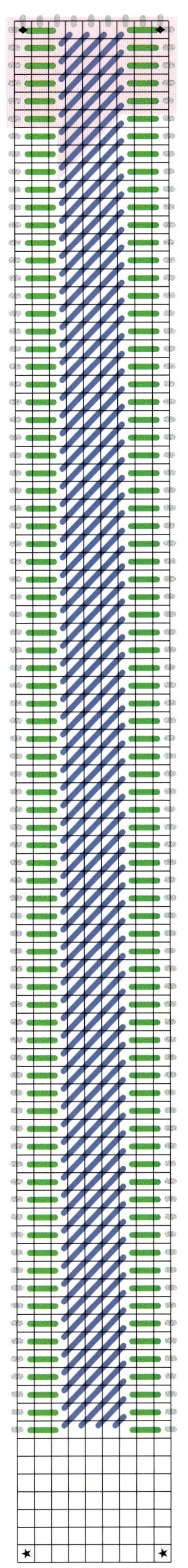

Handle (88 x 10 threads) (cut 2)
Stack and stitch through two thicknesses of canvas.

MOBILE

(Shown on page 9.)
Skill Level: Beginner
Size: 11"w x 26¼"h
Supplies: Worsted weight yarn (refer to color key), two 10½" x 13½" sheets of clear 7 mesh plastic canvas, #16 tapestry needle, one 1" dia. bone ring, nylon line, one ¾" pink pom-pom, one ½" pink pom-pom, one ¼" pink pom-pom, and craft glue.

Stitches Used: Backstitch, Diagonal Mosaic Stitch, French Knot, Fringe Stitch, Gobelin Stitch, Overcast Stitch, Scotch Stitch, and Tent Stitch.

Instructions: Follow charts to cut and stitch Mobile pieces, working backstitches, French knots, and Fringe stitches last. For bangs on Babies, separate each strand of Fringe into plies. With wrong sides together, use gold overcast stitches to join Baby Hair to Baby On Swing. Tack Baby to wrong side of Cloud A; tack Cloud A and Baby to Moon. Cut two 8" lengths of green yarn. Knot one end of each yarn length. Thread yarn lengths through Baby On Swing and Large Star at ✖'s. Run loose ends of yarn under backs of stitches on wrong side of Large Star. Referring to Diagram, use nylon line to assemble Mobile pieces. Glue pom-poms to Moon and Large Star.

Cloud A (28 x 14 threads)

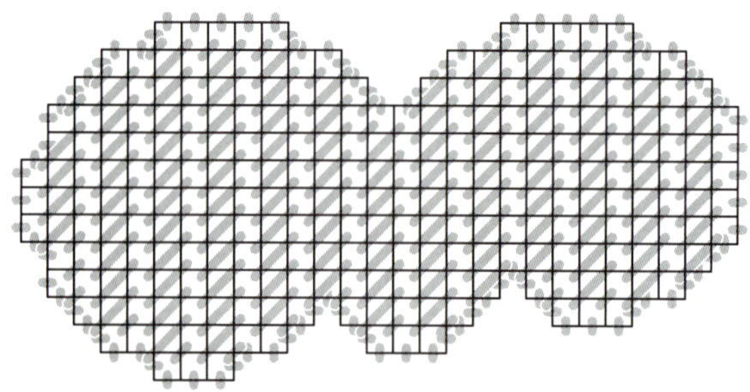

Cloud B (28 x 14 threads)

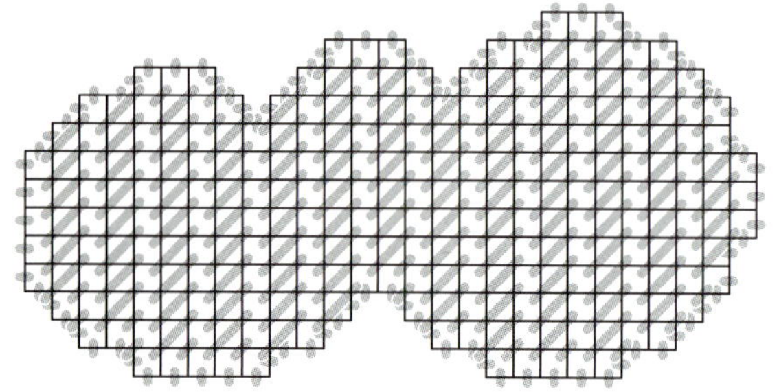

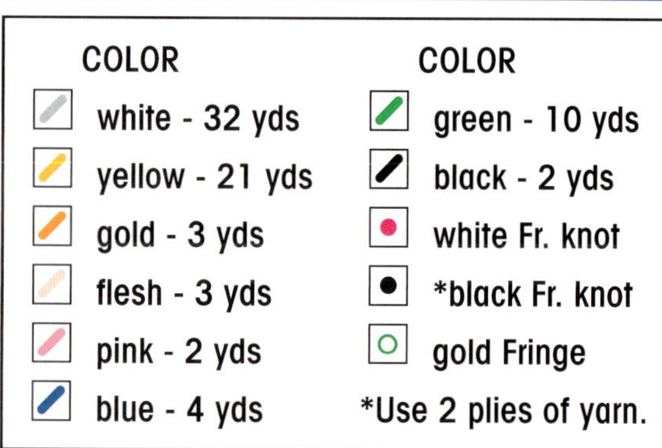

Cloud C (28 x 14 threads)

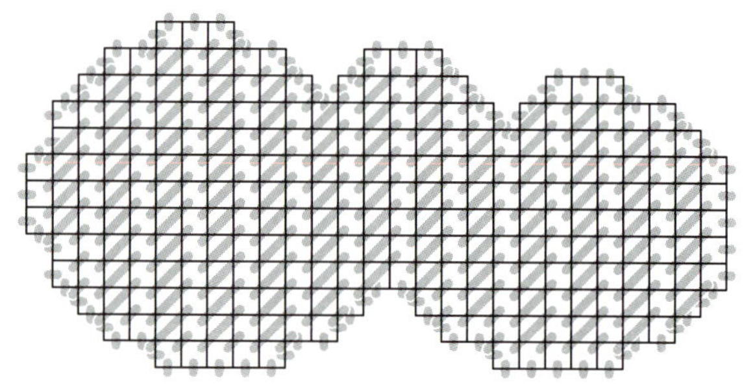

Diagram

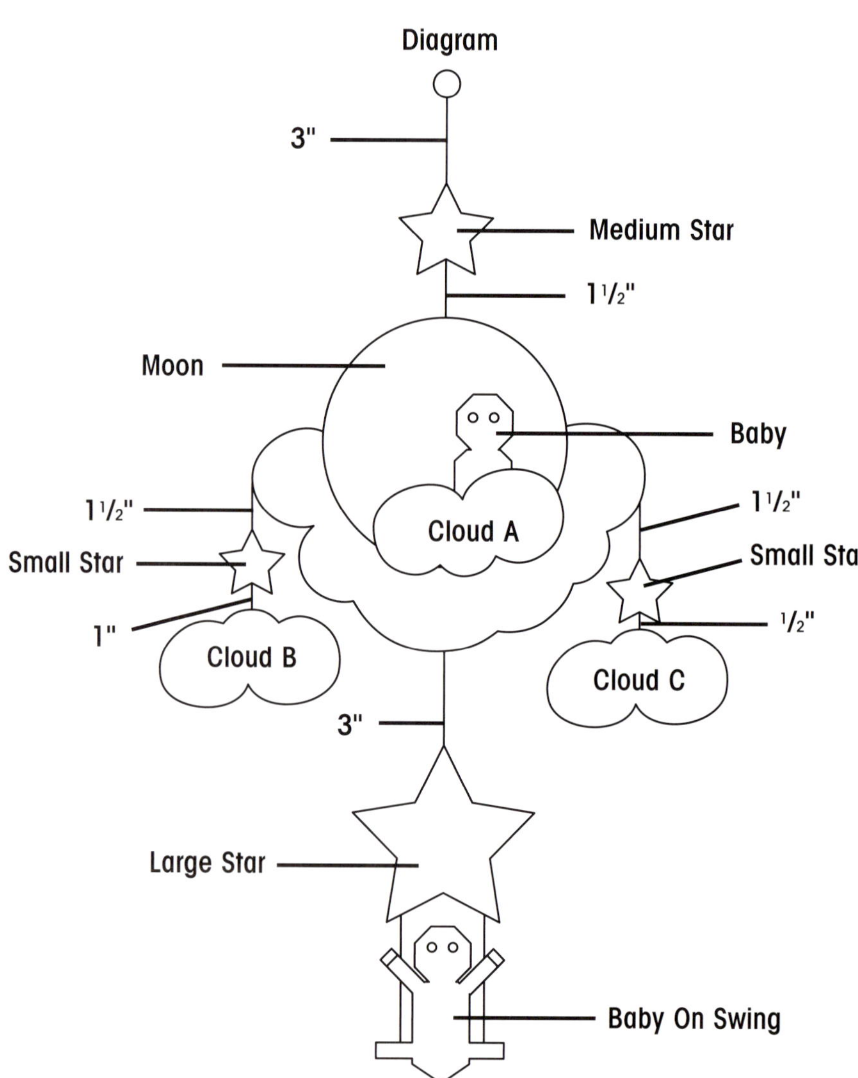

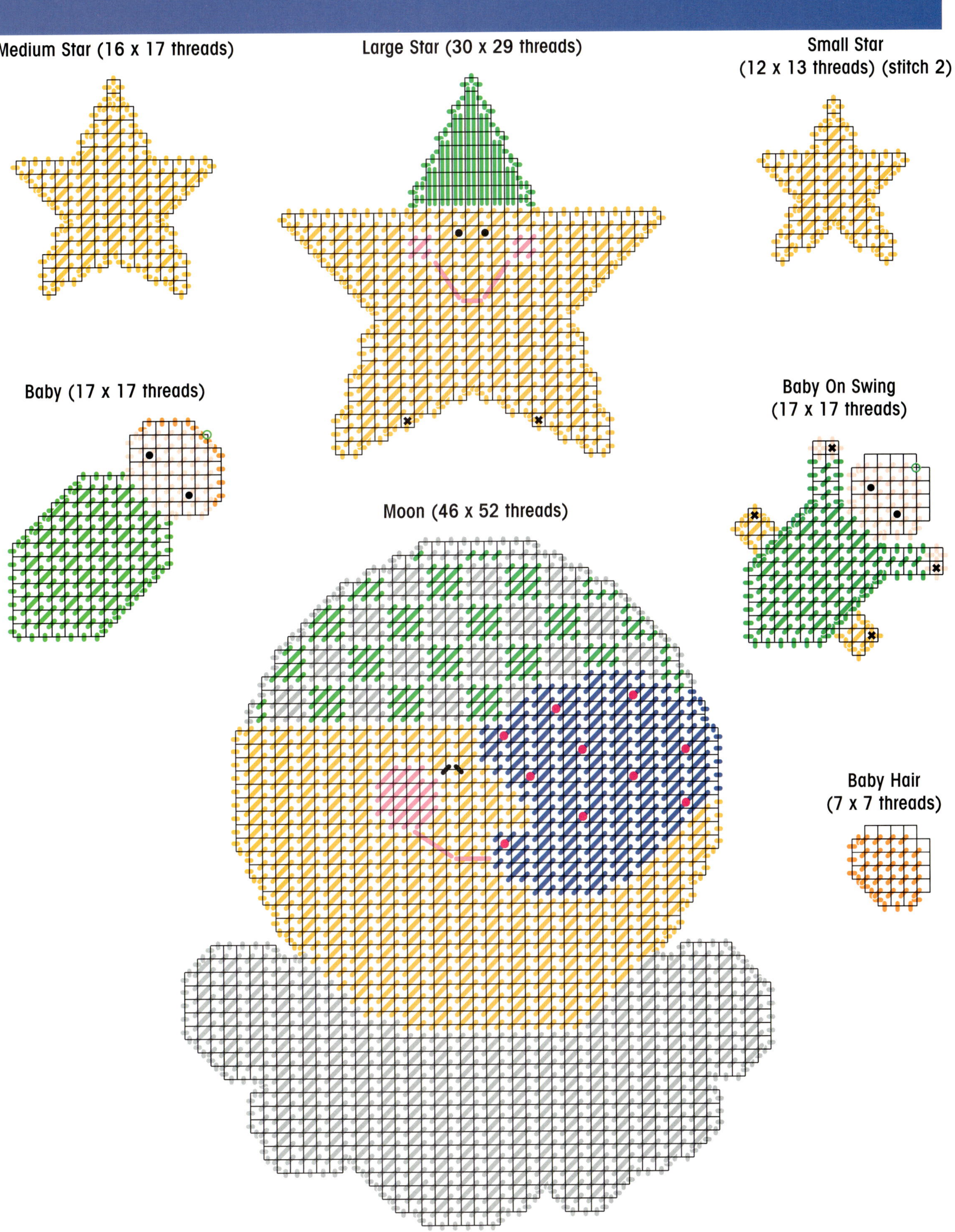

Medium Star (16 x 17 threads)
Large Star (30 x 29 threads)
Small Star
(12 x 13 threads) (stitch 2)
Baby (17 x 17 threads)
Baby On Swing
(17 x 17 threads)
Moon (46 x 52 threads)
Baby Hair
(7 x 7 threads)

GIFT-BASKET BUNNY

(Shown on page 10.)

Skill Level: Advanced

Size: 9"w x 10¹/₂"h x 9¹/₂"d

Supplies: Worsted weight yarn (refer to color keys), five 10¹/₂" x 13¹/₂" sheets of clear 7 mesh plastic canvas, #16 tapestry needle, one 2" white pom-pom, and craft glue.

Stitches Used: Backstitch, French Knot, Gobelin Stitch, Mosaic Stitch, Overcast Stitch, and Tent Stitch.

Instructions: For each Carrot Bottom, cut Carrot Top along blue cutting line and use only the lower portion of shape. Follow the charts to cut and stitch Basket pieces, working backstitches and French knots last and leaving blue shaded area on Carrot Bottoms only unworked. For Back, work Front, replacing facial features and inner ear stitches with white Gobelin stitches. With right sides up, match ■'s and work stitches in blue shaded areas to join Connector to Carrot Bottoms. Using matching color overcast stitches, join Carrot Tops above ✖'s. Join Carrot Tops to Carrot Bottoms and Connector along unworked edges. Tack Nose to Front. Join Front to Back above ★'s. Join Sides to Feet Back between ♦'s. Join Feet Front to Feet Back, leaving bottom edges open. Join Front and Back to Sides. For Bottom, cut a piece of plastic canvas 34 x 50 threads. Bottom is not worked. Join Bottom to Front, Back, Sides, Feet Front, and Feet Back. Place Sides between Carrot Tops and Carrot Bottoms. Tack Carrot Tops and Carrot Bottoms to Sides. Glue Arms to Sides and Carrot Tops. Glue Flowers to Feet Front and Sides. For tail, glue pom-pom to Back.

Front/Back (42 x 70 threads)
(cut 2) (stitch 1)

Lavender Flower
(8 x 8 threads)
(stitch 5)

Pink Flower
(8 x 8 threads)
(stitch 3)

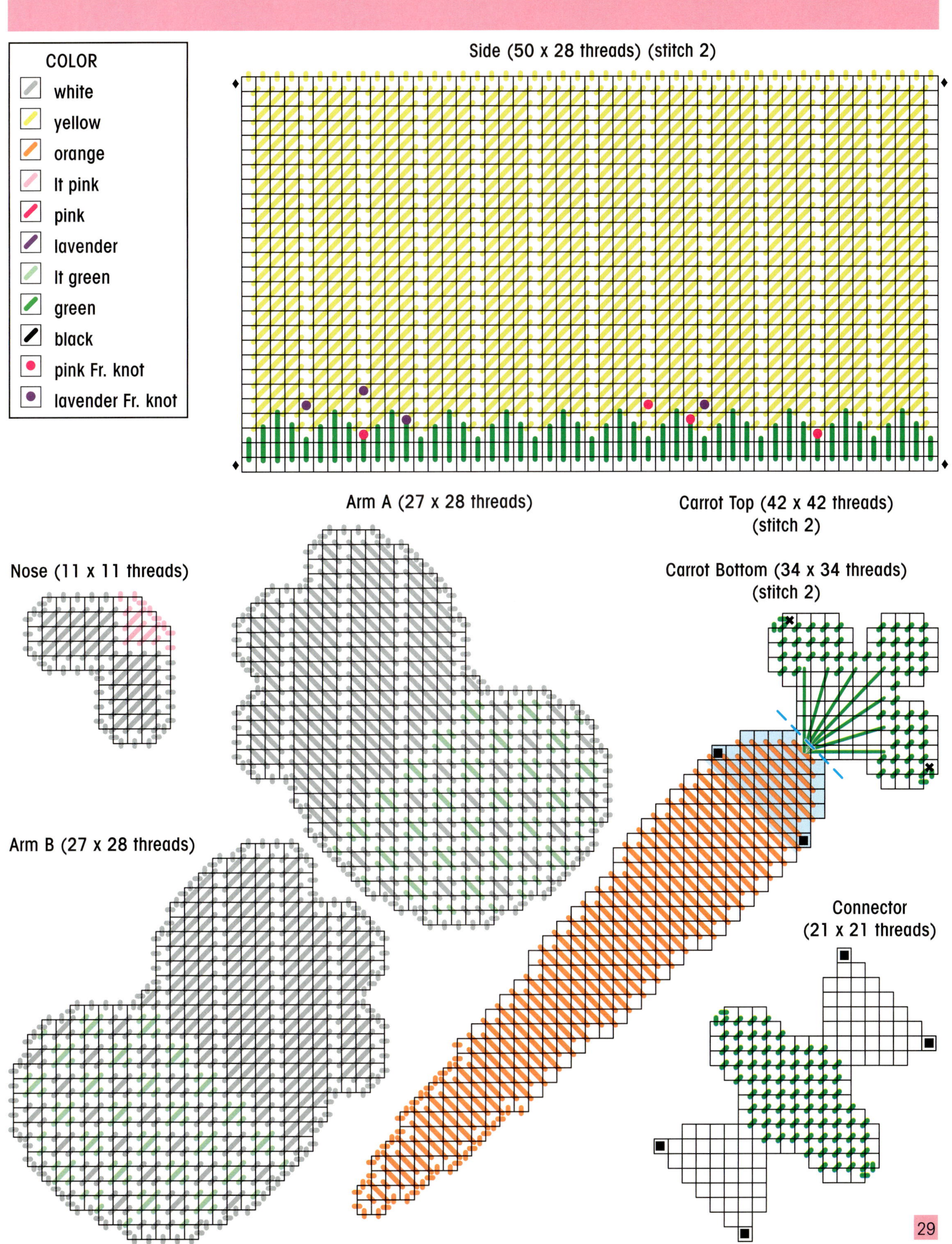COLOR
white
yellow
orange
lt pink
pink
lavender
lt green
green
black
pink Fr. knot
lavender Fr. knot
Side (50 x 28 threads) (stitch 2)
Arm A (27 x 28 threads)
Carrot Top (42 x 42 threads)
(stitch 2)
Nose (11 x 11 threads)
Carrot Bottom (34 x 34 threads)
(stitch 2)
Arm B (27 x 28 threads)
Connector
(21 x 21 threads)

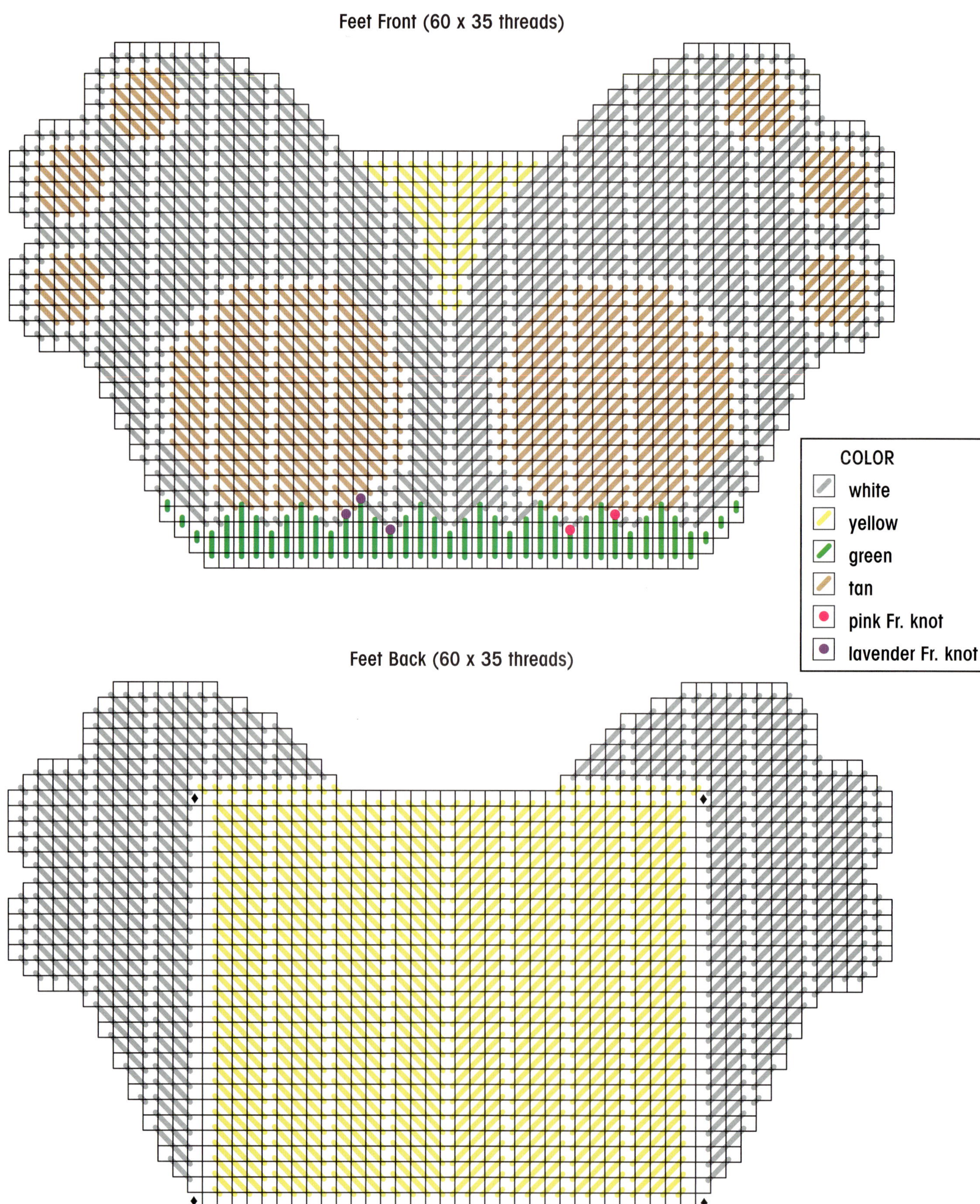

Feet Front (60 x 35 threads)
Feet Back (60 x 35 threads)
COLOR
white
yellow
green
tan
pink Fr. knot
lavender Fr. knot

BEAR SWITCH PLATE COVER

(Shown on page 11.)

Skill Level: Beginner

Size: 5¼"w x 6¾"h

Supplies: Worsted weight yarn (refer to color key), one 10½" x 13½" sheet of clear 7 mesh plastic canvas, and #16 tapestry needle.

Stitches Used: Backstitch, French Knot, Gobelin Stitch, Overcast Stitch, Reversed Tent Stitch, and Tent Stitch.

Instructions: Follow charts to cut and stitch Switch Plate Cover pieces, working backstitches and French knots last. Matching A to B and C to D, fold down top section of Nose. Using lt tan overcast stitches, join these sections. Matching ✘'s, join top edge of Nose to Body along unworked threads. Tack each side of Nose to Body. Matching ★'s, join Left Arm to Body along unworked edges. Matching ♥'s, join Right Arm to Body along unworked edges. Following Diagram for placement of stitches, use lt tan to join Flowers to Switch Plate Cover.

Small Flower (4 x 4 threads) (stitch 2)

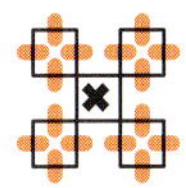

Large Flower (6 x 6 threads) (stitch 2)

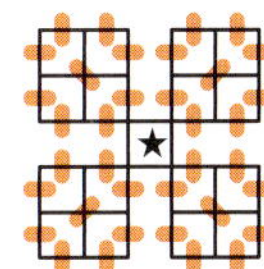

COLOR	
⊘	white
⊘	lt pink
⊘	pink
⊘	aqua
⊘	green
⊘	lt tan
⊘	tan
⊘	black
●	white Fr. knot

Nose (12 x 12 threads)

Body (50 x 50 threads)

Diagram

Right Arm (13 x 7 threads)

Left Arm (13 x 7 threads)

WALL HANGING

(Shown on page 11.)
Skill Level: Beginner
Size: 5¹/₄"w x 6³/₄"h
Supplies: Worsted weight yarn (refer to color key), two 10¹/₂" x 13¹/₂" sheets of clear 7 mesh plastic canvas, #16 tapestry needle, and sawtooth hanger.
Stitches Used: Backstitch, Gobelin Stitch, Overcast Stitch, Reversed Tent Stitch, and Tent Stitch.
Instructions: Follow charts to cut and stitch Wall Hanging pieces, working backstitches last. Matching A to B and C to D, fold down top section of Nose. Using lt tan overcast stitches, join these sections. Matching ✖'s, join top edge of Nose to Body along unworked threads. Tack each side of Nose to Body. Matching ■'s, use tan overcast stitches to join Left Ear to Body along unworked edges. Matching ▲'s, join Right Ear to Body along unworked edges. Matching ◗'s, join Left Arm to Body along unworked edges. Matching ★'s, join Right Arm to Body along unworked edges. Matching ♠'s, use white overcast stitches to join Left Leg to Body along unworked edges. Matching ♦'s, join Right Leg to Body along unworked edges. For drawstring on each Leg, follow Diagram to weave white yarn back and forth across bootie. Matching ♣'s, join Diaper to Body along unworked edges of Diaper. Using aqua overcast stitches, join Pin Head to Pin along unworked edges. To attach Pin to Diaper, match ♥'s and work three white Gobelin Stitches over Pin through Diaper and Body. Tack Wings to wrong side of Bee; tack Bee to Rattle. Tack Rattle to Right Arm. Securely attach hanger to wrong side of Body.

COLOR	
	white
	orange
	lt pink
	pink
	aqua
	lt tan
	tan
	black

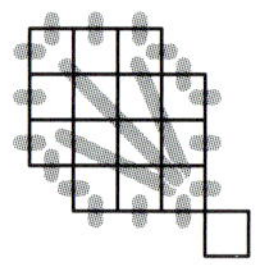

Bee Wing (6 x 6 threads)
(stitch 2)

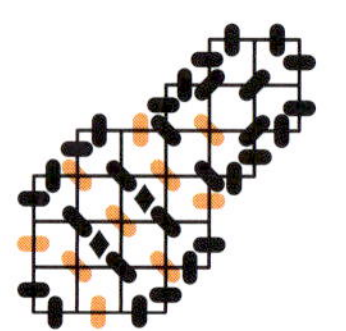

Bee (7 x 7 threads)

Right Arm (25 x 12 threads)

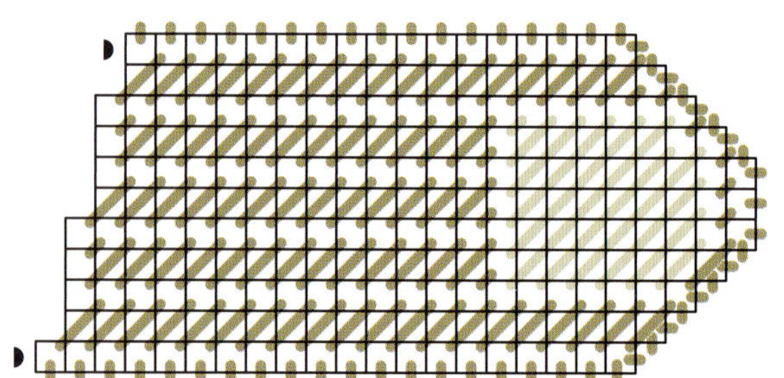

Left Arm (25 x 12 threads)

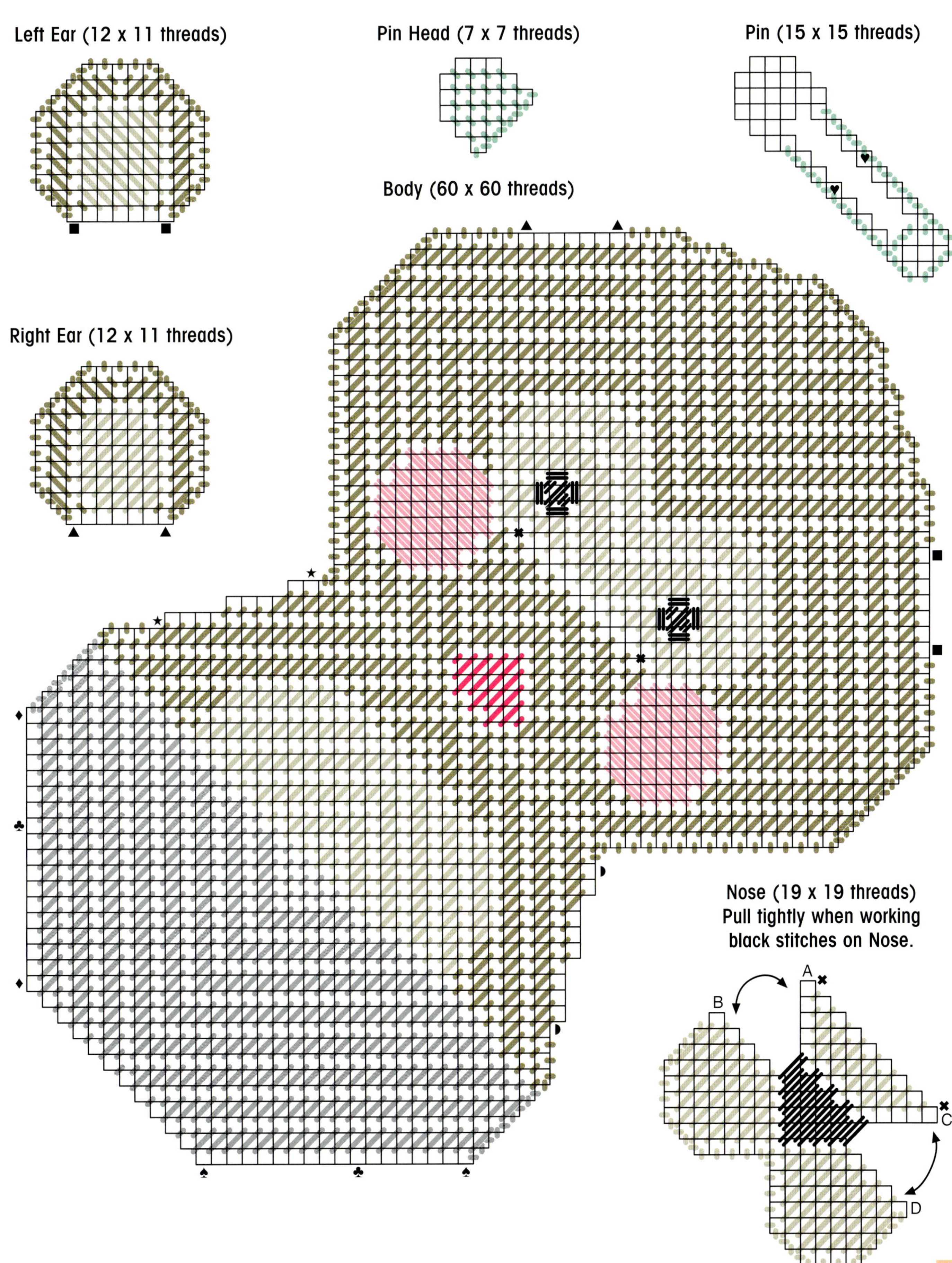

Left Ear (12 x 11 threads)
Right Ear (12 x 11 threads)
Pin Head (7 x 7 threads)
Pin (15 x 15 threads)
Body (60 x 60 threads)
Nose (19 x 19 threads)
Pull tightly when working
black stitches on Nose.
A
B
C
D

COLOR	
	white
	aqua
	lt tan
	tan
	black

Diaper (24 x 24 threads)

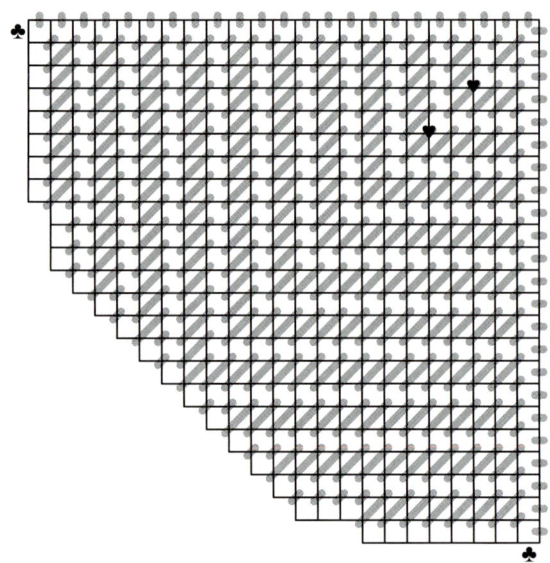

Rattle (22 x 22 threads)

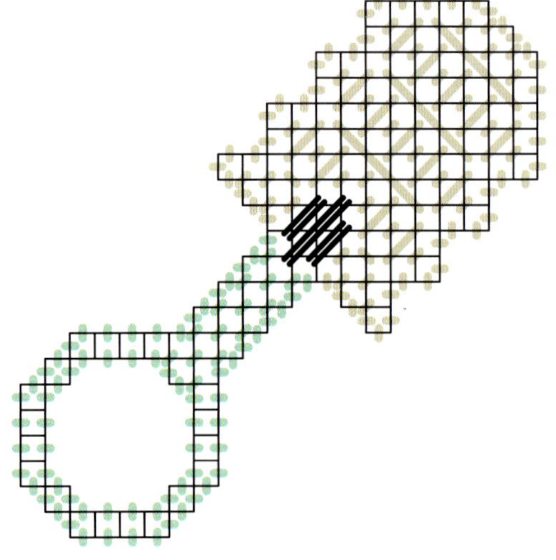

Left Leg (32 x 19 threads)

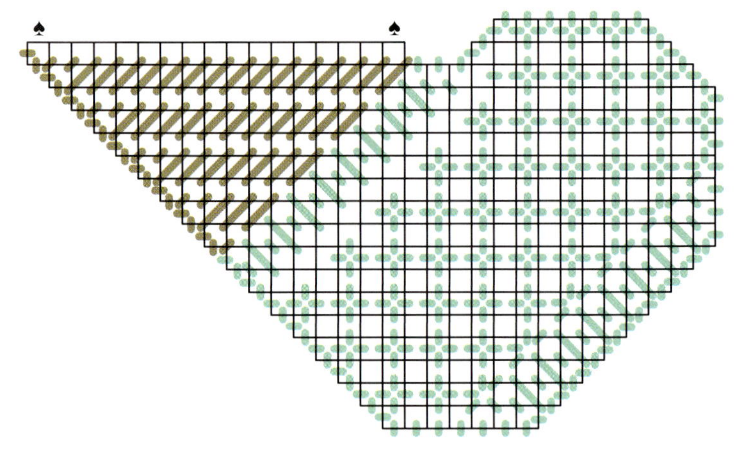

Right Leg (32 x 19 threads)

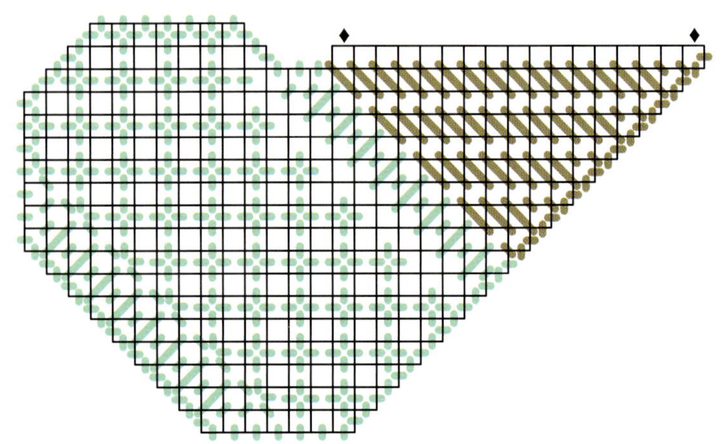

Diagram

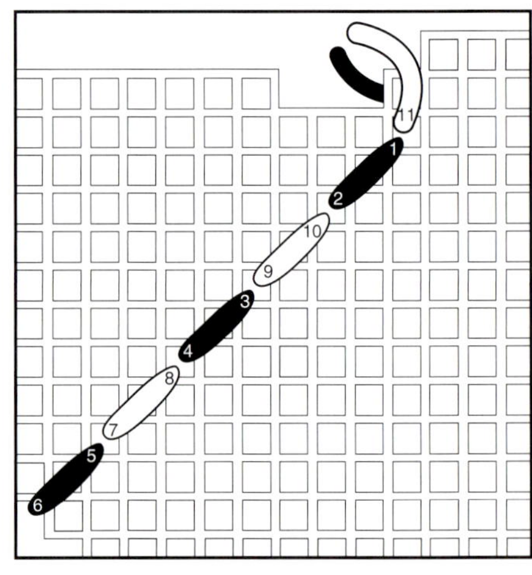

STORAGE BOX

(Shown on page 11.)

Skill Level: Beginner

Size: 3¼"w x 3¼"h 3¼"d

Supplies: Worsted weight yarn (refer to color key), one 10½" x 13½" sheet of clear 7 mesh plastic canvas, and #16 tapestry needle.

Stitches Used: Backstitch, Cross Stitch, Eyelet Stitch, French Knot, Gobelin Stitch, Overcast Stitch.

Instructions: Follow charts to cut and stitch Box pieces, working backstitches and French knots last. Using aqua overcast stitches, join Front and Back to Sides. Join Bottom to Front, Back, and Sides. Join Top to unworked edge of Back. Cover remaining unworked edges.

COLOR	
	yellow
	orange
	lt pink
	pink
	purple
	aqua
	lt tan
	tan
	black
●	pink Fr. knot
●	*black Fr. knot

*Use 2 plies of yarn.

Top/Bottom (22 x 22 threads)
(cut 2) (stitch 1)

Front/Back/Side
(22 x 22 threads) (stitch 4)
Complete background with yellow backstitches as indicated on chart.

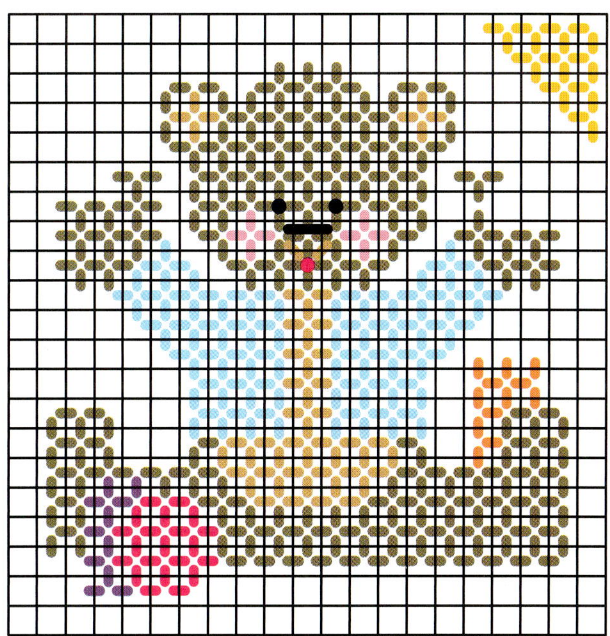

PHOTO FRAME

(Shown on page 12.)
Skill Level: Beginner
Size: 7¹/₂"w x 13¹/₄"h
(Fits a 5"w x 7"h photograph.)
Supplies: Worsted weight yarn (refer to color key), two 10¹/₂" x 13¹/₂" sheets of clear 7 mesh plastic canvas, #16 tapestry needle, and one sawtooth hanger.
Stitches Used: French Knot, Gobelin Stitch, Overcast Stitch, Reversed Tent Stitch, Tent Stitch, and Upright Cross Stitch.
Instructions: Follow charts to cut and stitch Photo Frame pieces, working French knots last. Tack Flowers to Front. Tack hanger to Back. Referring to photo for yarn colors, use overcast stitches to join Front to Back. Cut an 8" length of blue yarn. Tie yarn in bow around bear's neck and trim ends.

Front (50 x 88 threads)

COLOR	
/	white
/	yellow
/	pink
/	blue
/	green
/	lt tan
/	tan
/	black
●	gold Fr. knot
●	pink Fr. knot
●	green Fr. knot
●	black Fr. knot

Flower (4 x 4 threads) (stitch 4)

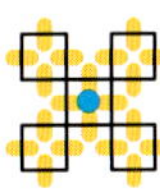

Back (50 x 88 threads)

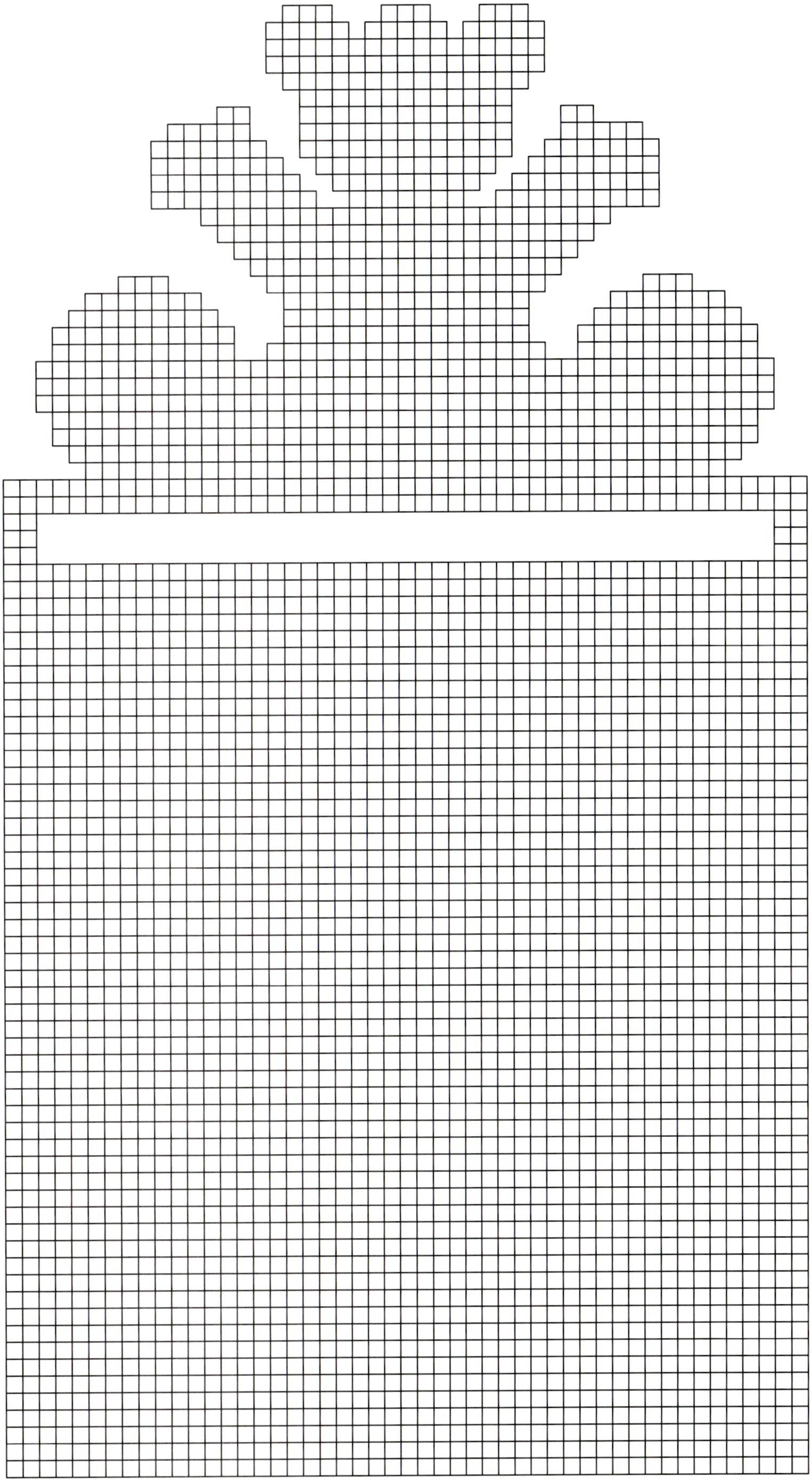

WIPE COVER

(Shown on page 12.)

Skill Level: Beginner

Size: 6¼"h x 4¾" dia.

(Fits a 7"h x 4½" dia. baby wipe container.)

Supplies: Worsted weight yarn (refer to color key), one 12" x 18" sheet of clear 7 mesh plastic canvas, and #16 tapestry needle.

Stitches Used: French Knot, Gobelin Stitch, Mosaic Stitch, Overcast Stitch, Scotch Stitch, Reversed Tent Stitch, Tent Stitch, and Upright Cross Stitch.

Instructions: Follow charts to cut and stitch Wipe Cover pieces, working French knots last. Matching ♥'s and ★'s, use tan overcast stitches to join Arm A to Side. Matching ▲'s and ■'s, join Arm B to Side. Tack Flowers to Side. Using blue overcast stitches, join short edges of Side, forming a cylinder. Slide stitched piece over wipe container.

COLOR	
⁄	white
⁄	yellow
⁄	pink
⁄	blue
⁄	green
⁄	lt tan
⁄	tan
⁄	black
●	gold Fr. knot
●	black Fr. knot

Side (98 x 42 threads)

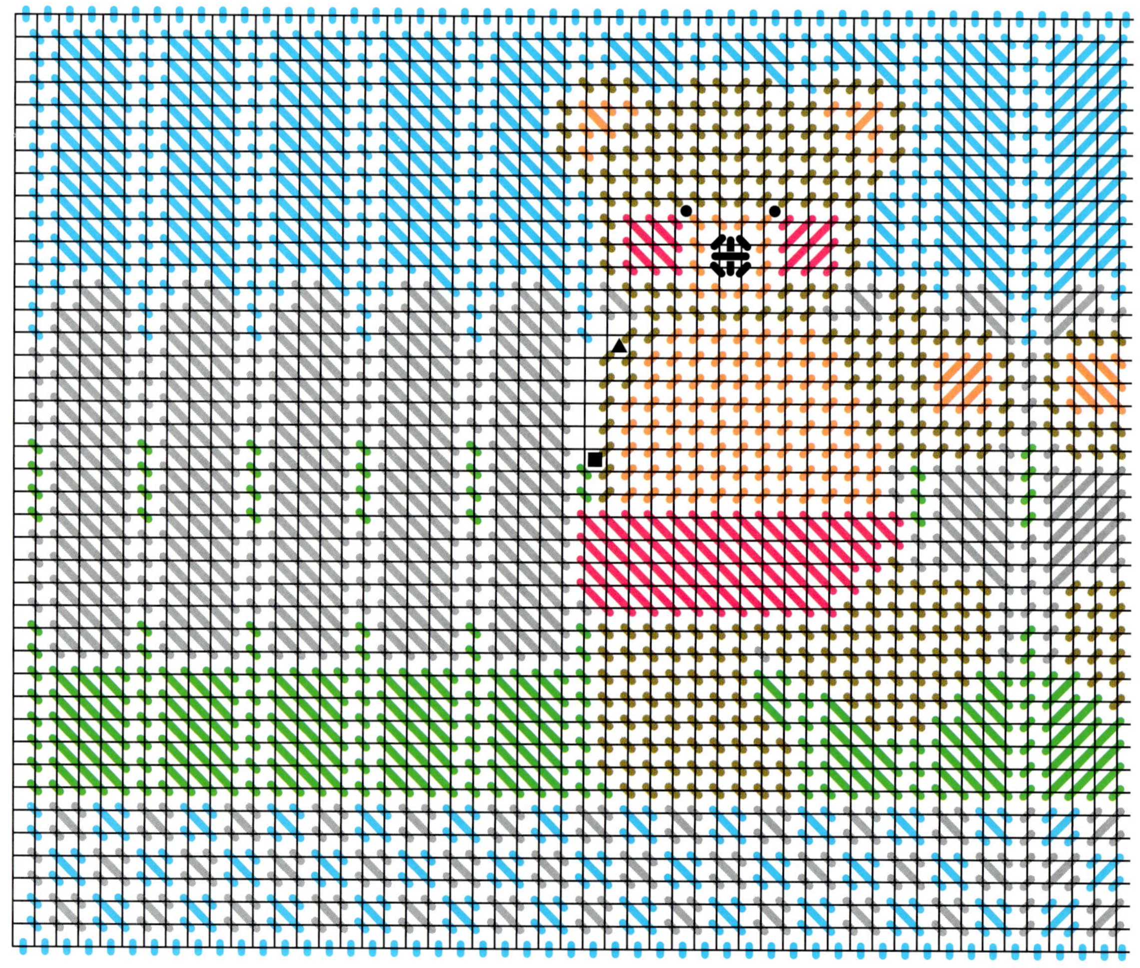

Flower (4 x 4 threads) (stitch 5)

Arm A (13 x 10 threads)

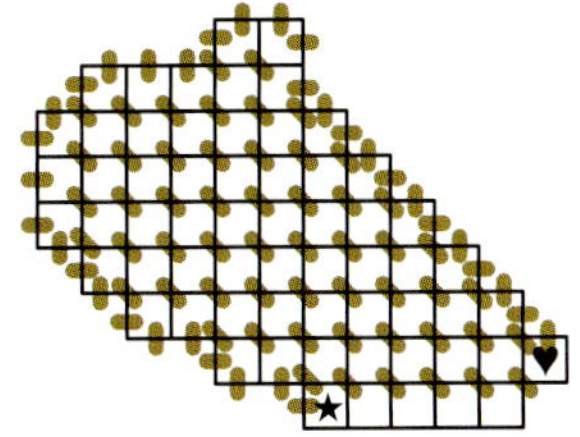

Arm B (13 x 10 threads)

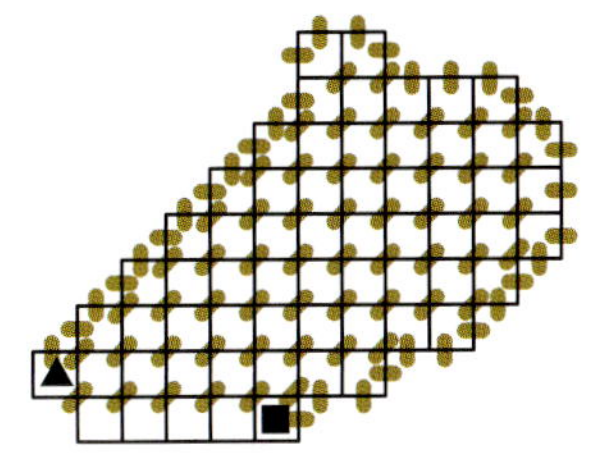

Chart Note: This chart of the Side represents one 98 x 42 thread canvas piece. It is spread across two pages to make it large enough to be followed easily. No threads or stitches are repeated from one page to the next.

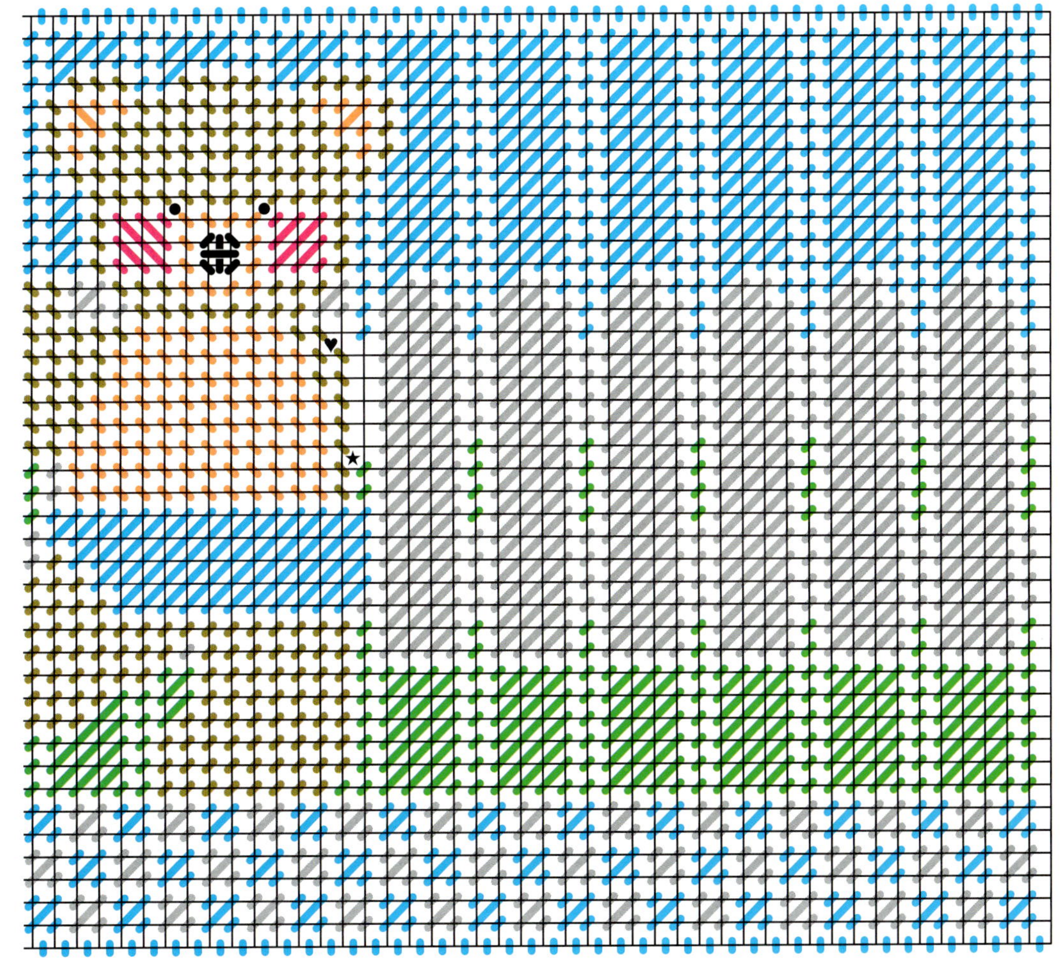

"BEARY" CUTE PARADE

(Shown on page 15.)
Skill Level: Beginner
Size: 4³/₄"w x 5¹/₂"h x 4³/₄"d
(Fits a 4¹/₄"w x 5¹/₄"h x 4¹/₄"d boutique tissue box.)
Supplies: Worsted weight yarn and DMC Embroidery Floss (refer to color key), two 10¹/₂" x 13¹/₂" sheets of clear 7 mesh plastic canvas, and #16 tapestry needle.
Stitches Used: Backstitch, French Knot, Gobelin Stitch, Overcast Stitch, and Tent Stitch.
Instructions: Follow charts to cut and stitch Tissue Box Cover pieces, working backstitches and French knots last. Using matching color overcast stitches, join Sides along long edges. Join Top to Sides.

COLOR (YARN)	COLOR (YARN)
ecru	*lt blue
yellow	*lt blue Fr. knot
peach	*black Fr. knot
pink	
purple	**COLOR (FLOSS)**
lt blue	†black (310)
green	*Use 2 plies of yarn.
brown	†Use 1 strand of floss.
black	

Top (32 x 32 threads)

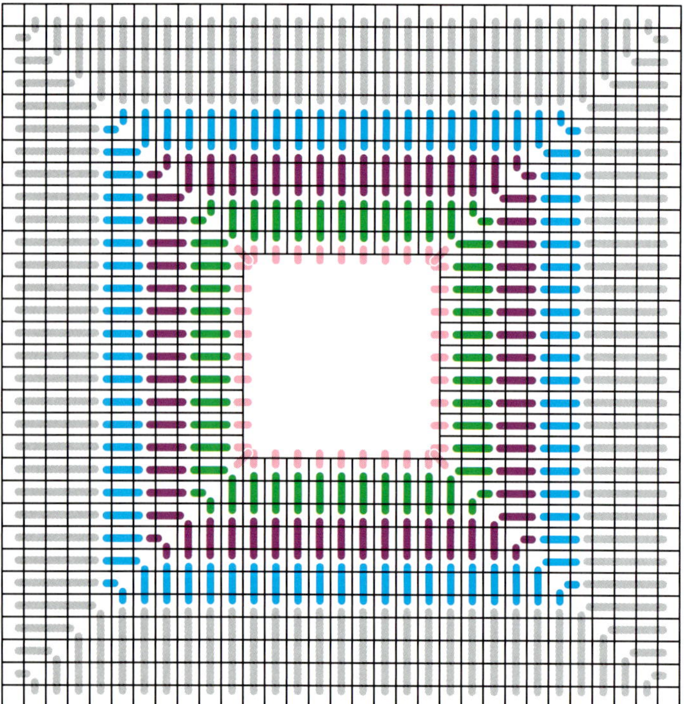

Side (32 x 38 threads) (stitch 4)

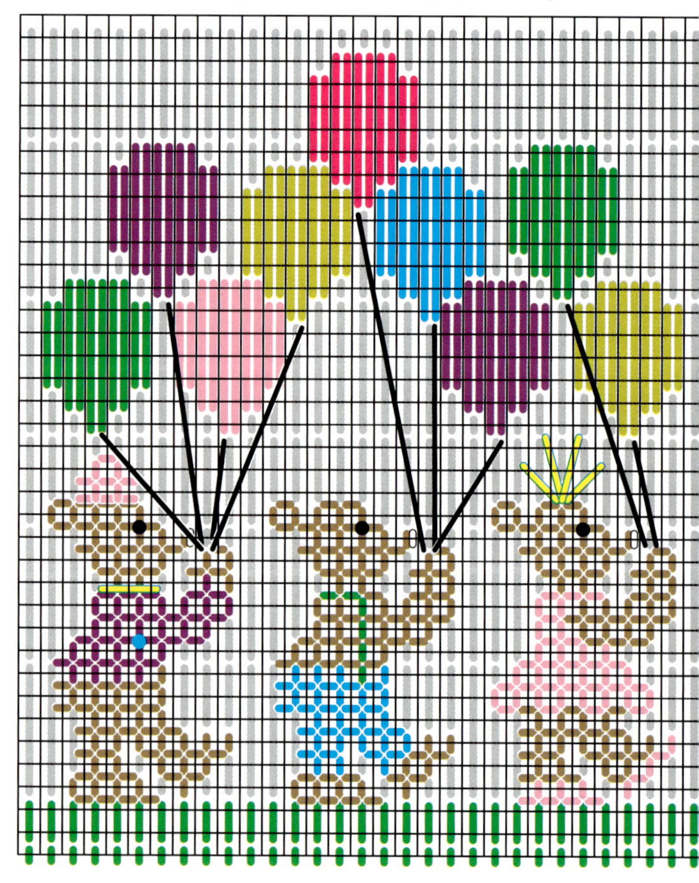

(Shown on page 7.)
Skill Level: Beginner
Size: 5¾"w x 10"h x 10"d
Supplies: Worsted weight yarn (refer to color keys), four 10½" x 13½" sheets of clear 7 mesh plastic canvas, #16 tapestry needle, and craft glue.
Stitches Used: Backstitch, Cross Stitch, Gobelin Stitch, Overcast Stitch, Reversed Tent, and Tent Stitch.
Instructions: Follow the charts to cut and stitch Basket pieces, working backstitches last and leaving lavender shaded areas unworked. Glue Muzzle to Head Front. Matching ▲'s, use pink overcast stitches to join Hat Trim to Head Front. Repeat to join Hat Trim to Head Back. Matching ♥'s, join Collar to Head Front. Repeat to join Collar to Head Back. With wrong sides together, match ♦'s and use matching color overcast stitches to join Head Front to Head Back along unworked edges, leaving edges below ♦'s unworked. Matching ★'s, place Handle Supports on wrong side of Side A and Side B. Work stitches in lavender shaded areas through two thicknesses of canvas to join Sides to Handle Supports. With wrong sides together, use yellow overcast stitches to join Handle pieces along long edges, leaving stitches between ■'s and ♣'s unworked. Matching ■'s and ♣'s, place Handle Supports between Handle pieces. Using yellow overcast stitches, work through three thicknesses of canvas to join Handle pieces to Handle Supports. Working through four thicknesses of canvas, join Handle pieces to Sides and Handle Supports. Matching ♠'s, join Foreleg A to Side A. Matching ◗'s, join Foreleg B to Side B. Tack Cuffs to Forelegs and Sides. With wrong sides together, use aqua overcast stitches to join Wagon Handle Front to Wagon Handle Back, leaving stitches between ✖'s unworked. Matching ✖'s, join Wagon Handle to End along unworked edge of Wagon Handle. Tack Wagon Handle to End. Using matching color overcast stitches, join Sides to End. Working through three thicknesses of canvas, use matching color overcast stitches to join Head Front and Head Back to Sides. Using lt green overcast stitches, join Basket Bottom to unworked edges of Basket. Glue Wheels to Sides.

COLOR	
/	yellow
/	pink
/	aqua
/	tan
/	black

Collar (24 x 6 threads) (stitch 2)

Hat Trim (18 x 5 threads) (stitch 2)

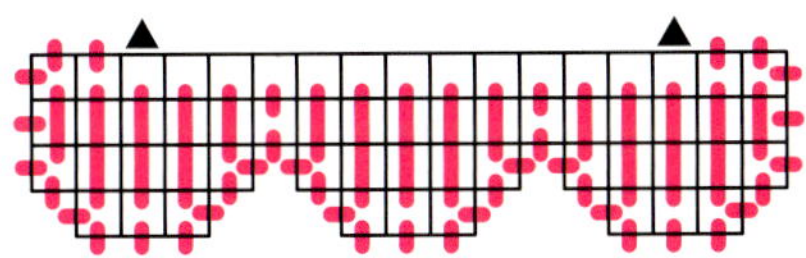

Wheel (14 x 14 threads) (stitch 4)

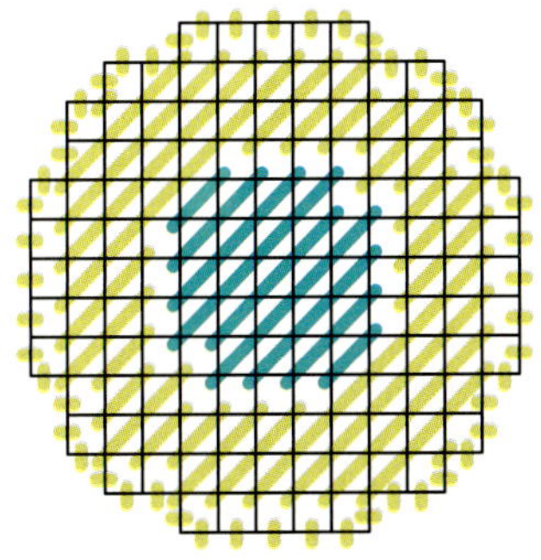

Muzzle (10 x 8 threads)

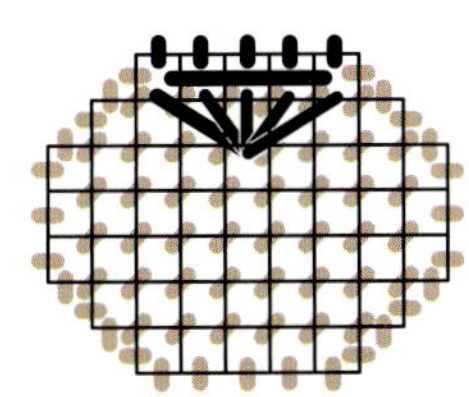

COLOR

- yellow
- pink
- aqua
- lt green
- tan
- brown
- black

Head Front (38 x 67 threads)

**Wagon Handle Front/Back
(14 x 35 threads) (stitch 2)**

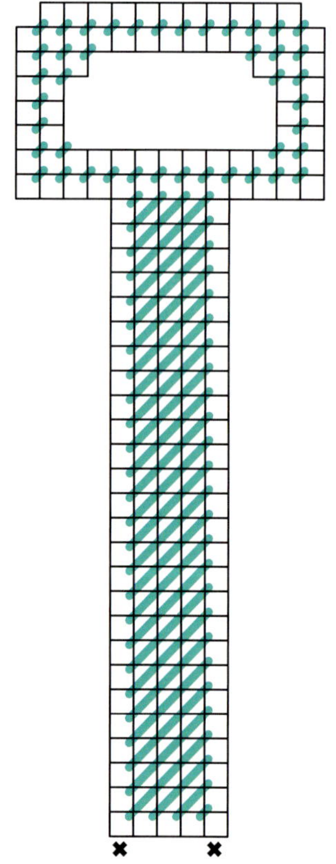

Cuff (12 x 5 threads) (stitch 4)

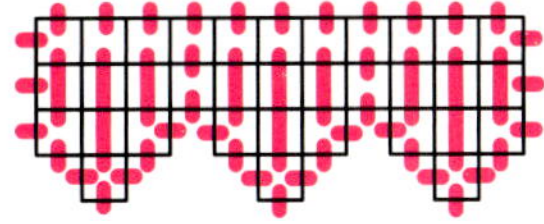

Head Back (38 x 67 threads)

Foreleg A (26 x 19 threads)

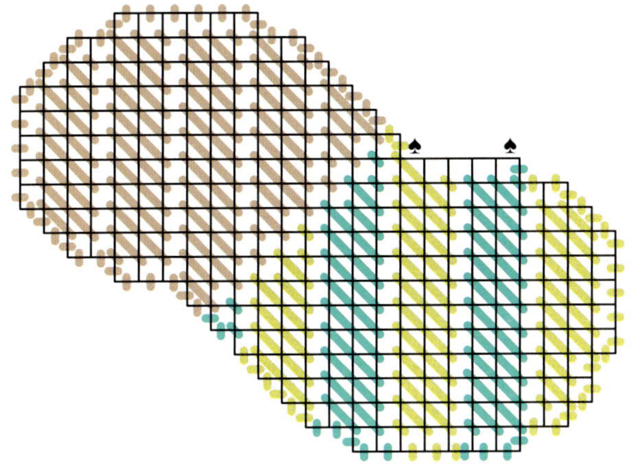

Foreleg B (26 x 19 threads)

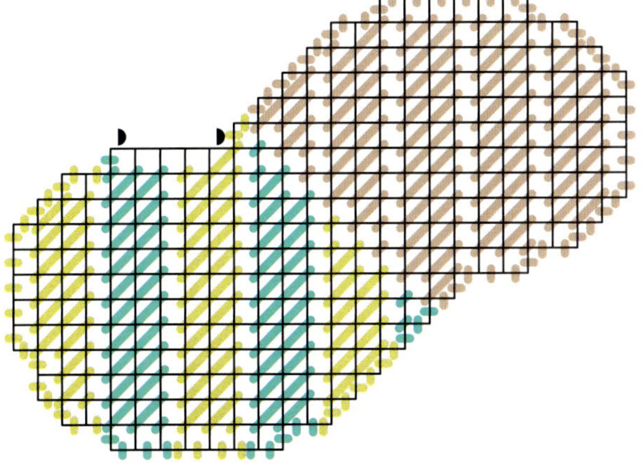

Side A (50 x 34 threads)

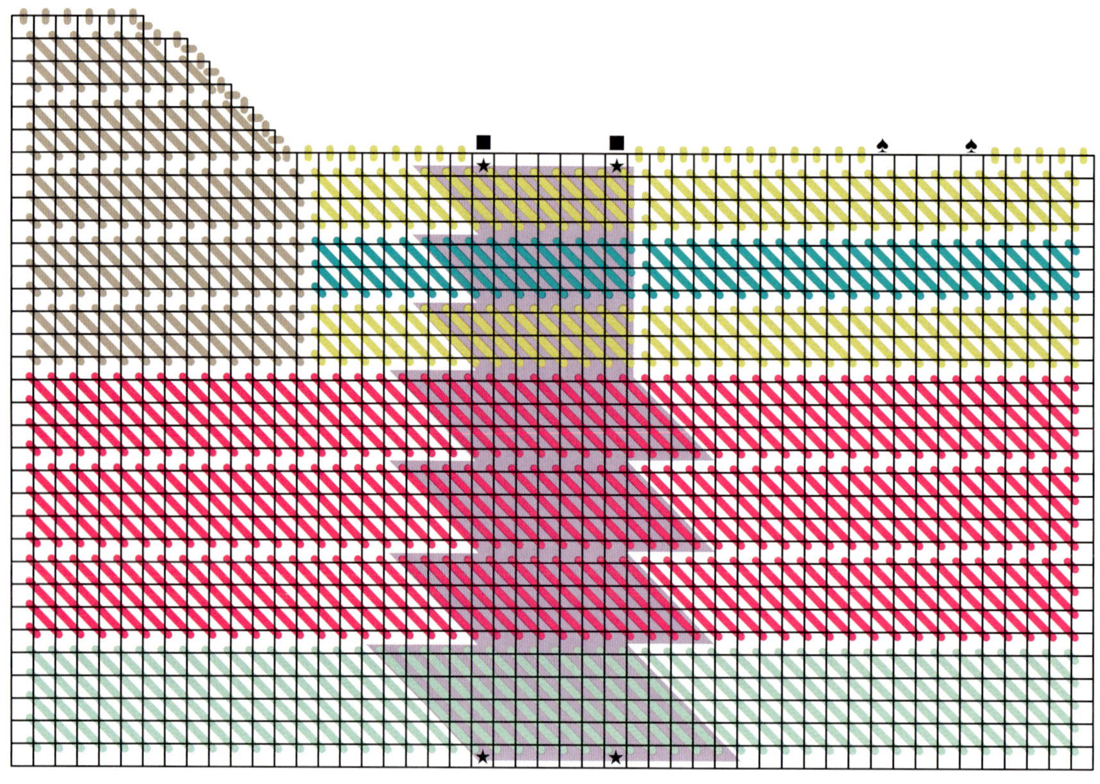

Side B (50 x 34 threads)

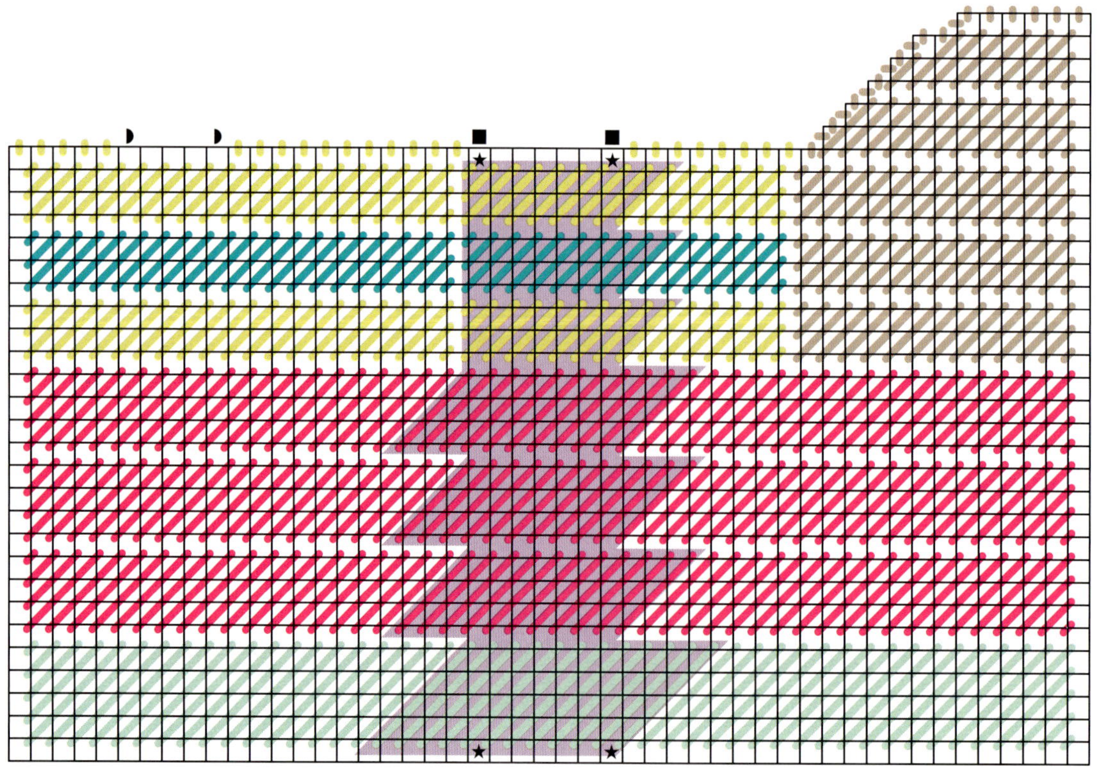

Handle Support (8 x 35 threads) (cut 2)

Handle (8 x 80 threads) (stitch 2)

End (34 x 34 threads)

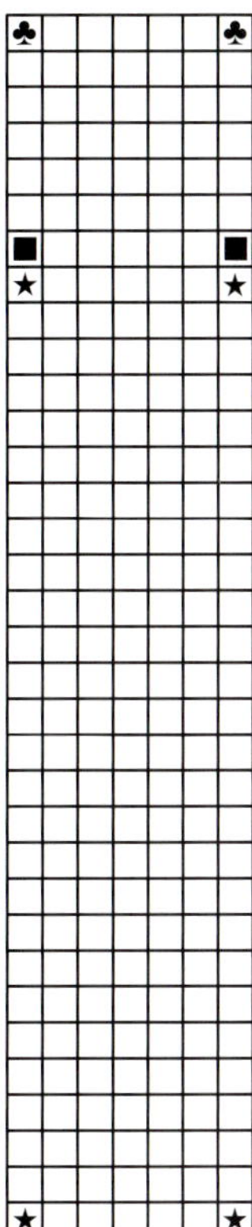

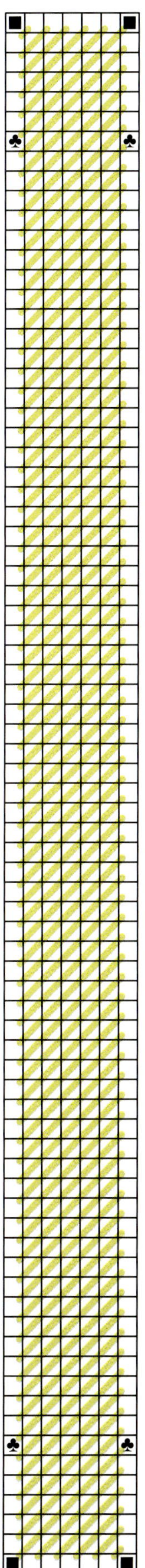

COLOR
It green

Basket Bottom (50 x 34 threads)

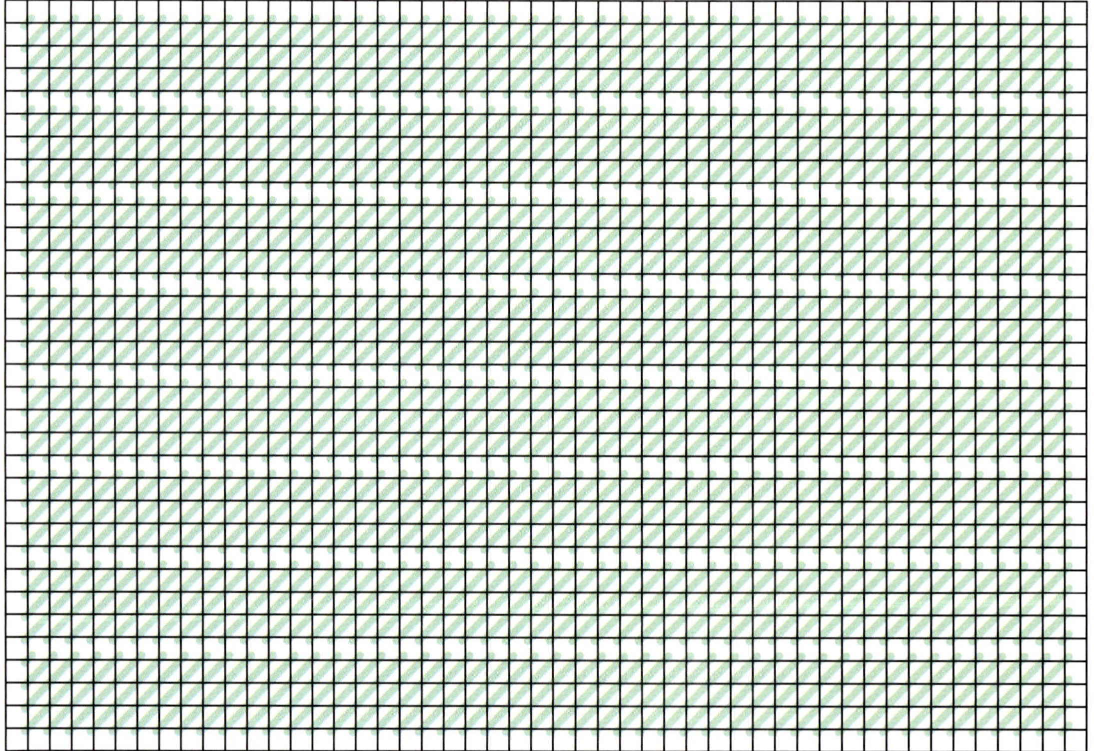

FOR A LITTLE LAMB

(Shown on page 13.)
Skill Level: Beginner
Size: 7¼"w x 8¾"h x 8"d
Supplies: Worsted weight yarn (refer to color keys), three 10½" x 13½" sheets of clear 7 mesh plastic canvas, #16 tapestry needle, polyester fiberfill, nylon line, eleven ¾" white pom-poms, and craft glue.
Stitches Used: Backstitch, Gobelin Stitch, Overcast Stitch, Reversed Tent, and Tent Stitch.
Instructions: Follow the charts to cut and stitch Basket pieces, working backstitches last and leaving grey shaded areas unworked. Glue Muzzle to Head Front. With right sides facing up, match ■'s and use lt green overcast stitches to join Head Back to Basket Back along bottom edge of Head Back. With wrong sides together, use matching color overcast stitches to join Head Front to Head Back and Basket Back along unworked edges of Head Front. Lightly stuff Lamb with fiberfill. Use nylon line to join short edges of Basket Front to short edges of Basket Back, forming a cylinder. Matching ♥'s, place Handle Supports on wrong side of Basket Front and Basket Back. Work stitches in grey shaded areas through two thicknesses of canvas to join Basket Front and Basket Back to Handle Supports. Cover unworked areas at seams with yellow Gobelin stitches. With wrong sides together, use yellow overcast stitches to join Handle pieces along long edges, leaving stitches between ✖'s and ★'s unworked. Matching ✖'s and ★'s, place Handle Supports between Handle pieces. Using yellow overcast stitches, work through three thicknesses of canvas to join Handle pieces to Handle Supports. Working through four thicknesses of canvas, join Handle pieces to Basket Front, Basket Back, and Handle Supports. Using lavender overcast stitches, join Basket Bottom to unworked edges of Basket Front and Basket Back. Matching ♦'s, join Foreleg A to Basket Back. Matching ♣'s, join Foreleg B to Basket Back. Glue Forelegs to Handle. Matching ▲'s, join Hind Leg A to Basket Front. Matching ♠'s, join Hind Leg B to Basket Front. Glue pom-poms to Head Front, Forelegs, and Hind Legs.

Basket Bottom (44 x 44 threads)

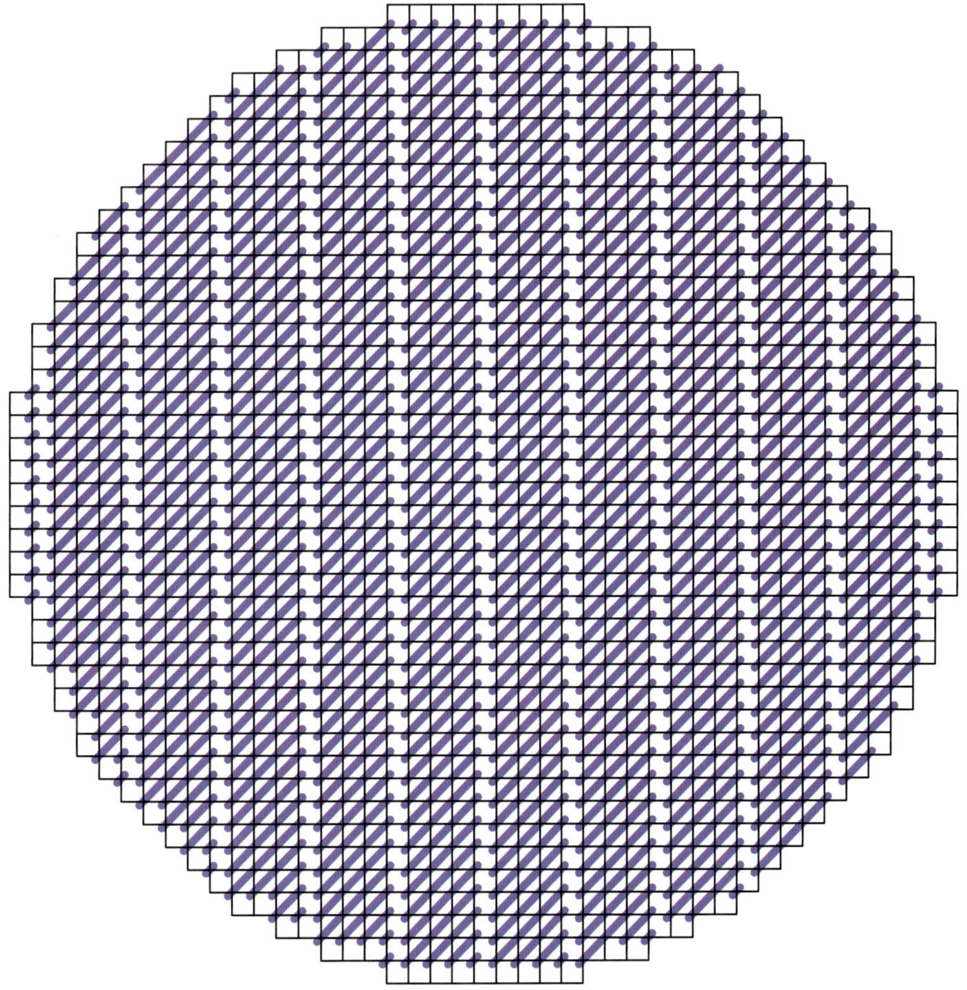

COLOR	
◪	lavender

COLOR
- white
- yellow
- lt pink
- lt green
- black
- *black

*Use 2 plies of yarn.

Muzzle (6 x 6 threads)

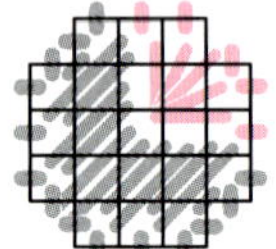

**Handle Support
(7 x 35 threads)
(cut 2)**

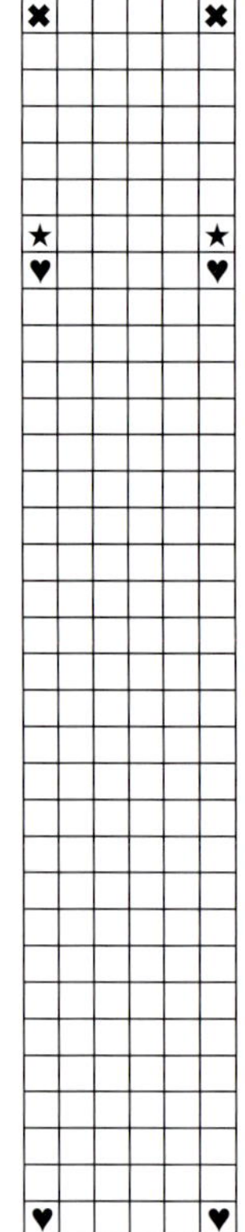

**Handle
(7 x 75 threads)
(stitch 2)**

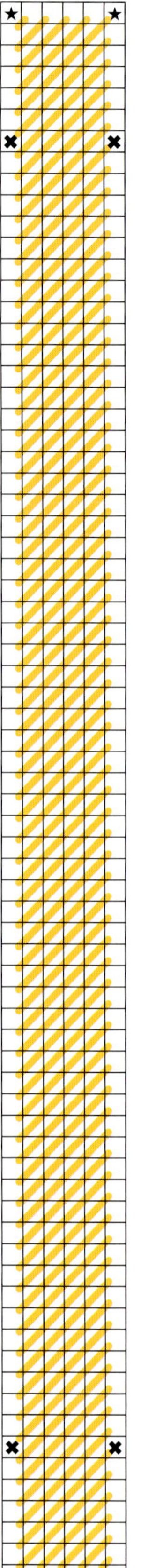

Head Front (44 x 35 threads)

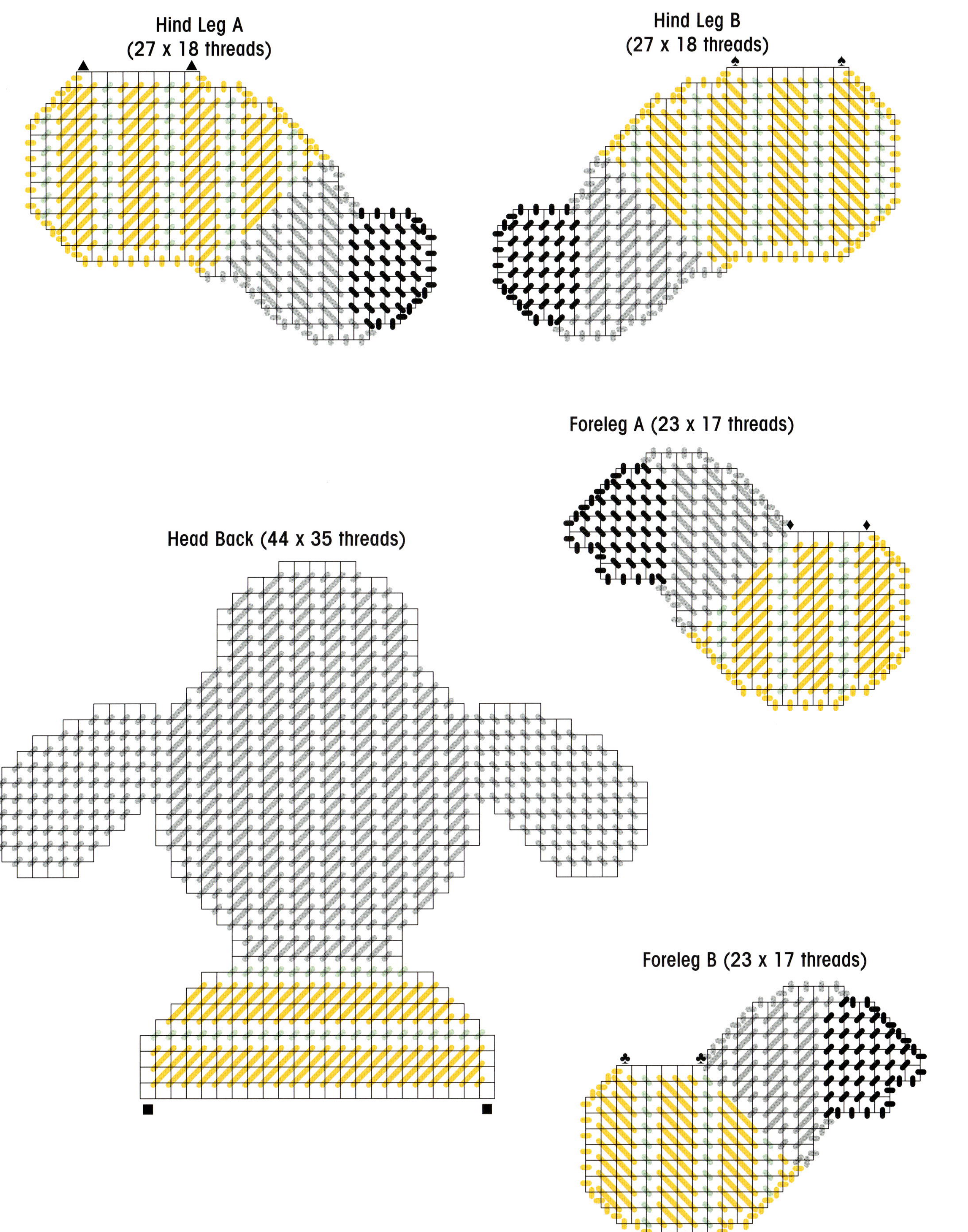

Hind Leg A
(27 x 18 threads)
Hind Leg B
(27 x 18 threads)
Foreleg A (23 x 17 threads)
Head Back (44 x 35 threads)
Foreleg B (23 x 17 threads)

Basket Front (68 x 28 threads)

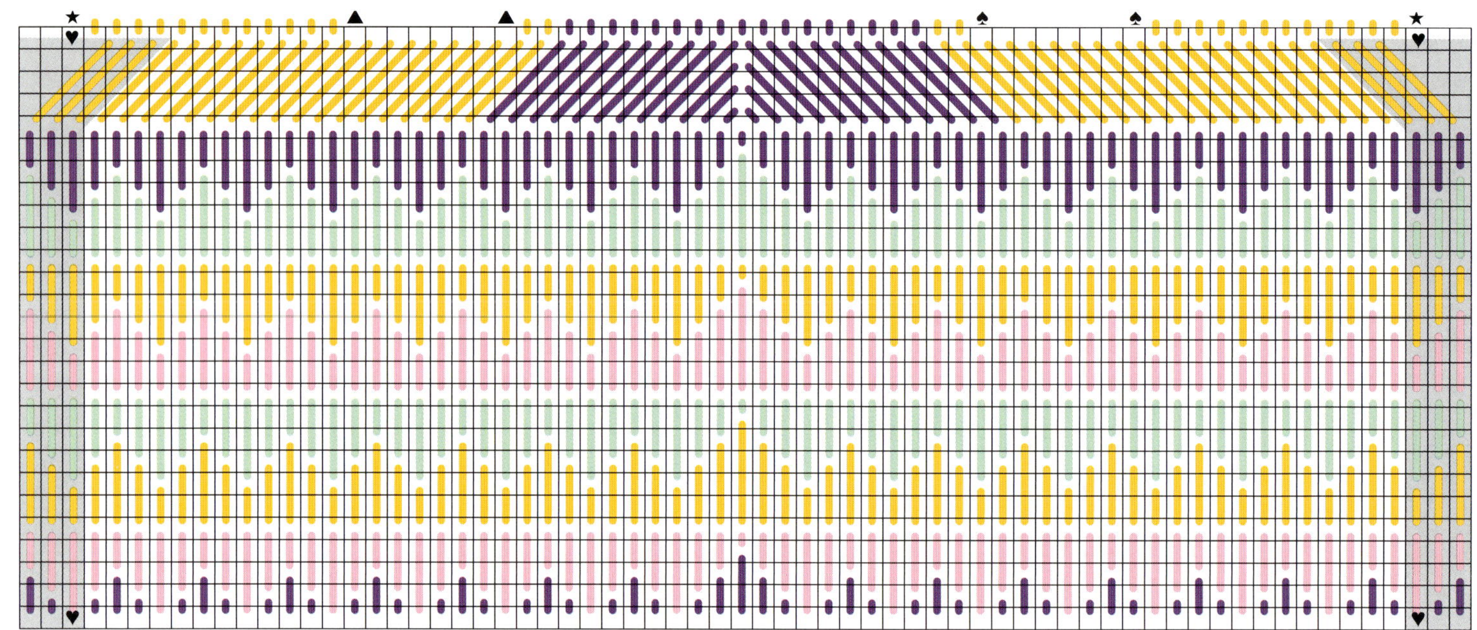

Basket Back (68 x 28 threads)

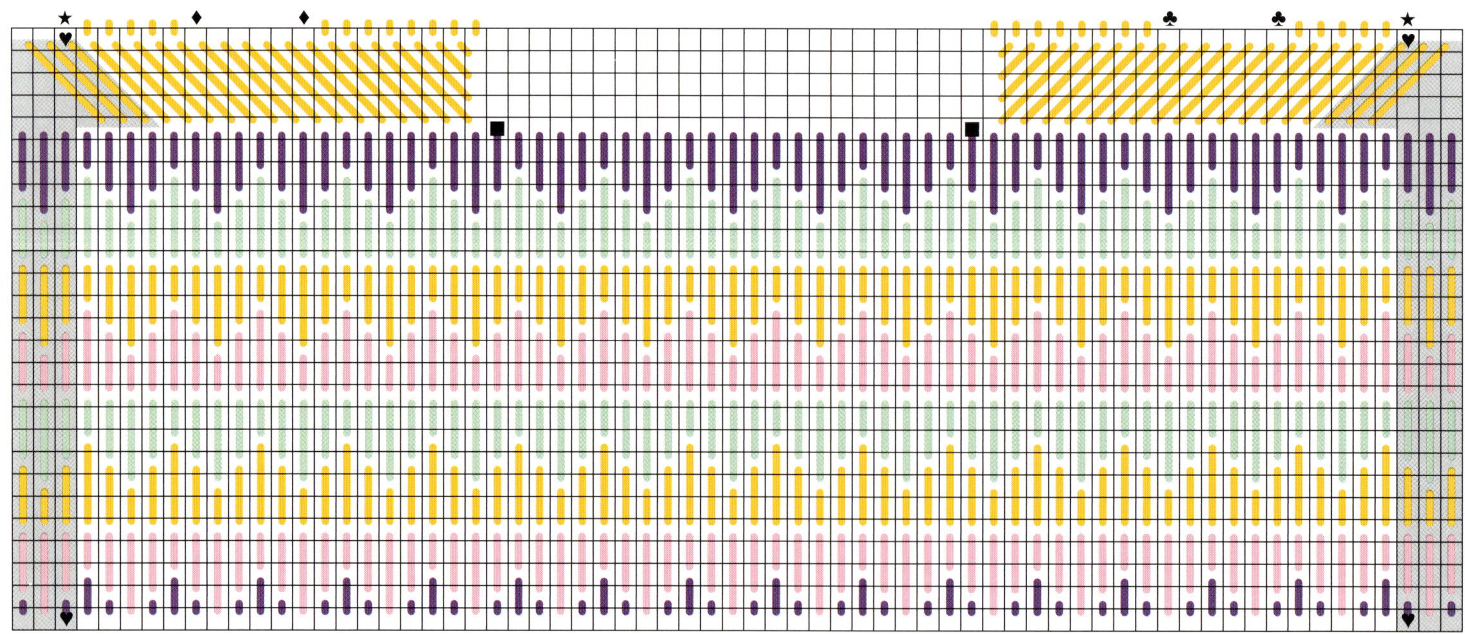

LOVABLE LAMBS

(Shown on page 15.)
Skill Level: Beginner
Size: 4³/₄"w x 5¹/₂"h x 4³/₄"d
(Fits a 4¹/₄"w x 5¹/₄"h x 4¹/₄"d boutique tissue box.)
Supplies: Worsted weight yarn (refer to color key), two 10¹/₂" x 13¹/₂" sheets of clear 7 mesh plastic canvas, #16 tapestry needle, and craft glue.
Stitches Used: Backstitch, French Knot, Gobelin Stitch, Overcast Stitch, and Tent Stitch.
Instructions: Follow charts to cut and stitch Tissue Box Cover pieces, working backstitches and French knots last. Using matching color overcast stitches, join Sides along long edges. Join Top to Sides. Glue Flowers to Sides.

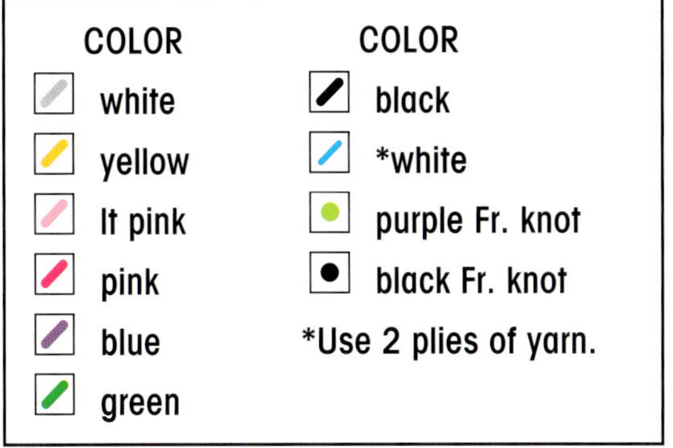

Flower (4 x 4 threads)
(stitch 12)

Top (32 x 32 threads)

Side (32 x 38 threads) (stitch 4)

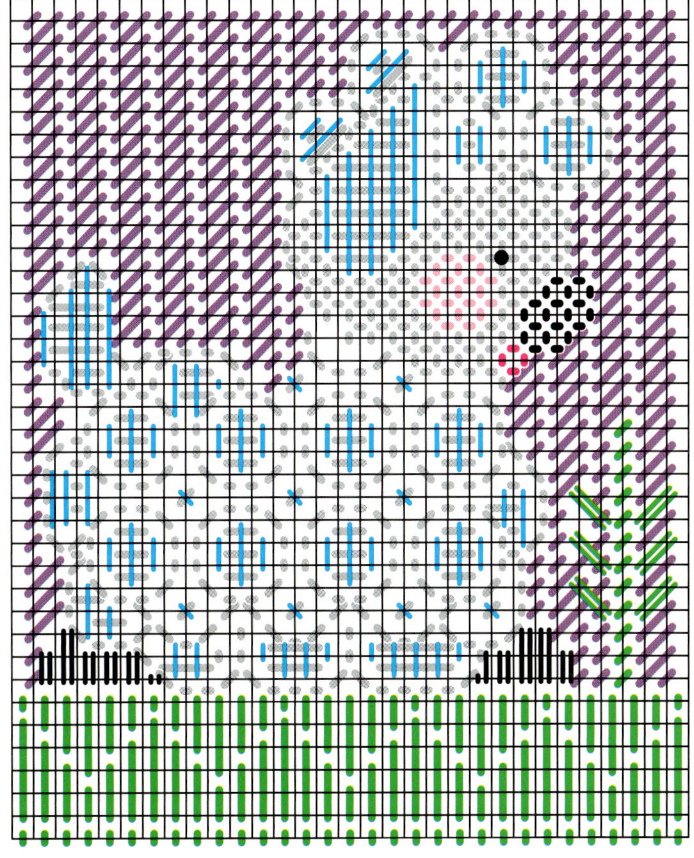

PRECIOUS CARRIAGE

(Shown on page 14.)
Skill Level: Intermediate
Size: 6$\frac{1}{2}$"w x 9$\frac{1}{2}$"h x 9"d
(Fits a 4$\frac{1}{4}$"w x 5$\frac{1}{4}$"h x 4$\frac{1}{4}$"d boutique tissue box.)
Supplies: Worsted weight yarn (refer to color keys), three 10$\frac{1}{2}$" x 13$\frac{1}{2}$" sheets of clear 7 mesh plastic canvas, #16 tapestry needle, and craft glue.
Stitches Used: Backstitch, Cross Stitch, French Knot, Gobelin Stitch, Overcast Stitch, Reversed Tent, Tent Stitch, and Turkey Loop Stitch.
Instructions: Follow charts to cut and stitch Tissue Box Cover pieces, working backstitches, French knots, and Turkey loops last. Matching ✖'s, use ecru overcast stitches to join Lace Front and Lace Back to Front and Back along blue shaded thread. Matching ✖'s, join Lace Side pieces to Sides along blue shaded thread. Matching ★'s, tack Baby to Pillow. Matching ■'s and working through three layers of canvas as necessary, join Pillow and Baby to Top. Matching ♥'s, join Blanket to Top along unworked edges of Blanket. Matching ♣'s, join Hood to Hood Back. Matching ♦'s, join Hood Lace to Hood. Matching ♠'s, join Hood and Hood Back to Top. Using matching color overcast stitches, join Front and Back to Sides. Join Top to Front, Back, and Sides. With wrong sides together, join Handle pieces. Tack Handle to Handle Sides A and B. With wrong sides together, join remaining Handle Side A to Handle Side B attached to Handle. With wrong sides together, join remaining Handle Side B to Handle Side A attached to Handle. Tack Handle Sides to Sides. Glue Flowers to Wheels. Glue Wheels to Sides. For hair, cut Turkey loops and separate yarn into plies. Cut an 8" length of green yarn. Tie yarn in a bow and trim ends. Glue bow to Baby.

<table>
<tr><td colspan="2">COLOR</td></tr>
<tr><td>◪</td><td>ecru</td></tr>
<tr><td>◪</td><td>green</td></tr>
<tr><td>●</td><td>yellow Fr. knot</td></tr>
</table>

Pillow (24 x 16 threads)

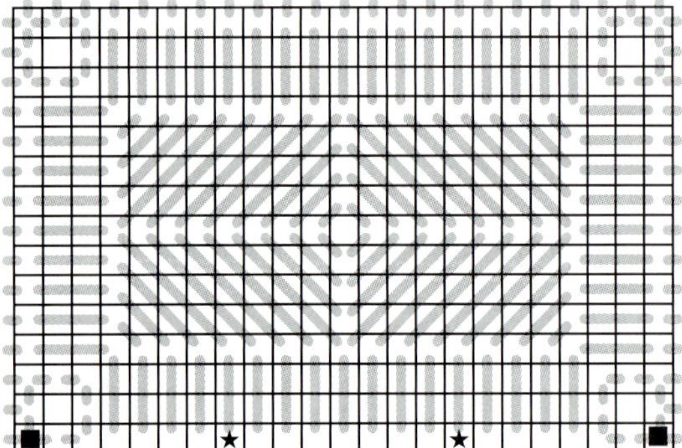

Blanket (28 x 23 threads)

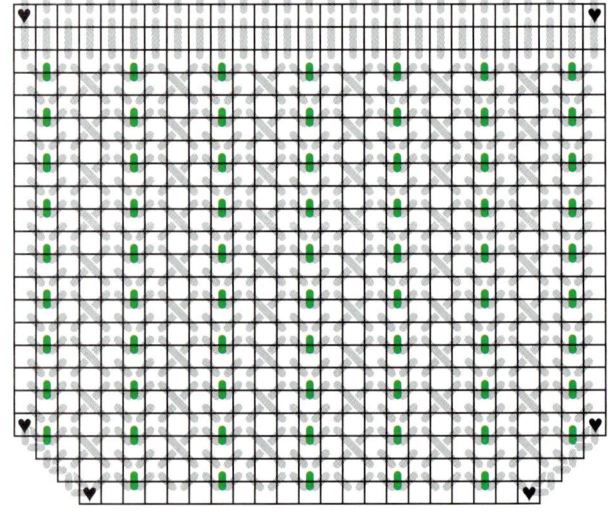

Side A/B (38 x 32 threads) (stitch 2)

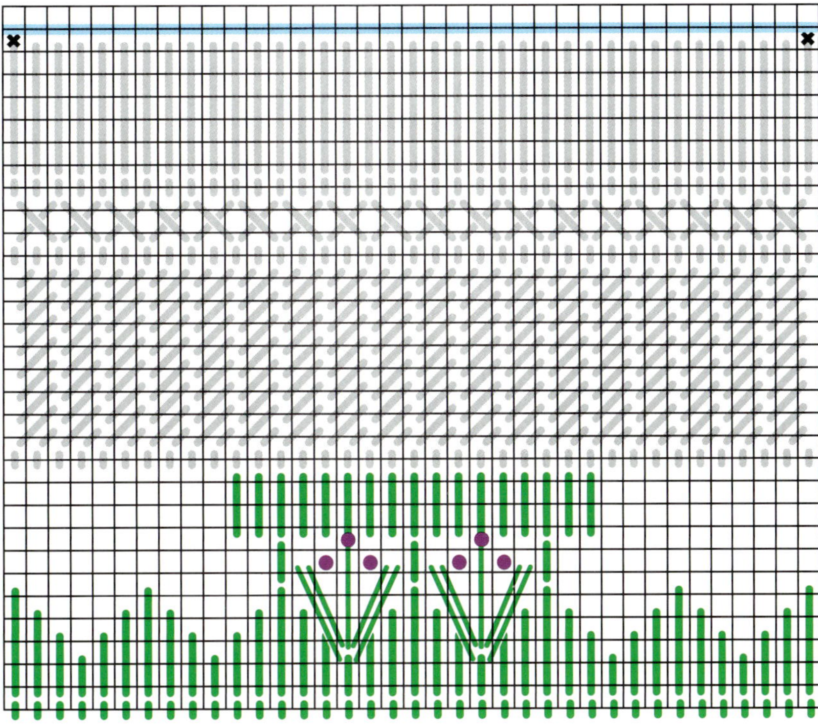

Front (32 x 32 threads)

Back (32 x 32 threads)

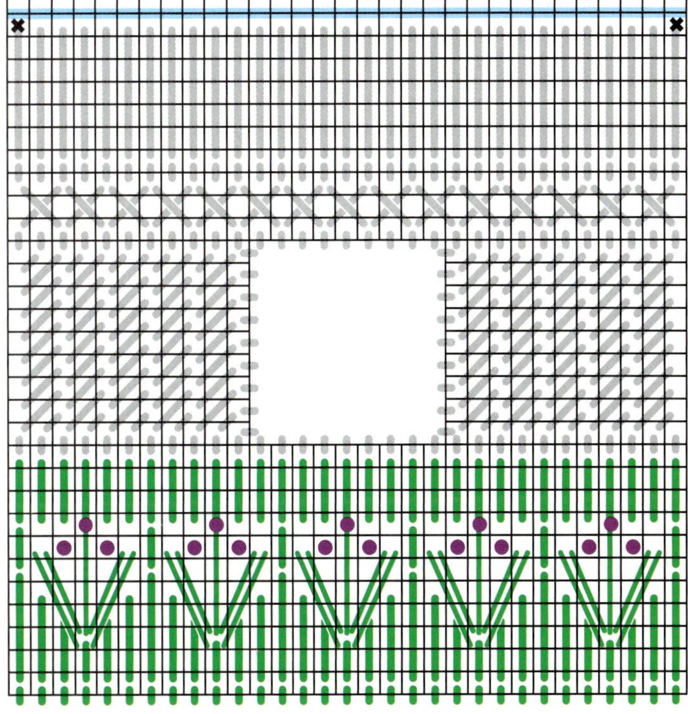

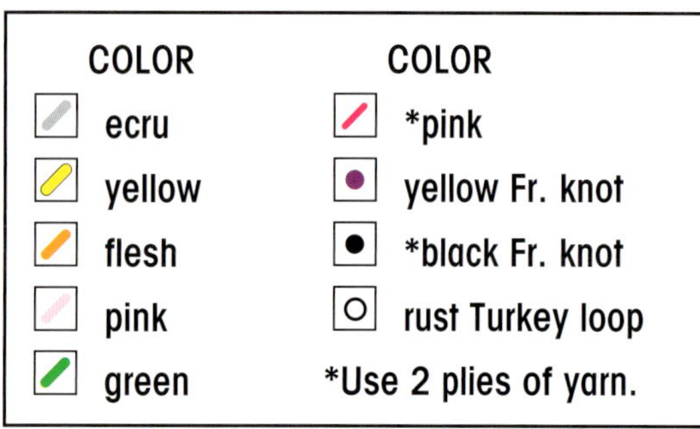

Wheel (20 x 20 threads) (stitch 4)

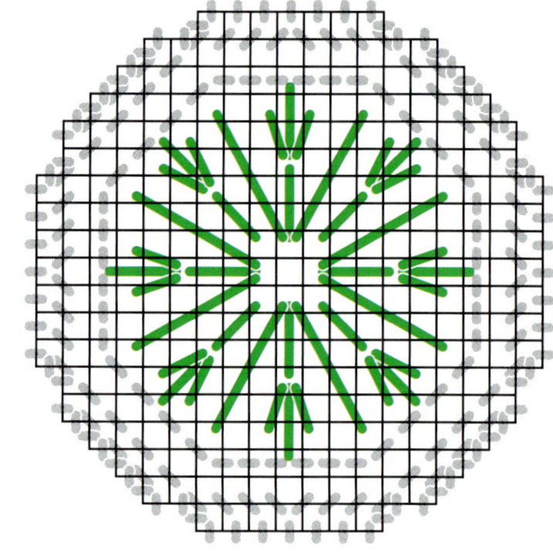

Lace Front/Back (32 x 6 threads)

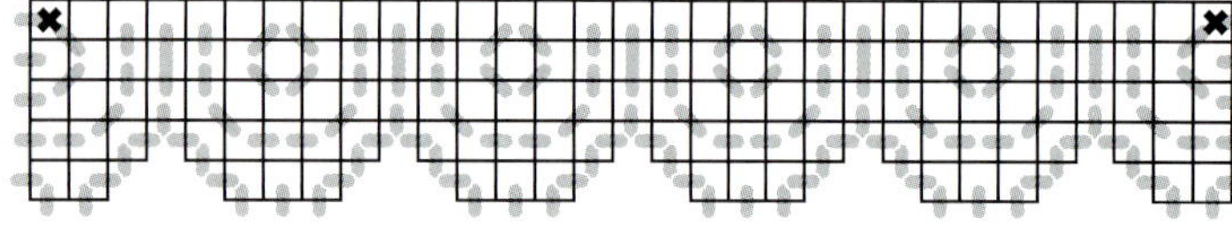

Lace Side (38 x 6 threads) (stitch 2)

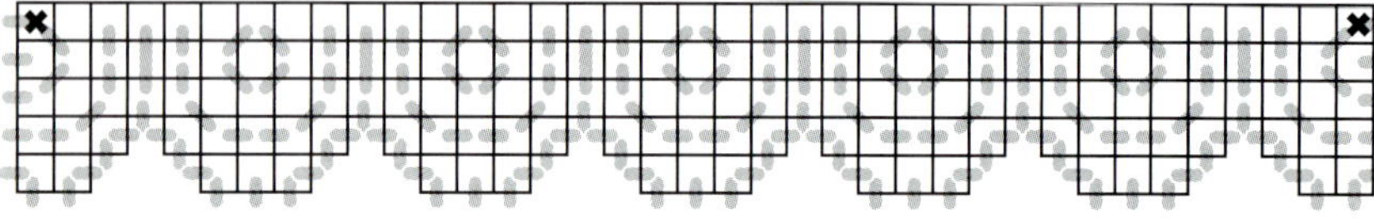

Flower (10 x 10 threads)
(stitch 4)

Top (32 x 38 threads)

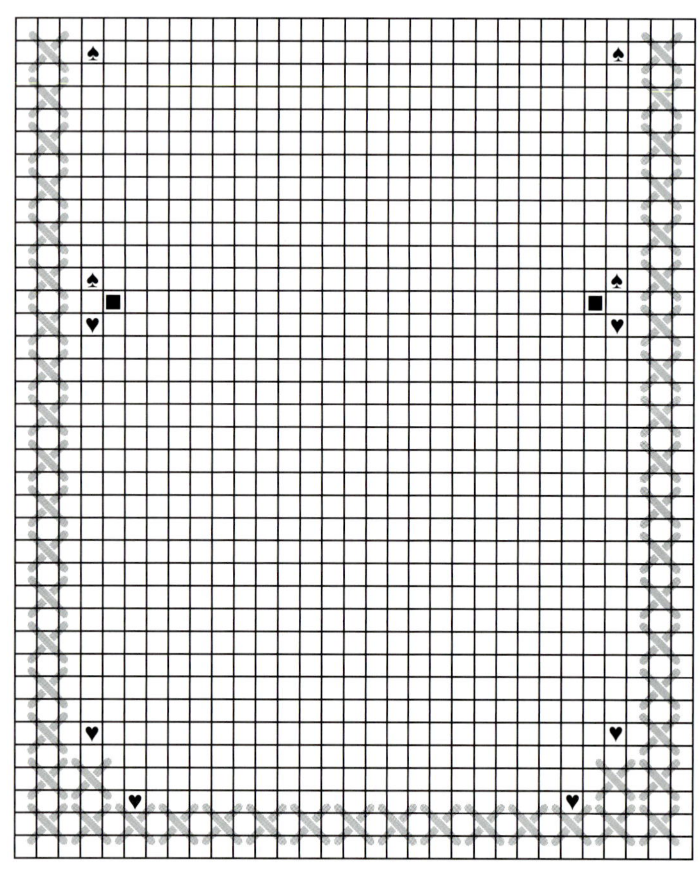

Baby (20 x 18 threads)

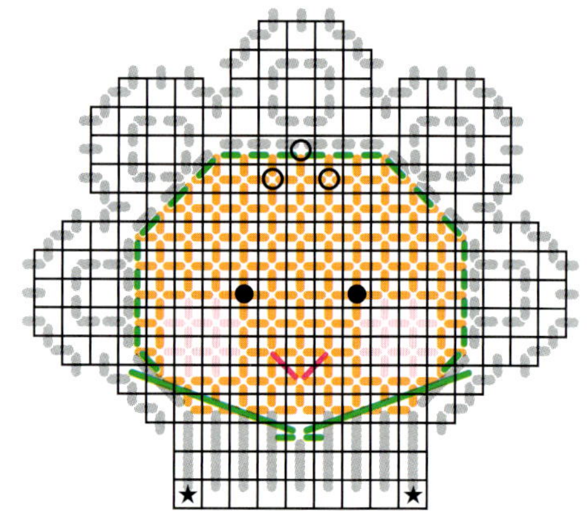

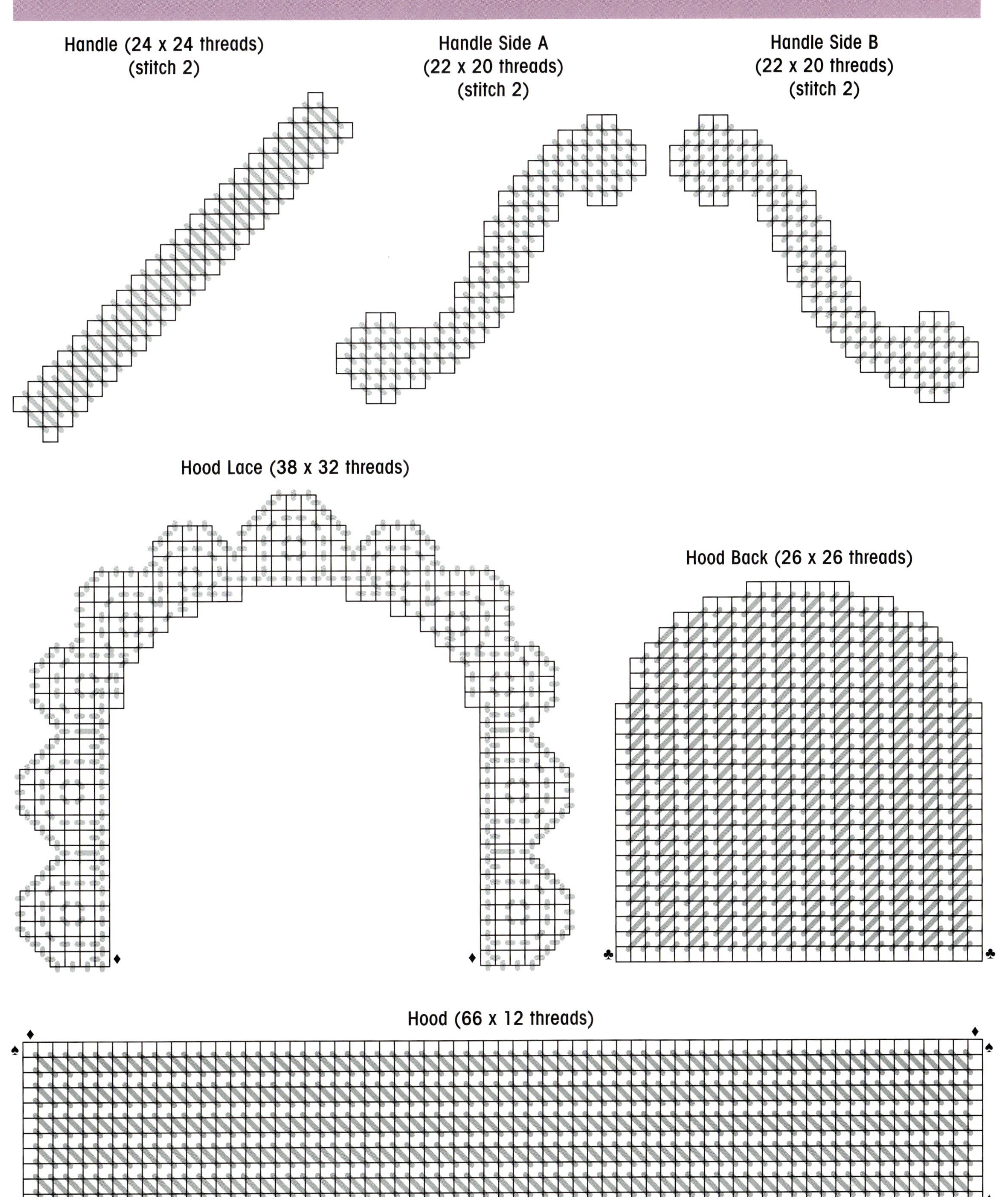

Handle (24 x 24 threads)
(stitch 2)

Handle Side A
(22 x 20 threads)
(stitch 2)

Handle Side B
(22 x 20 threads)
(stitch 2)

Hood Lace (38 x 32 threads)

Hood Back (26 x 26 threads)

Hood (66 x 12 threads)

KID STUFF

Kids love to fill their rooms with bright, fun accents, and we've got just the things! They can even make some of the projects themselves. Step back in time with this prehistoric desk set! The Jurassic creatures rule on a tissue box cover, a pencil holder, and a bookend.

FROM A TO Z

Encourage a youngster's love for reading with a set of these brightly colored bookend covers! Presented with several children's books, the clever projects are sure to stimulate a child's interest in learning about everything from apples to zebras!

Instructions on pages 70-71.

Instructions on page 73.

CLOWNING AROUND

We're not clowning around; kids will love these funny-face characters! The jovial set — a handy bookend, a switch plate cover, and a tissue topper — will brighten your child's room.

Instructions on pages 76-78.

PET KISSES

Make your child's day by giving them an easy-to-care-for pet! The cheeks of these whimsical dog and cat kisses can also be used to hold a special treat.

Instructions on pages 74-75.

LOVING HEARTS

Around every corner of this colorful photo cube, you'll find a heart-shaped cutout to frame a special snapshot. Having four of your favorite pictures on display together will be a heartwarming experience!

Instructions on page 72.

SO-SWEET TIC-TAC-TOE

Take the "board-om" out of rainy afternoons with this so-sweet tic-tac-toe game. There's even a storage box for the cookie O's and peppermint X's.

Instructions on page 79.

FUN FOR LUNCH

Carrying a lunch to school can be lots of fun with this colorful lunch sack! Stitched with bright designs, our unique tote features convenient handles that are just right for little ones to hold.

SPLASHES OF COLOR

Ideal for adding splashes of color to message boards or school lockers, these bright magnets are sure to catch your child's attention. The butterfly, dinosaurs, and rainbow are simple enough for kids to make themselves!

Instructions on page 65.

SPLASHES OF COLOR

(Shown on page 64.)

Skill Level: Beginner

Approx. Size: 3½"w x 3"h each

Supplies: Worsted weight yarn (refer to color key), one 10½" x 13½" sheet of white 7 mesh plastic canvas, #16 tapestry needle, magnetic strip, and craft glue.

Additional supplies for each Dinosaur Magnet: One black bead and black sewing thread and needle.

Stitches Used: Backstitch, Gobelin Stitch, Reversed Tent Stitch, and Tent Stitch.

Instructions: Follow chart to cut and stitch desired Magnet. Glue magnetic strip to back of Magnet. For Dinosaurs, sew bead to Magnet at ✪.

Butterfly Magnet
(27 x 27 threads)

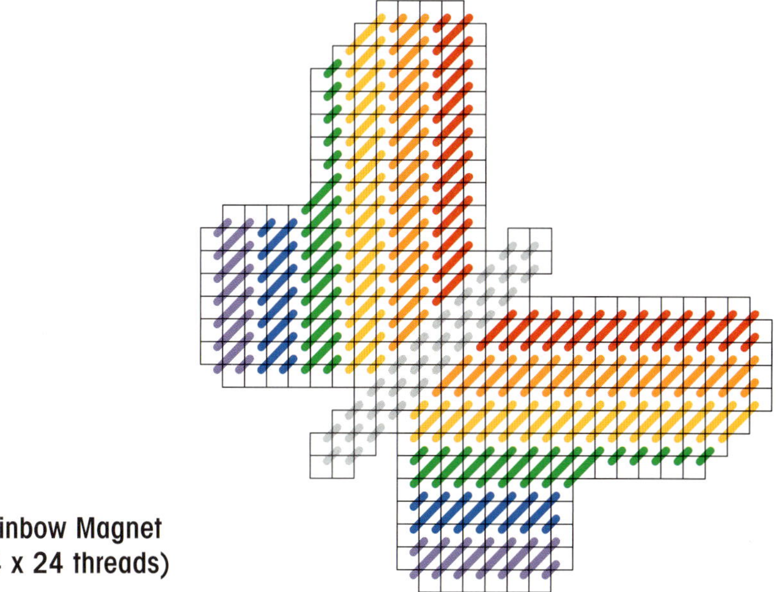

COLOR	
	white
	yellow
	orange
	red
	purple
	blue
	dk green

Rainbow Magnet
(24 x 24 threads)

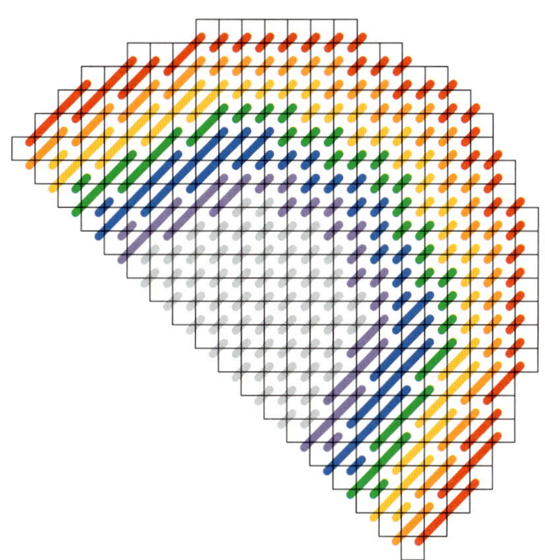

Purple Dinosaur Magnet
(20 x 22 threads)

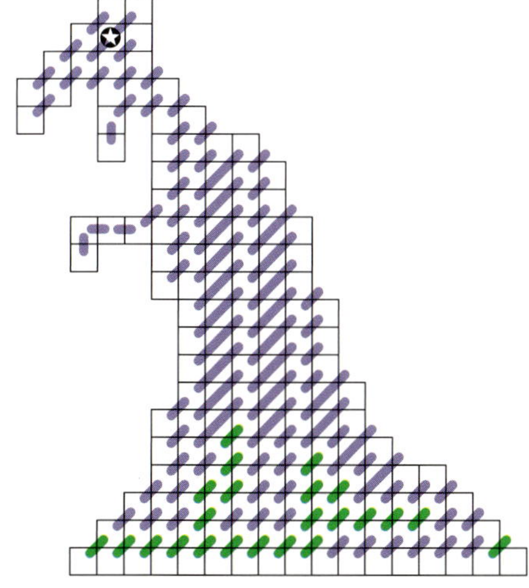

Orange Dinosaur Magnet
(23 x 20 threads)

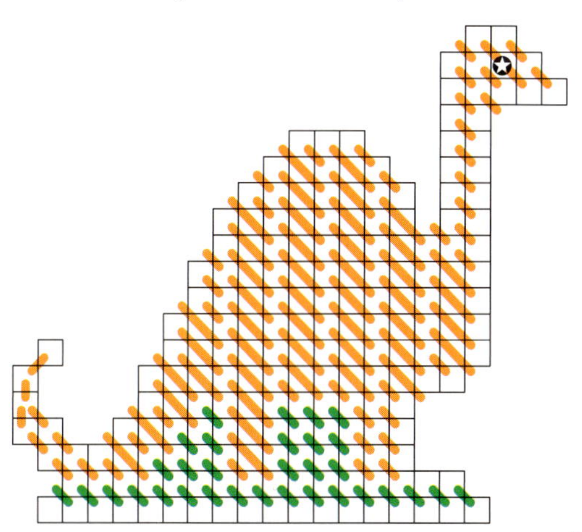

PENCIL CUP

(Shown on page 57.)
Skill Level: Beginner
Size: 5"w x 4¹/₄"h
Supplies: Worsted weight yarn (refer to color key), one 10¹/₂" x 13¹/₂" sheet of clear 7 mesh plastic canvas, #16 tapestry needle, and an empty 6 oz. frozen juice can.
Stitches Used: French Knot, Gobelin Stitch, Overcast Stitch, and Tent Stitch.
Instructions: Follow charts to cut and stitch Pencil Cup pieces, working French knot last and leaving blue shaded area unworked. Matching ■'s, work stitches in blue shaded area to join short edges of Side, forming a cylinder. Matching ♦'s, tack Dinosaur to Side. Slide stitched piece over juice can.

COLOR	
╱	yellow
╱	red
╱	purple
╱	green
╱	black
●	black Fr. knot

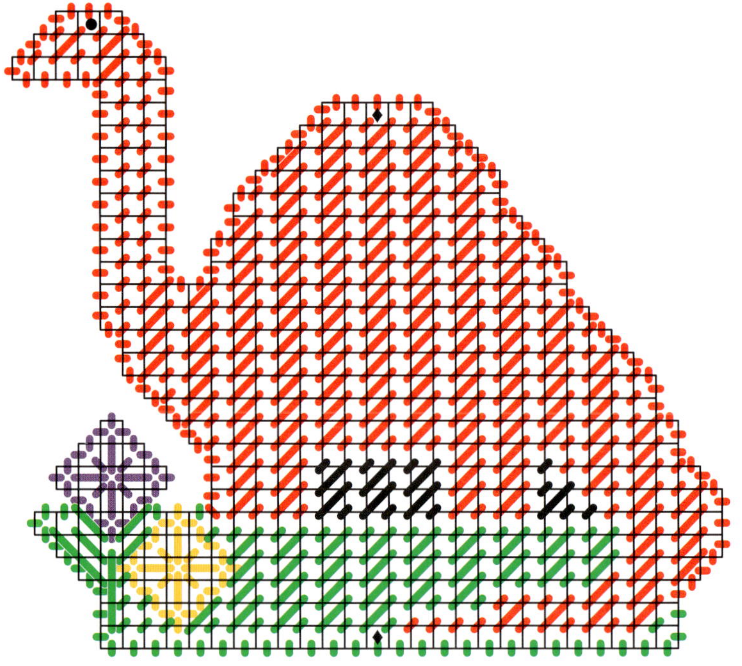

Dinosaur (33 x 29 threads)

Side (52 x 25 threads)

TISSUE BOX COVER

(Shown on page 56.)

Skill Level: Beginner

Size: 4$\frac{1}{2}$"w x 5$\frac{3}{4}$"h x 4$\frac{1}{2}$"d

(Fits a 4$\frac{1}{4}$"w x 5$\frac{1}{4}$"h x 4$\frac{1}{4}$"d boutique tissue box.)

Supplies: Worsted weight yarn (refer to color keys), two 10$\frac{1}{2}$" x 13$\frac{1}{2}$" sheets of clear 7 mesh plastic canvas, and #16 tapestry needle.

Stitches Used: Backstitch, French Knot, Gobelin Stitch, Overcast Stitch, and Tent Stitch.

Instructions: Follow charts to cut and stitch Tissue Box Cover pieces, working backstitches and French knots last. Using matching color overcast stitches and alternating Side A and Side B, join Sides along long edges. Using yellow overcast stitches, join Top to Sides. Tack Dragonflies, Flowers, and Buds to Sides.

COLOR	
	yellow
	red
	purple
	green
	brown
●	black Fr. knot

Top (30 x 30 threads)

Side A (30 x 38 threads) (stitch 2)

Side B (30 x 38 threads) (stitch 2)

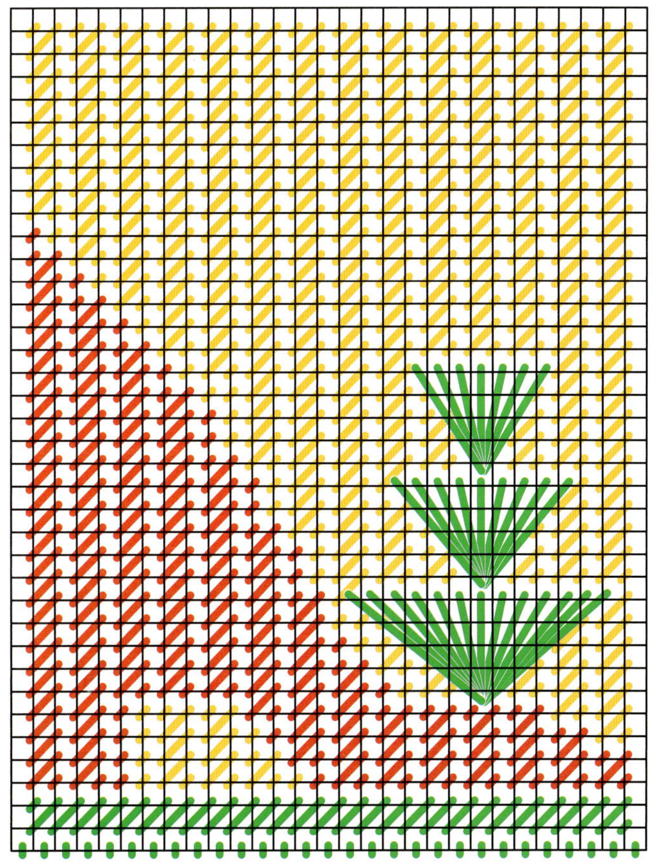

COLOR
- ⟋ orange
- ⟋ purple
- ⟋ lt blue

Bud (11 x 11 threads) (stitch 2)

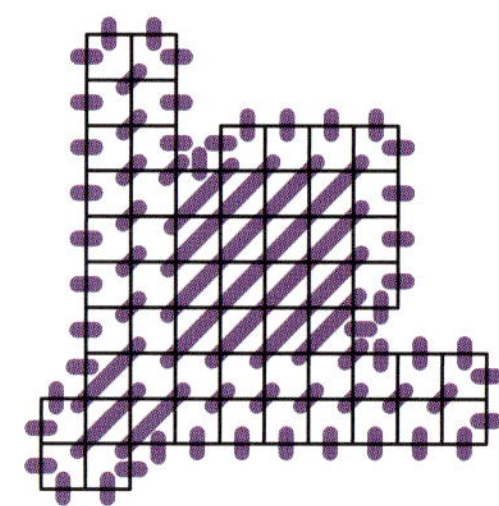

Dragonfly (19 x 19 threads) (stitch 2)

Flower (8 x 8 threads) (stitch 2)

BOOKEND COVER

(Shown on page 57.)

Skill Level: Beginner

Size: 6¹⁄₂"w x 8"h

Supplies: Worsted weight yarn (refer to color key), two 10¹⁄₂" x 13¹⁄₂" sheets of clear 7 mesh plastic canvas, #16 tapestry needle, and one 4³⁄₄"w x 5"h x 5¹⁄₄"d metal bookend.

Stitches Used: Backstitch, French Knot, Gobelin Stitch, Overcast Stitch, and Tent Stitch.

Instructions: Follow charts to cut and stitch Bookend Cover pieces, working backstitches and French knots last. Matching ▲'s, use green overcast stitches to join Front to Base. Stacking Front and Back, match ✖'s and join Foliage to Front and Back along unworked edges of Foliage. Tack Foliage to Base. Using matching color overcast stitches, join Front to Back along remaining unworked edges of Front.

Foliage (39 x 21 threads)

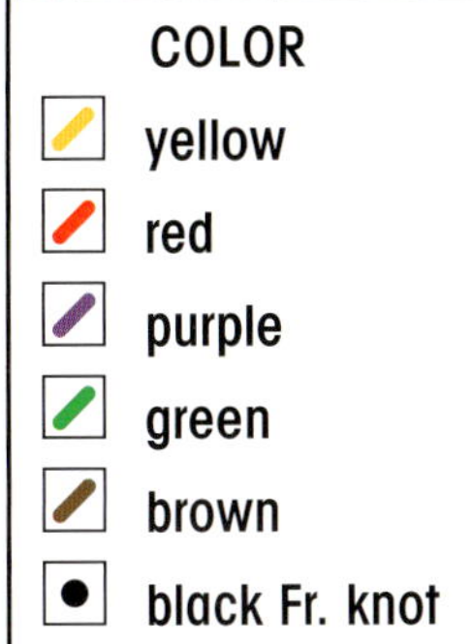

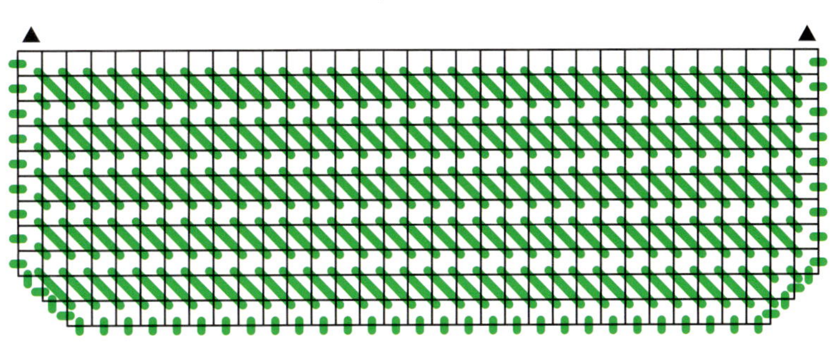

Front/Back (44 x 53 threads) (cut 2) (stitch 1)

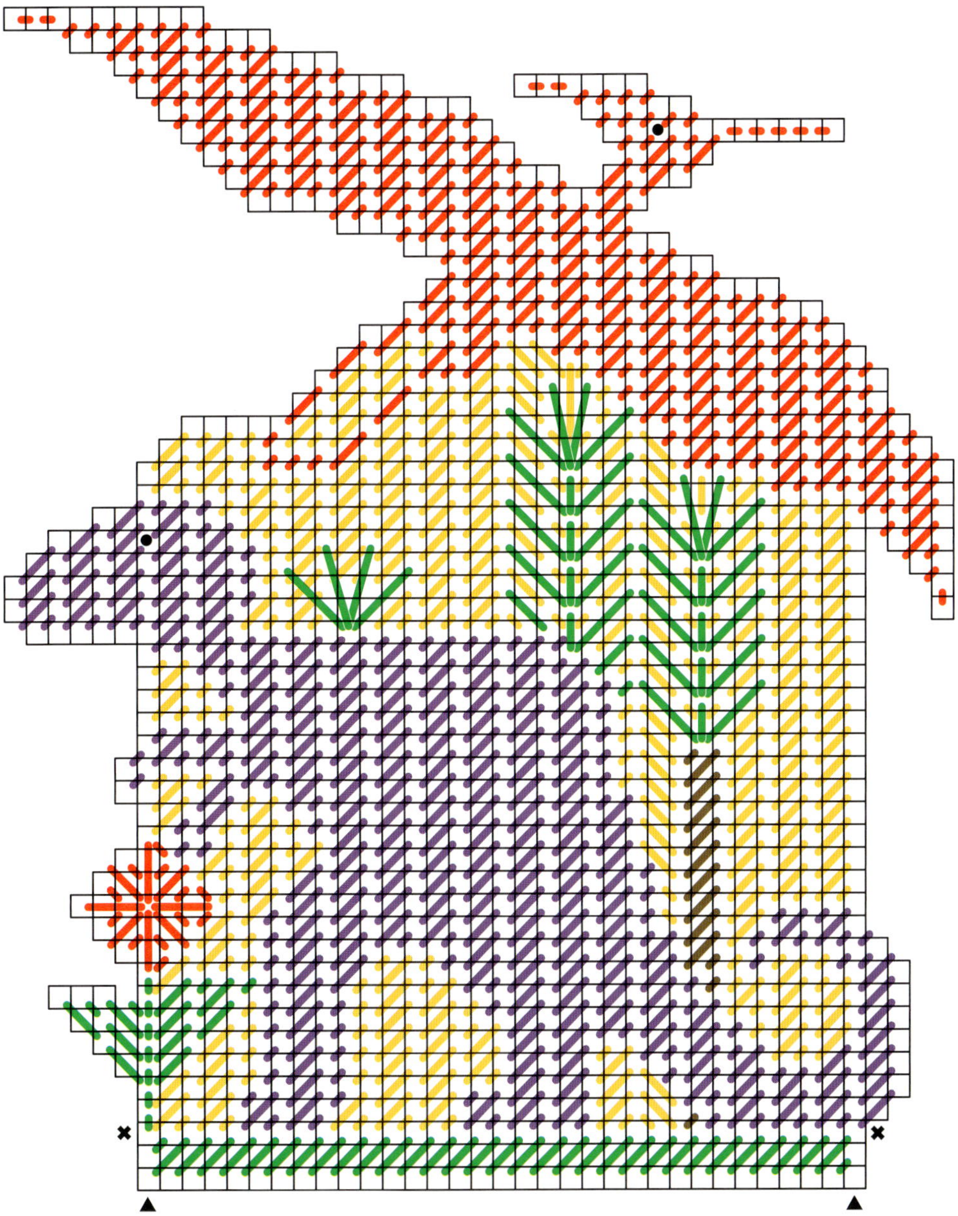

(Shown on page 58.)
Skill Level: Intermediate
Size: 5"w x 5¹/₂"h x 2"d
Supplies: Worsted weight yarn (refer to color key), two 10¹/₂" x 13¹/₂" sheets of clear 7 mesh plastic canvas, #16 tapestry needle, two 4³/₄"w x 5"h x 5¹/₄"d metal bookends, and craft glue.
Stitches Used: Backstitch, French Knot, Gobelin Stitch, Overcast Stitch, and Tent Stitch.
Instructions: Follow charts to cut and stitch Bookend Cover pieces, working backstitches and French knots last and leaving pink shaded area unworked. Matching ★'s, use green overcast stitches to join A Front to A Base. Tack Apple to A Front and A Base. Matching ✖'s, join Z Front to Z Base. With right sides up, match ▲'s and work stitches in pink shaded area through two thicknesses of canvas to join Zebra to Zebra Support. Matching ■'s, tack short edges of Zebra Support to Z Front. Tack Zebra to Z Base. Using matching color overcast stitches, join A Front to A Back. Join Z Front to Z Back. For tail, cut three 12" lengths and two 8" lengths of black yarn. Fold 12" lengths in half and secure fold with one 8" length. Braid for 2" and secure end of braid with remaining yarn length. Trim ends. Remove yarn securing fold. Glue folded end of tail to wrong side of Zebra.

A Front/Back
(34 x 37 threads) (cut 2) (stitch 1)

Apple (28 x 24 threads)

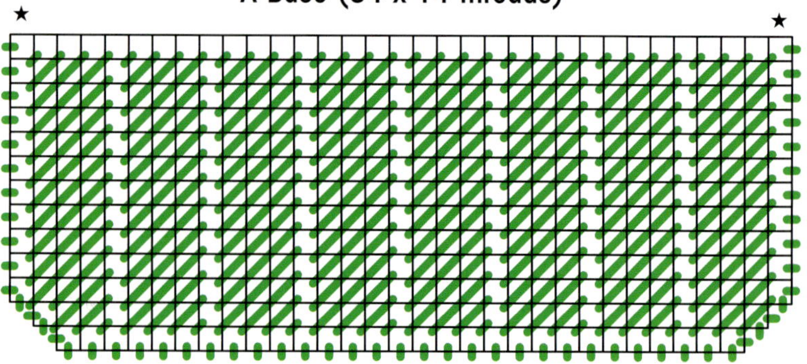

A Base (34 x 14 threads)

Z Front/Back
(34 x 37 threads) (cut 2) (stitch 1)

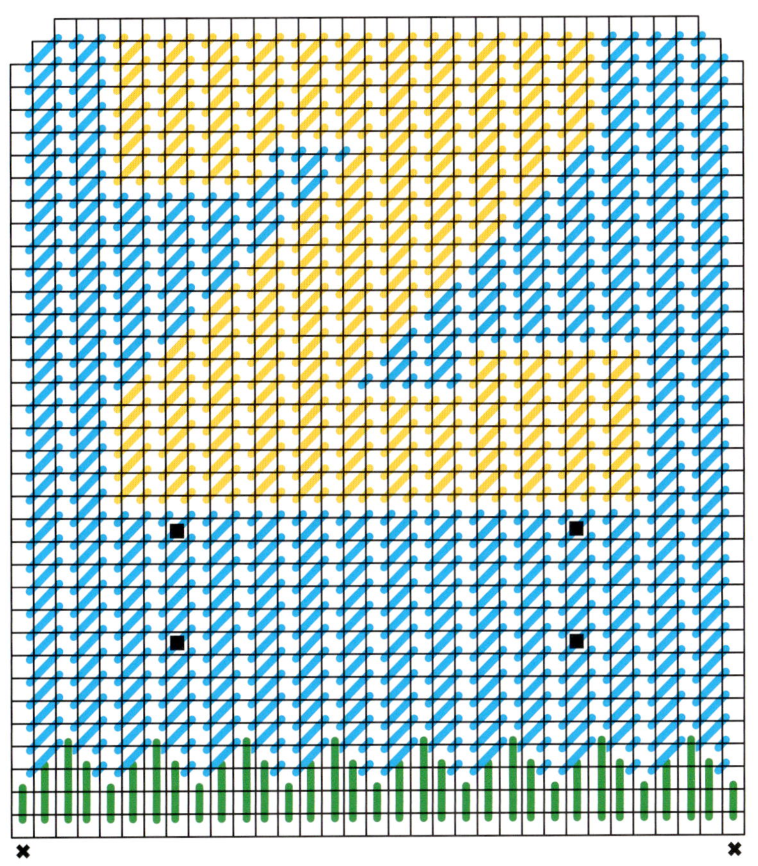

COLOR

╱	white - 4 yds
╱	yellow - 9 yds
╱	red - 4 yds
╱	blue - 20 yds
╱	green - 12 yds
╱	black - 5 yds
•	yellow Fr. knot
●	black Fr. knot

Zebra (27 x 25 threads)

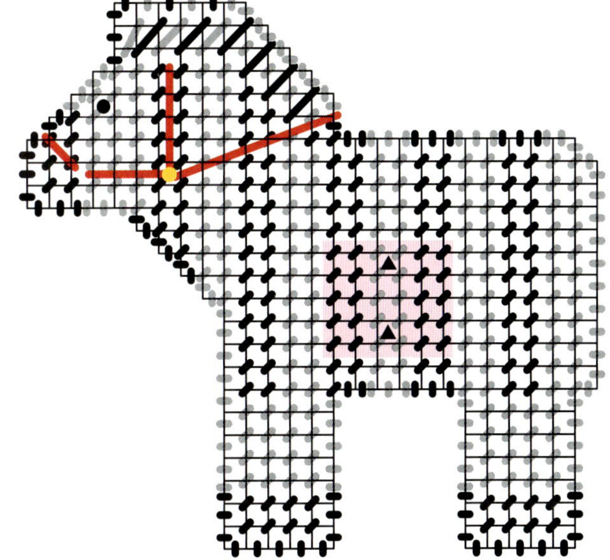

Z Base (34 x 14 threads)

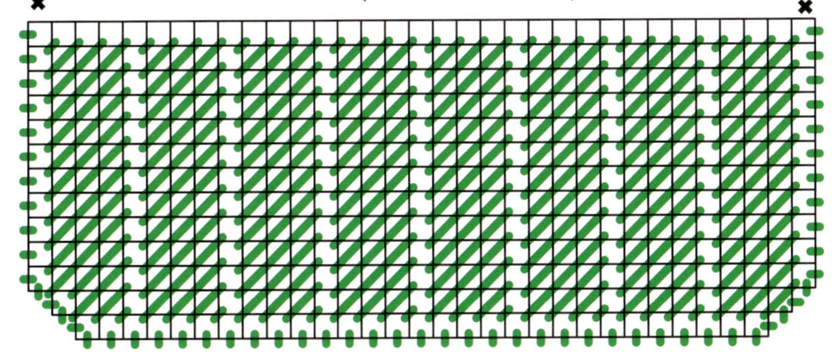

Zebra Support (24 x 7 threads)

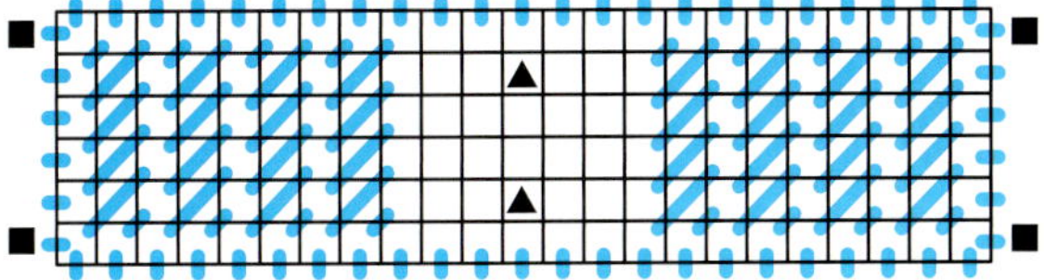

(Shown on page 61.)
Skill Level: Beginner
Size: 3¹/₂"w x 3¹/₂"h x 3¹/₂"d
Supplies: Worsted weight yarn (refer to color key), one 10¹/₂" x 13¹/₂" sheet of clear 7 mesh plastic canvas, and #16 tapestry needle.
Stitches Used: Overcast Stitch, Reversed Tent Stitch, and Tent Stitch.
Instructions: Follow charts to cut and stitch Photo Cube pieces. Using red overcast stitches, join red Side to blue Side. Using blue overcast stitches, join blue Side to yellow Side. Using yellow overcast stitches, join yellow Side to green Side. Using green overcast stitches, join green Side to red Side. Using yarn color to match Sides, join Top to Sides. For Inner Cube, cut six 21 x 21 thread pieces of plastic canvas. Join pieces to form a cube. Insert Inner Cube into Photo Cube to hold photos in place.

COLOR	
⬜	yellow
⬜	red
⬜	blue
⬜	green
⬜	Side color

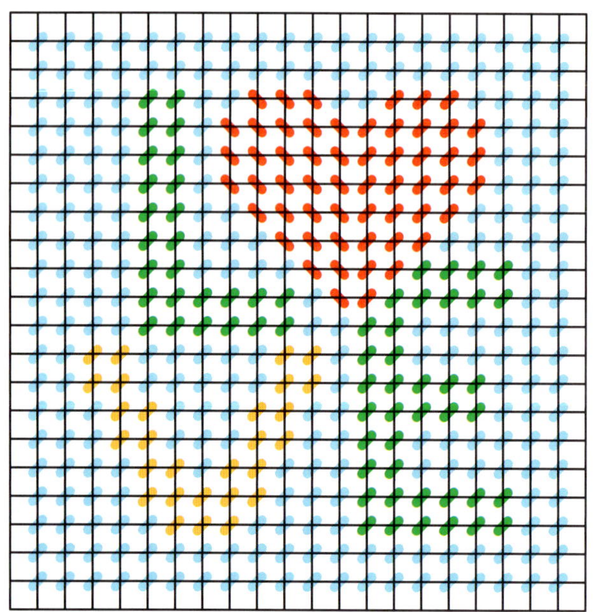

Top (22 x 22 threads)

Side (22 x 22 threads) (stitch 4)
Stitch one Side with yellow, one with red, one with blue, and one with green.

LITTLE MISS SUNSHINE

(Shown on page 59.)
Skill Level: Beginner
Size: 11 1/2"w x 16 1/2"h
Supplies: Worsted weight yarn (refer to color key), two 10 1/2" x 13 1/2" sheets of white 7 mesh plastic canvas, #16 tapestry needle, thirteen 1/2" yellow pom-poms, one 3/4" pink pom-pom, and craft glue.
Stitches Used: Gobelin Stitch, Overcast Stitch, Smyrna Cross Stitch, and Tent Stitch.
Instructions: Follow charts to cut and stitch Barrette Holder pieces, leaving pink shaded areas unworked. For Tails, cut two 4 x 43 thread pieces and one 4 x 34 thread piece of plastic canvas. Work stitches in pink shaded areas to join Tail pieces to Sunburst. Tack Daisy pieces to Sunburst. Glue yellow pom-poms to centers of Daisies. Glue pink pom-pom to center of Sunburst.

COLOR
- white
- dk yellow
- pink
- black

Daisy (10 x 10 threads) (cut 13)

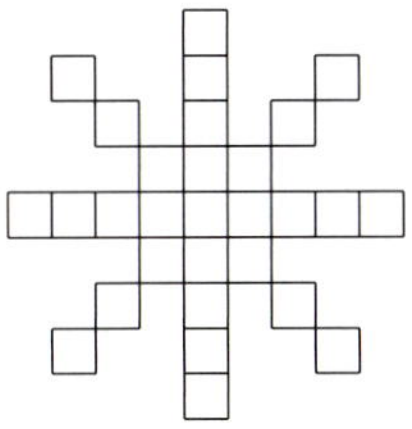

Sunburst (70 x 70 threads)

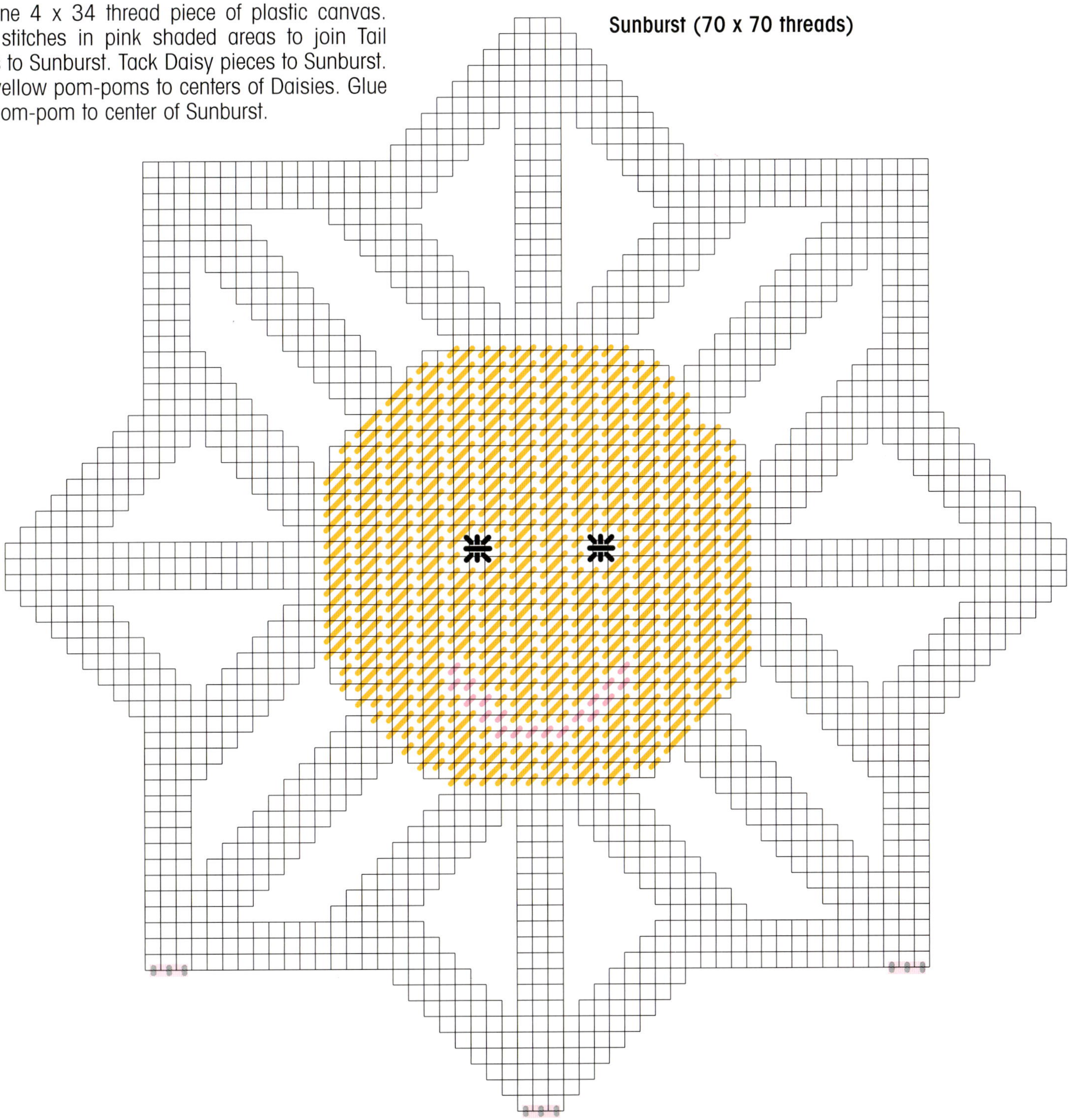

CAT KISS

(Shown on page 61.)
Skill Level: Intermediate
Size: 3½"w x 4"h
Supplies: Worsted weight yarn (refer to color key), one 10½" x 13½" sheet of clear 7 mesh plastic canvas, #16 tapestry needle, and craft glue.
Stitches Used: French Knot, Gobelin Stitch, Overcast Stitch, Scotch Stitch, and Tent Stitch.

Instructions: Follow charts to cut and stitch Cat Kiss pieces, working French knots last. Matching ▲'s, use lt tan overcast stitches to join Top to Back along unworked edges of Top. Matching ■'s, join Bottom to Back along unworked edges of Bottom. Matching ✖'s, tack Bow to Back. Matching ★'s and ♦'s, join Arm to Back along unworked threads. Tack Arm to Bow. Cut an 8" length of blue yarn. Tie bow and glue to Top; trim ends.

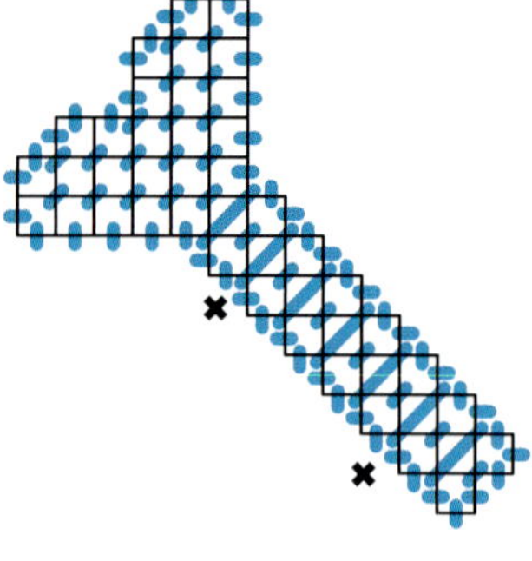

Bow (14 x 14 threads)

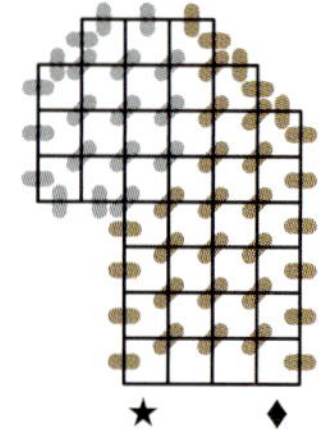

Arm (7 x 9 threads)

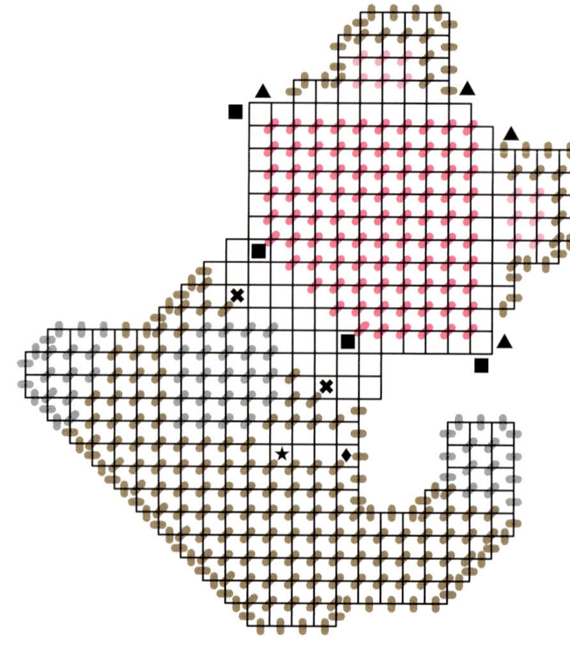

Back (26 x 28 threads)

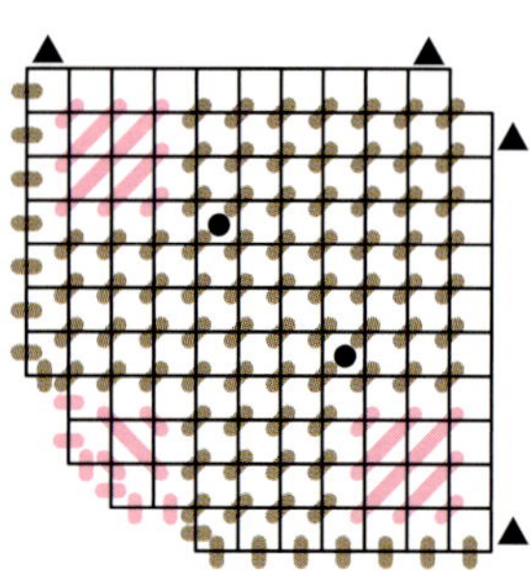

Top (12 x 12 threads)

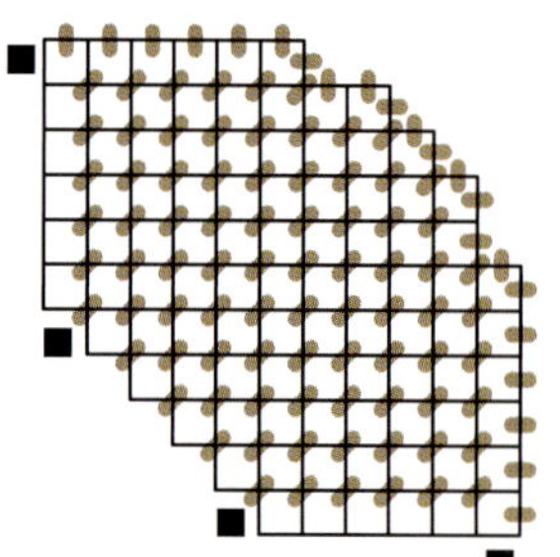

Bottom (12 x 12 threads)

DOG KISS

(Shown on page 61.)
Skill Level: Intermediate
Size: 3¹/₂"w x 4"h
Supplies: Worsted weight yarn (refer to color key), one 10¹/₂" x 13¹/₂" sheet of clear 7 mesh plastic canvas, #16 tapestry needle.
Stitches Used: Backstitch, French Knot, Overcast Stitch, Scotch Stitch, and Tent Stitch.
Instructions: Follow charts to cut and stitch Dog Kiss pieces, working backstitches and French knots last. Matching ▲'s, use lt tan overcast stitches to join Top to Back along unworked edges of Top. Matching ✖'s, join Bottom to Back along unworked edges of Bottom. Matching ★'s, join Arm to Back along unworked threads. Tack Arm to Back.

COLOR	
	white
	red
	pink
	lt tan
	brown
	black
●	black Fr. knot

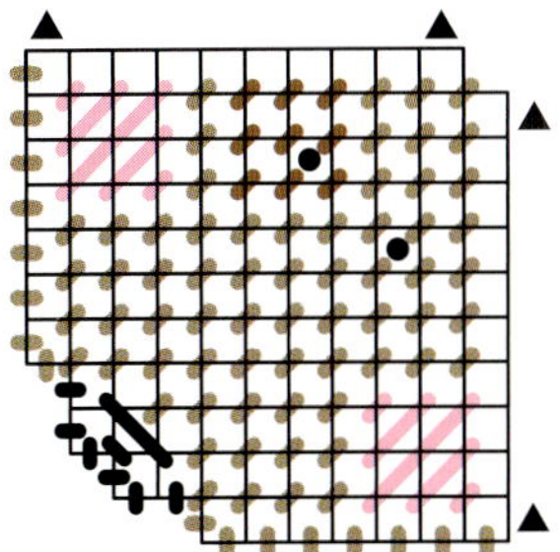

Top (12 x 12 threads)

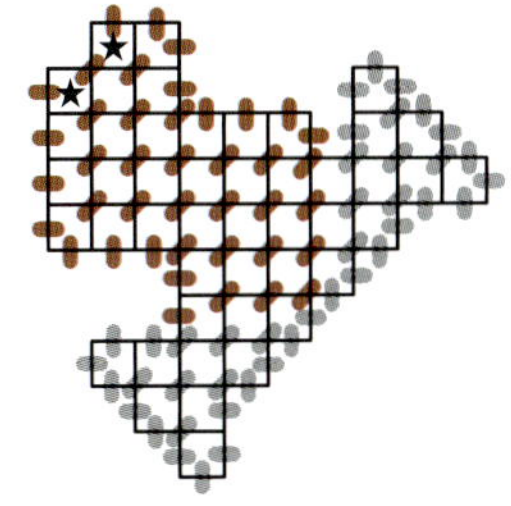

Arm (11 x 11 threads)

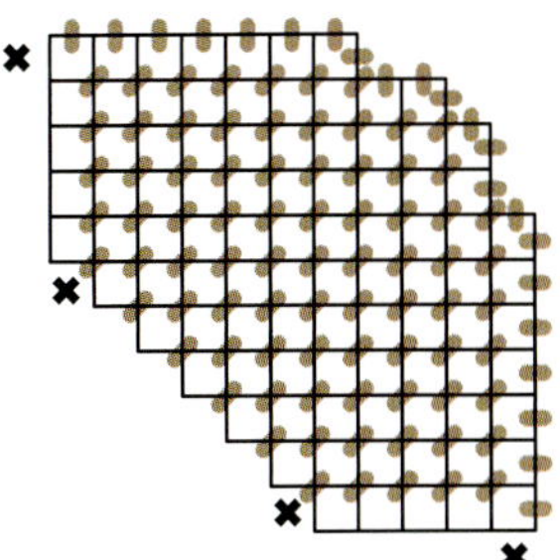

Bottom (12 x 12 threads)

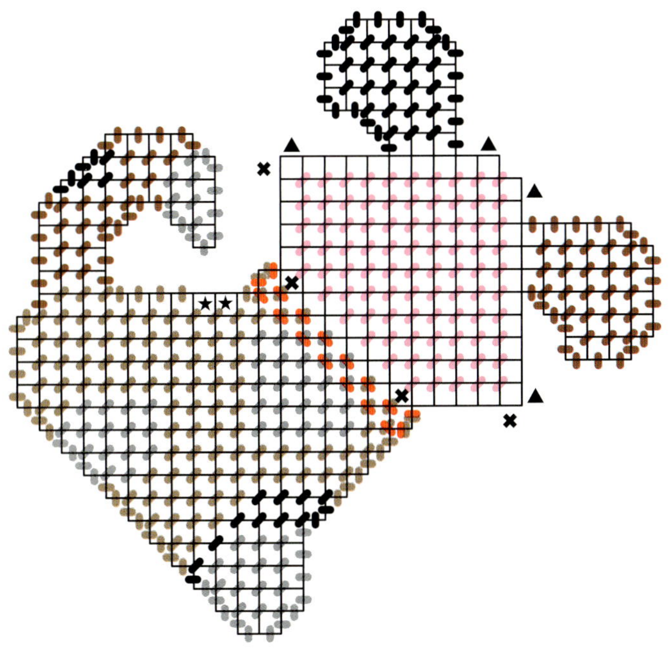

Back (30 x 28 threads)

BOOKEND COVER

(Shown on page 60.)

Skill Level: Beginner

Size: 6¼"w x 8¾"h

Supplies: Worsted weight yarn (refer to color key), two 10½" x 13½" sheets of clear 7 mesh plastic canvas, #16 tapestry needle, three wooden toothpicks, three ¾" yellow pom-poms, one 4¾"w x 5"h x 5¼"d metal bookend, and craft glue.

Stitches Used: Backstitch, Cross Stitch, French Knot, Gobelin Stitch, Overcast Stitch, Reversed Tent Stitch, and Tent Stitch.

Instructions: Follow charts to cut and stitch Bookend Cover pieces, working backstitches and French knots last. For Back, cut a 34 x 32 thread piece of plastic canvas. Back is not worked. Matching ★'s, use black overcast stitches to join Clown Support to Front. Matching ✖'s, use yellow overcast stitches to join Base to Front. Join Back to Front along unworked edges of Front. Using matching color overcast stitches, join each Flag to a toothpick. Glue toothpicks to wrong side of Bookend Cover. Attach Clown to Clown Support by inserting unworked points of Clown Support into slits in Clown. Glue pom-poms to Clown.

**Bookend Cover
Clown (32 x 32 threads)**

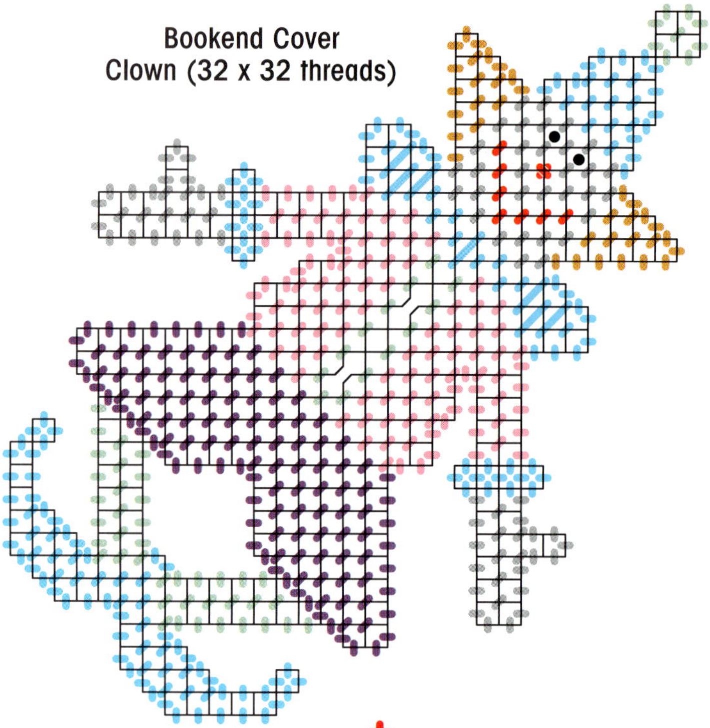

**Bookend Cover
Front (38 x 48 threads)**

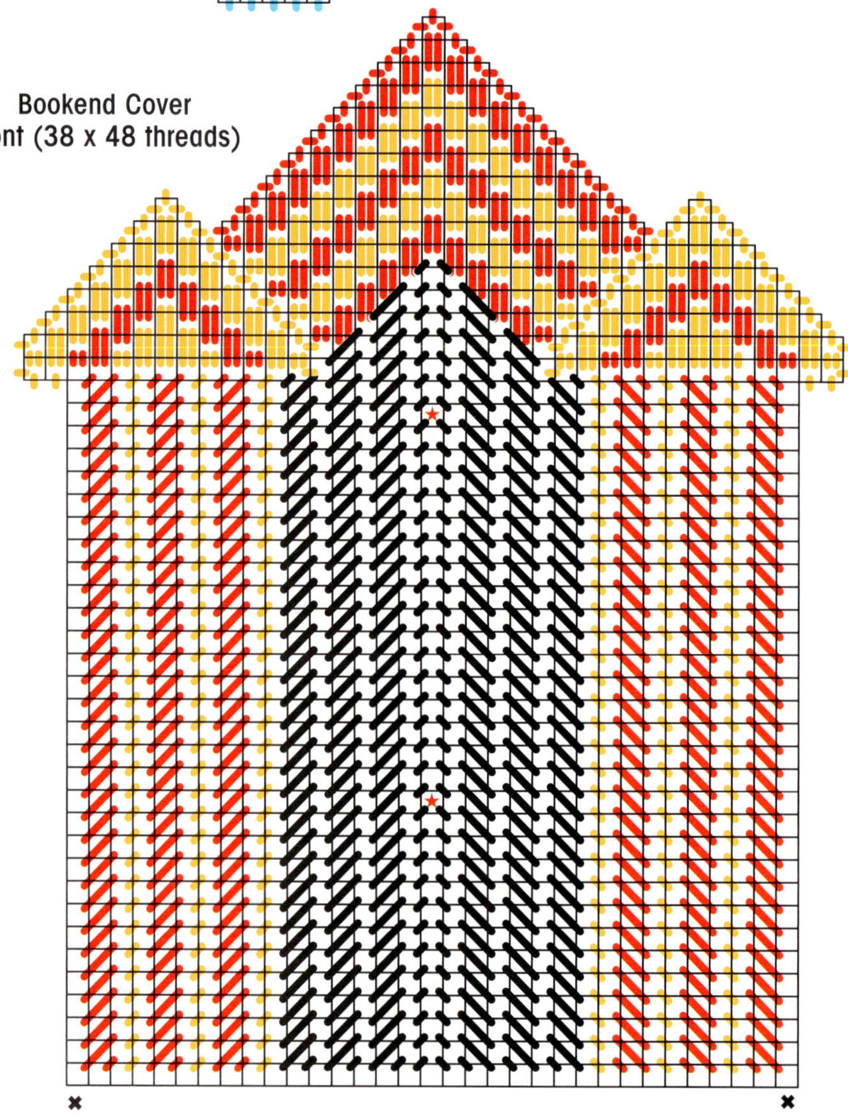

**Bookend Cover
Clown Support (13 x 13 threads)**

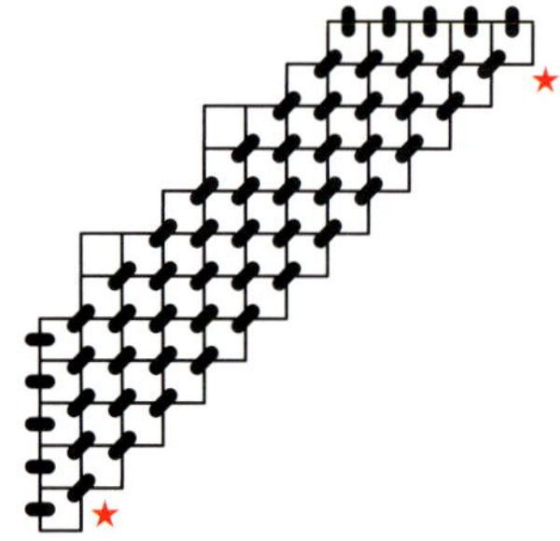

**Bookend Cover
Flags (8 x 10 threads) (stitch 3)
Stitch one with pink, one with lt blue,
and one with lt green.**

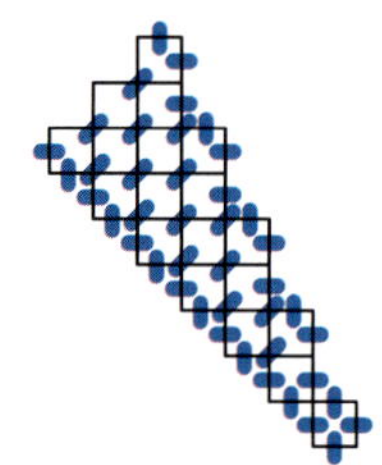

COLOR

- white - 2 yds
- yellow - 16 yds
- dk yellow - 1 yd
- pink - 3 yds
- red - 13 yds
- purple - 2 yds
- lt blue - 3 yds
- lt green - 3 yds
- black - 10 yds
- Flag color
- *black Fr. knot

*Use 2 plies of yarn.

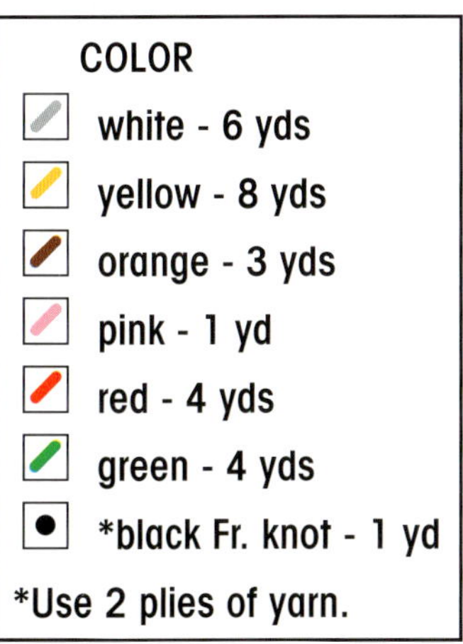

Bookend Cover
Base (34 x 19 threads)

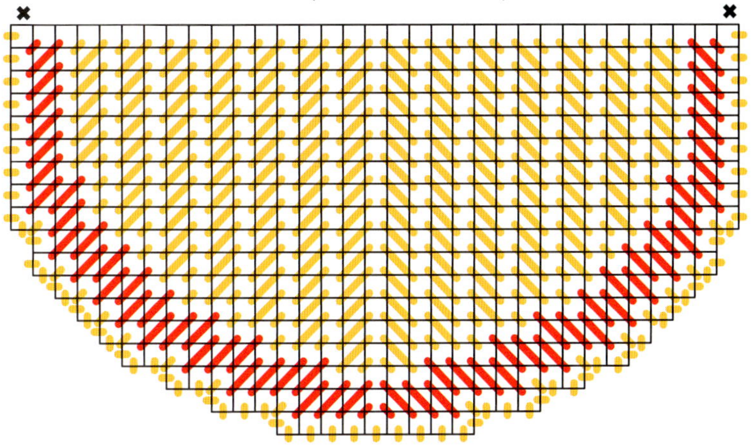

SWITCH PLATE COVER

(Shown on page 60.)
Skill Level: Beginner
Size: 5 1/4"w x 9 1/4"h
Supplies: Worsted weight yarn (refer to color key), one 10 1/2" x 13 1/2" sheet of clear 7 mesh plastic canvas, #16 tapestry needle, four 1" yellow pom-poms, and craft glue.
Stitches Used: French Knot, Gobelin Stitch, Overcast Stitch, Reversed Tent Stitch, and Tent Stitch.
Instructions: Follow chart to cut and stitch Switch Plate Cover piece, working French knots last. Glue pom-poms to Switch Plate Cover.

Switch Plate Cover
(34 x 55 threads)

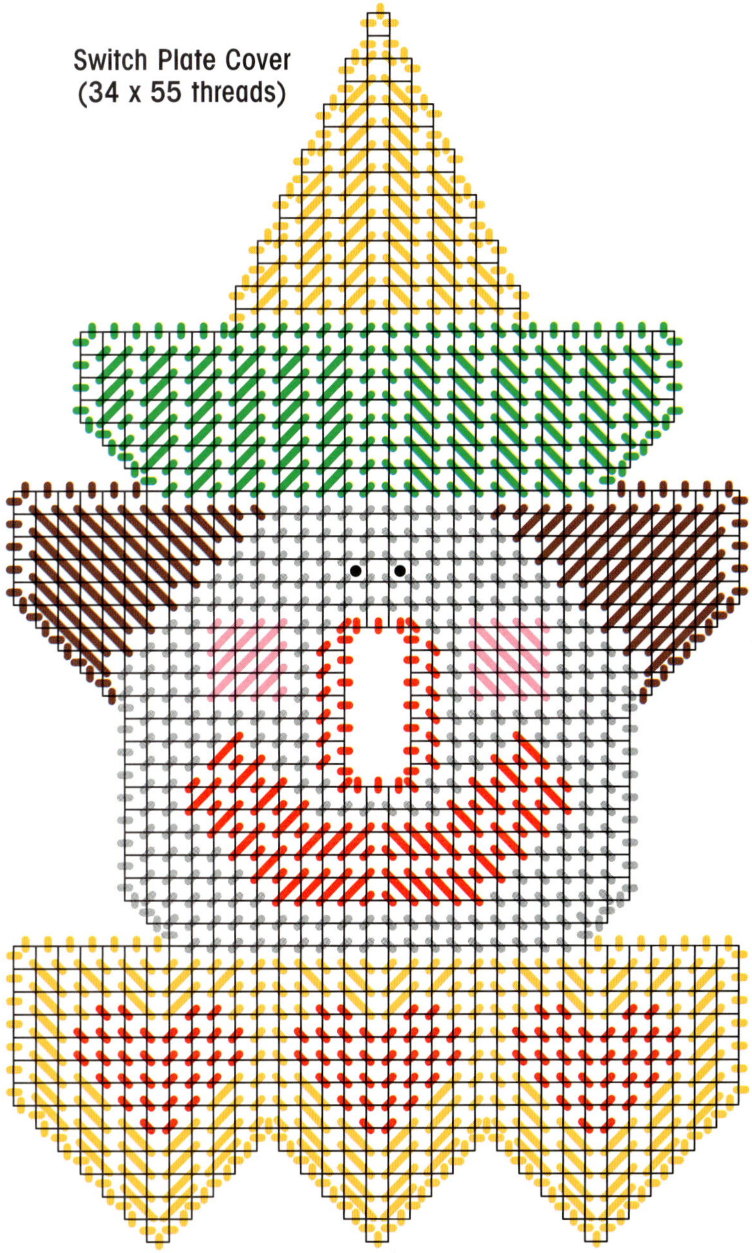

COLOR

- white - 6 yds
- yellow - 8 yds
- orange - 3 yds
- pink - 1 yd
- red - 4 yds
- green - 4 yds
- *black Fr. knot - 1 yd

*Use 2 plies of yarn.

TISSUE BOX COVER

(Shown on page 60.)

Skill Level: Beginner

Size: 6³/₄"w x 5³/₄"h x 6³/₄"d

(Fits a 4¹/₄"w x 5¹/₄"h x 4¹/₄"d boutique tissue box.)

Supplies: Worsted weight yarn (refer to color key), two 10¹/₂" x 13¹/₂" sheets of clear 7 mesh plastic canvas, #16 tapestry needle, sixteen 1" yellow pom-poms, four ³/₄" red pom-poms, and craft glue.

Stitches Used: French Knot, Gobelin Stitch, Overcast Stitch, Reversed Tent Stitch, and Tent Stitch.

Instructions: Follow charts to cut and stitch Tissue Box Cover pieces, working French knots last. Matching ✖'s, use yellow overcast stitches to join Collars to Sides along unworked threads. Tack Brims to Sides. Using matching color overcast stitches, join Sides along long edges. Using green overcast stitches, join Top to Sides. Glue yellow pom-poms to Collars and Sides. For nose, glue one red pom-pom to each Side.

COLOR	
	white - 18 yds
	yellow - 25 yds
	dk yellow - 10 yds
	orange - 6 yds
	pink - 2 yds
	red - 15 yds
	purple - 25 yds
	green - 30 yds
●	*black Fr. knot - 1 yd

*Use 2 plies of yarn.

Brim (16 x 4 threads) (stitch 4)

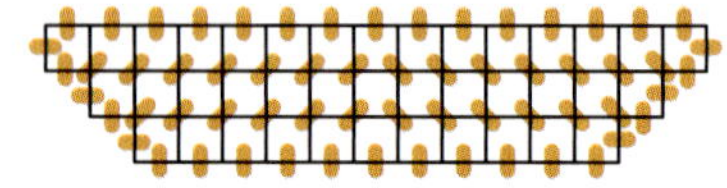

Collar (30 x 9 threads) (stitch 4)

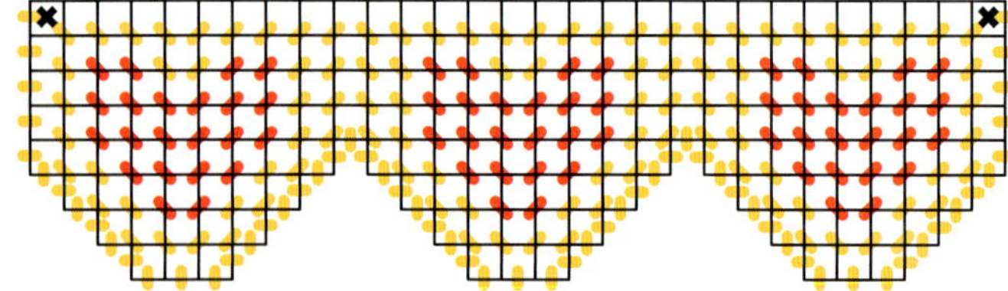

Top (30 x 30 threads)

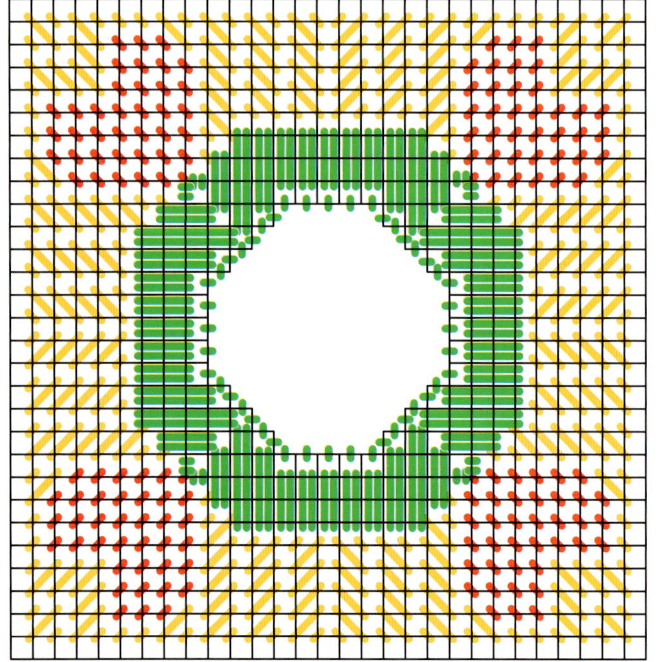

Side (30 x 38 threads) (stitch 4)

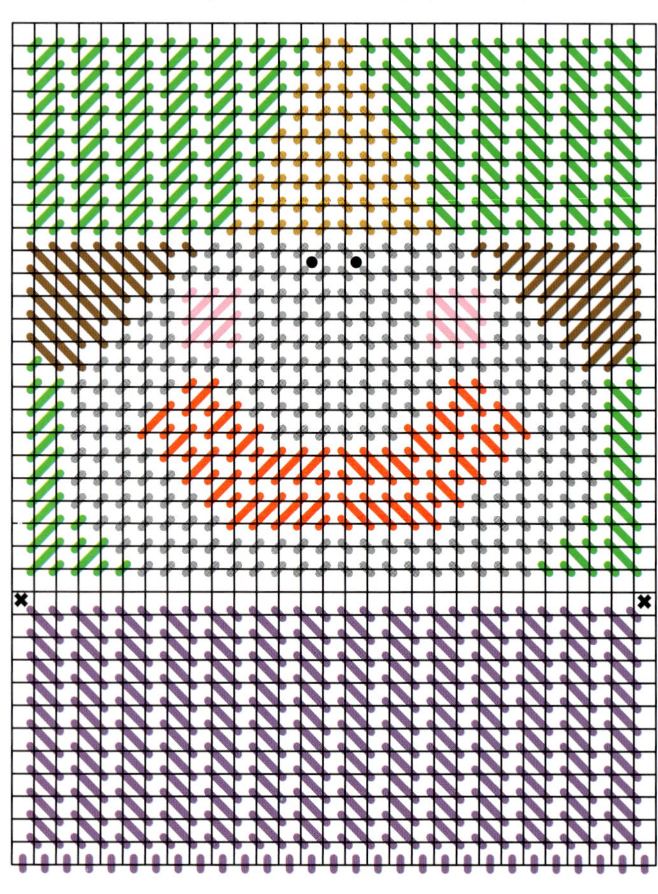

SO-SWEET TIC-TAC-TOE

(Shown on page 62.)
Skill Level: Beginner
Game Board Size: 4³/₄"w x 4³/₄"h
Box Size: 3¹/₄"w x 1¹/₂"h x 1¹/₂"d
Supplies: Worsted weight yarn (refer to color key), one 10¹/₂" x 13¹/₂" sheet of white 7 mesh plastic canvas, one 10¹/₂" x 13¹/₂" sheet of brown 7 mesh plastic canvas, #16 tapestry needle, and craft glue.
Stitches Used: Backstitch, Gobelin Stitch, Overcast Stitch, Reversed Tent Stitch, and Tent Stitch.
Instructions: Follow charts to cut and stitch Tic-Tac-Toe pieces, working backstitches last and leaving pink shaded areas unworked. For each Cookie, stack one white Cookie piece between two brown Cookie pieces. Work stitches in pink shaded area on Cookie through all three thicknesses. For each Candy, stack two Candy pieces together. Work stitches in pink shaded area on Candy through both thicknesses. Using white overcast stitches, join Box Front and Box Back to Box Sides along short edges. Join Box Bottom to Box Front, Box Back, and Box Sides. Matching ★'s, join Box Top to Box Back.

COLOR	
╱	white
╱	yellow
╱	red
╱	dk green
╱	brown

Cookie (8 x 8 threads)
Cut 14 from brown plastic canvas.
Cut 7 from white plastic canvas.

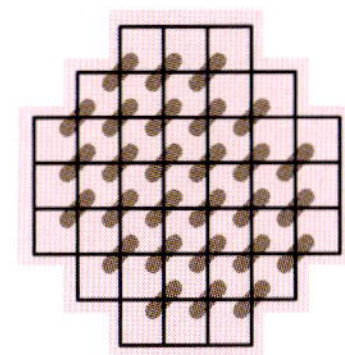

Candy (6 x 6 threads)
Cut 14 from white plastic canvas.

Box Side
(10 x 10 threads) (stitch 2)
Cut from white plastic canvas.

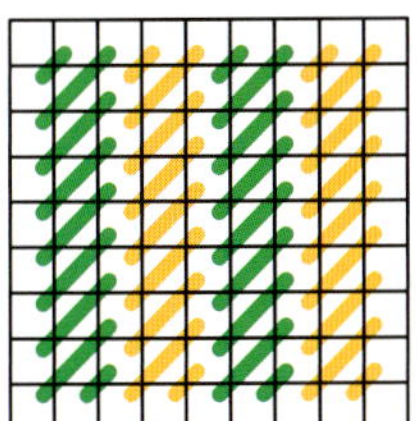

Box Bottom
(22 x 10 threads)
Cut from white plastic canvas.

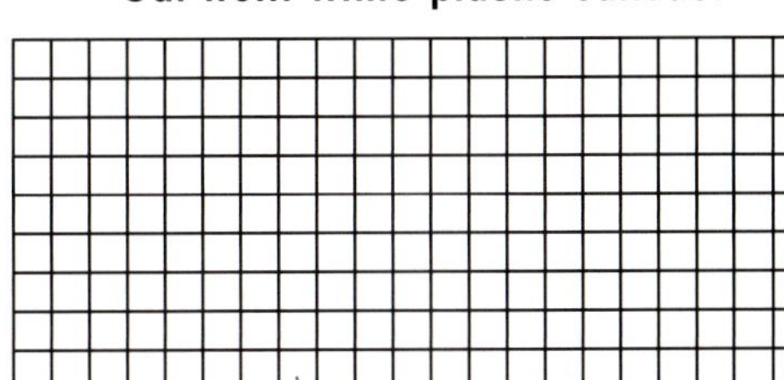

Box Top (24 x 11 threads)
Cut from white plastic canvas.

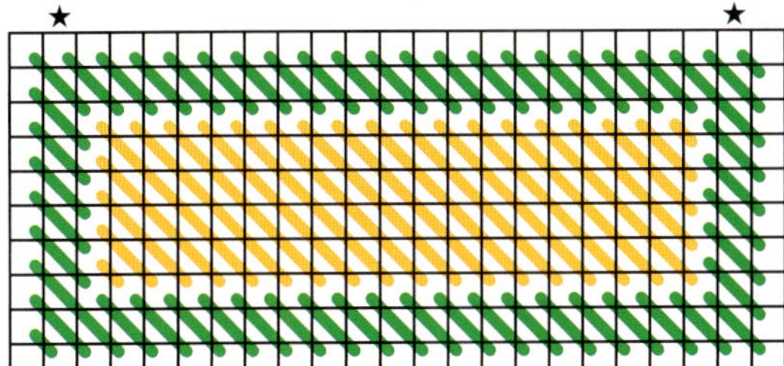

Game Board (32 x 32 threads)
Cut from white plastic canvas.

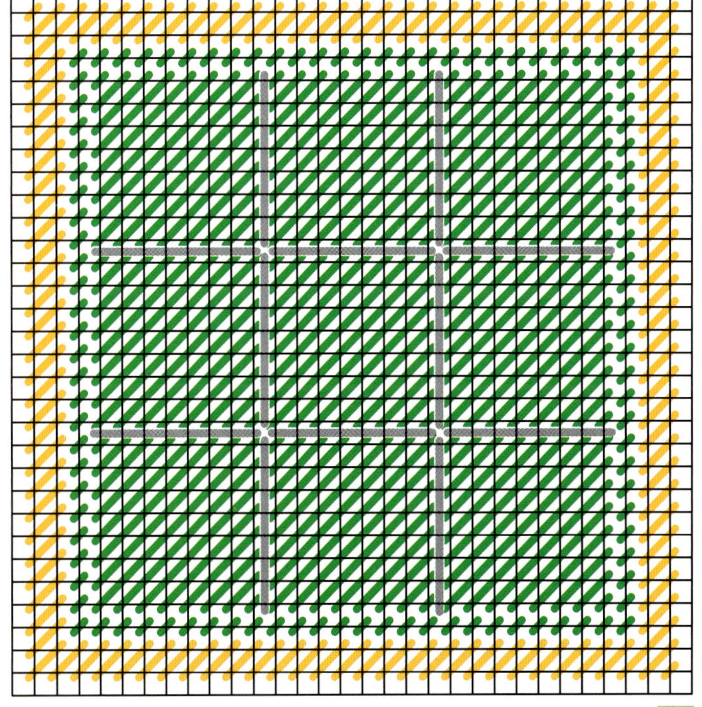

Box Front/Back
(22 x 10 threads) (stitch 2)
Cut from white plastic canvas.

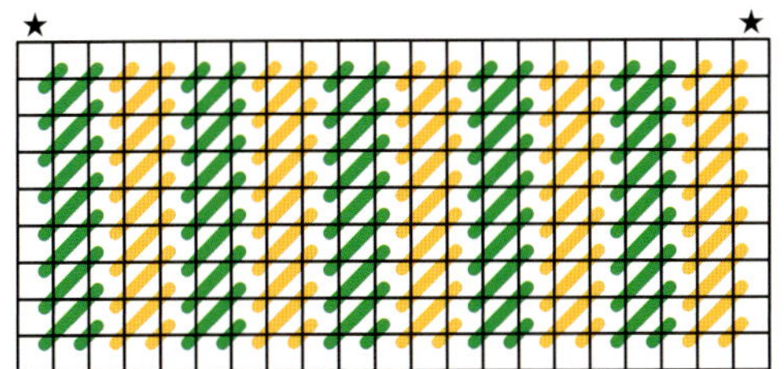

(Shown on page 63.)
Skill Level: Intermediate
Size: 5½"w x 10¼"h x 3¼"d
Supplies: Worsted weight yarn (refer to color key), two 10½" x 13½" sheets of clear 7 mesh plastic canvas, and #16 tapestry needle.
Stitches Used: Backstitch, Gobelin Stitch, Overcast Stitch, Reversed Tent Stitch, and Tent Stitch.
Instructions: Follow charts to cut and stitch Lunch Sack pieces, working backstitches last and leaving green shaded areas unworked. For Bottom, cut a 36 x 21 thread piece of plastic canvas. Cover Bottom with blue tent stitches. Matching ✖'s and ✖'s, work stitches in green shaded area to join Front to Handle Support through two thicknesses of canvas; repeat to join Back to Handle Support. Using matching color overcast stitches, join Front and Back to Sides along long edges. Join Bottom to Front, Back, and Sides. Fold down sections of Sides, joining sections where indicated by heavy black lines.

	COLOR
	white
	yellow
	*red
	blue
	green
	brown
	black

***Use two strands of yarn.**

Handle Support (26 x 17 threads) (cut 2)

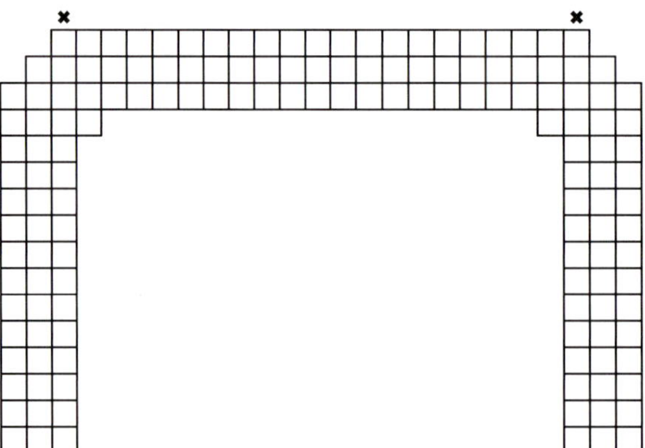

Side (21 x 57 threads) (stitch 2)

Front/Back (36 x 71 threads) (stitch 2)

GROWN-UP APPEAL

Whether made for yourself or someone dear, these creations are packed with grown-up appeal! Charming flower-of-the-month boxes are ideal for birthday gifts or any occasion. You can present your loved one's traditional birthday blossom or simply choose her favorite flower. To sweeten the surprise, tuck a little treat or trinket inside the box.

Instructions on pages 110-113.

WEDDING KEEPSAKE

Highlighted with pearls and satin ribbon, this exquisite frame offers a beautiful way to display a wedding invitation. As a keepsake for the parents or a gift for a bride, this lovely piece will hold lasting memories of that special day.

Instructions on pages 102-103.

NOVEL GIFTS

Friends and family members who love to read will treasure these novel bookmarks!
Tuck the gift inside a book to make your presentation twice as nice.

Instructions on pages 104-105.

THINKING OF DAD

Make Father's Day or any day more special by letting your dad know how much you care!
Embellished with mallards and cattails, this familiar saying is sure to touch his heart.

Instructions on pages 106-107.

HANDSOME DUCK

Resting peacefully in the marsh, this wild duck makes a handsome doorstop.
The sportsman is sure to find it an ideal accent for his office.

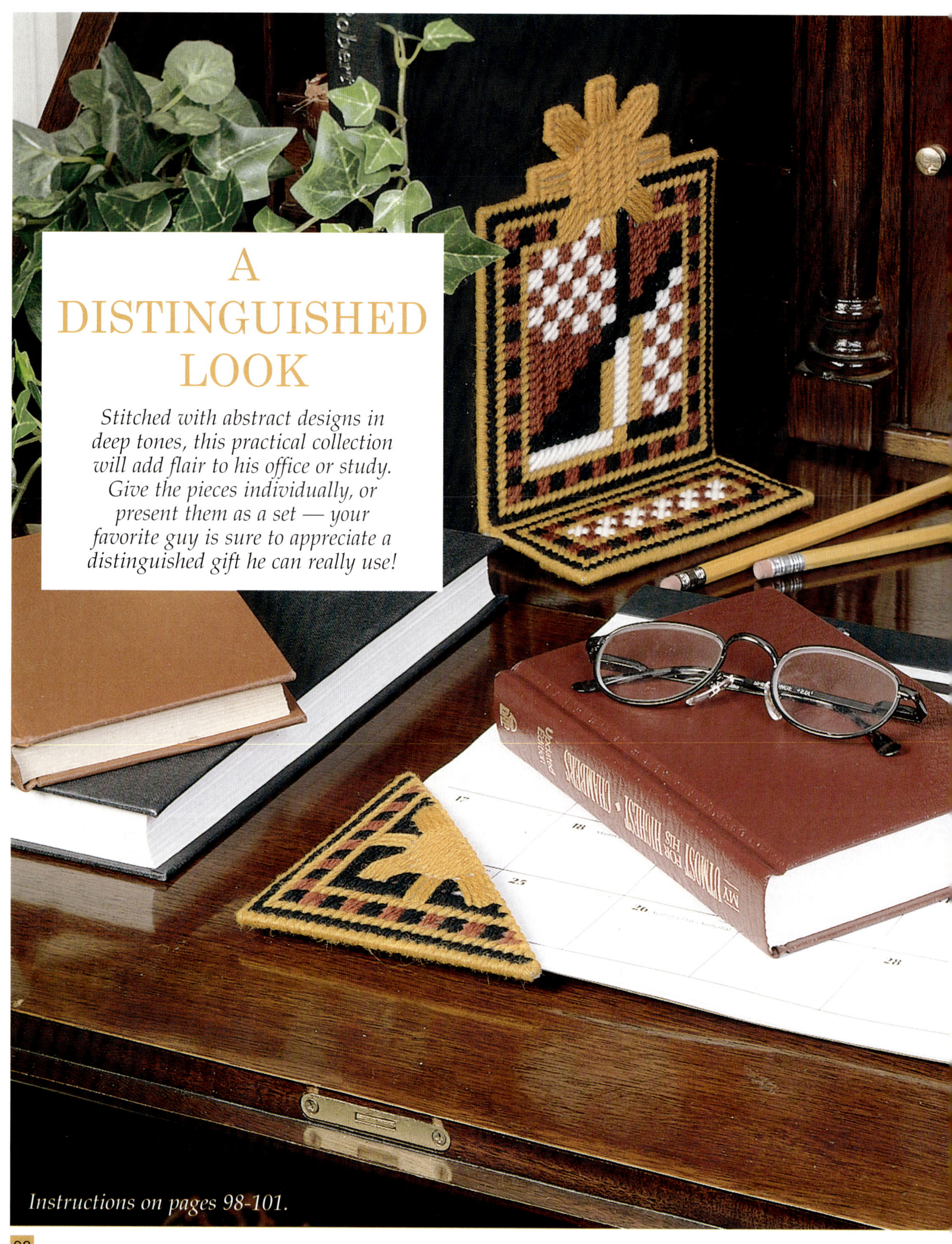

A DISTINGUISHED LOOK

Stitched with abstract designs in deep tones, this practical collection will add flair to his office or study. Give the pieces individually, or present them as a set — your favorite guy is sure to appreciate a distinguished gift he can really use!

Instructions on pages 98-101.

Instructions on page 124.

BLUEBIRDS OF HAPPINESS

Greet visitors to your "nest" with our little bluebirds of happiness. The friendly fliers adorn a heart-shaped door hanger.

Instructions on page 97.

Instructions on page 121.

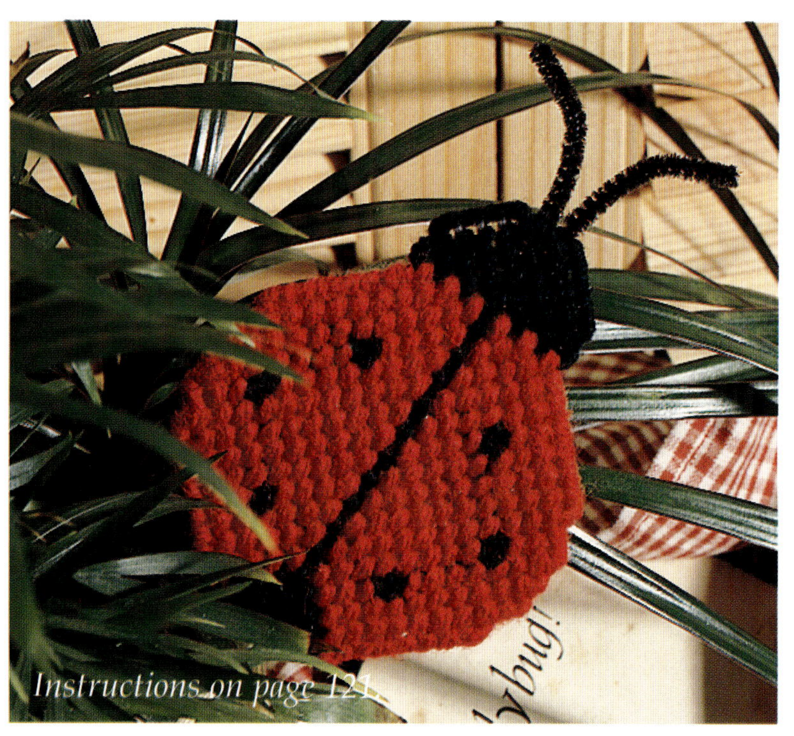

LI'L LADYBUG

For a nice gift in a hurry, dress up a potted plant with our whimsical ladybug plant poke. The fast-to-finish project adds a personal touch to your presentation.

FUN TEACHER'S DESK

Score high marks from a favorite teacher by stitching up a handy desk set. The apple-shaped pencil holder features eye-catching dimension, and our noteworthy storage box is ideal for storing miscellaneous supplies.

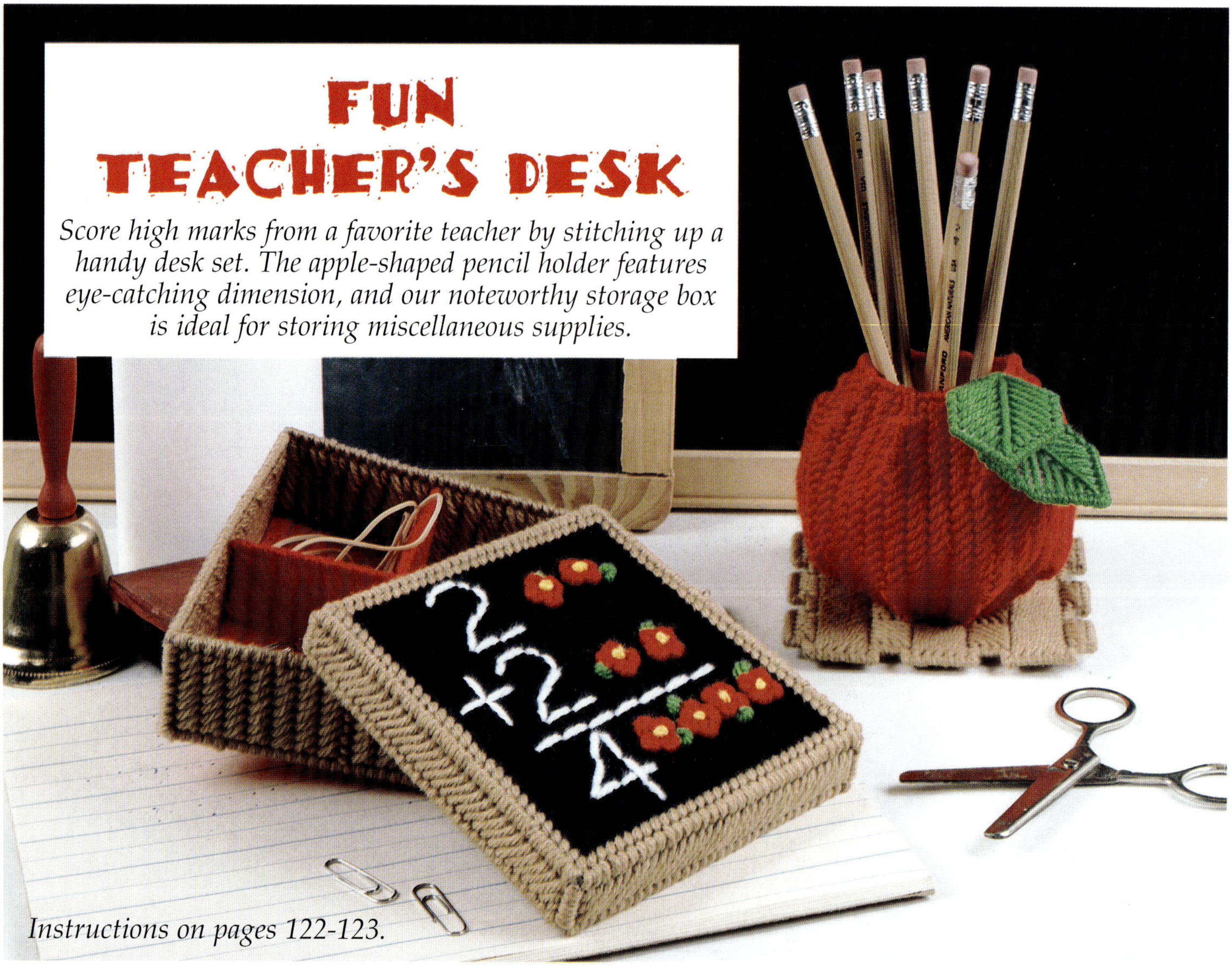

Instructions on pages 122-123.

THRU THE SEASONS

No matter what the season, you'll want to keep photos of your loved ones close at hand! This perky photo album cover is dressed in the symbols of each season so it can be enjoyed throughout the year.

Instructions on pages 114-115.

HOMEGROWN GOODNESS

*This cute, roadside vegetable stand is a sure pick for storing your tissues,
which are dispensed through a clever opening just above the lettuce and tomatoes.*

Instructions on pages 119-121.

TROPICAL FISH

Don't let water stains ruin your furniture — let our colorful sea creatures drink it up, instead! Adding a splash of tropical flair, these fish coasters are ideal for the living room or the patio.

Instructions on page 118.

SPRING BOUQUET

Plant a garden of sunshine in your message center. A trio of potted tulips will add a touch of spring all year 'round as they draw your attention to important reminders.

Instructions on page 118.

CHEERFUL GERANIUMS

Need to brighten a spot in your home? Then "plant" a pot of our cheery geraniums on a door sign, a switch plate cover, or a magnet for an instant room revitalizer.

Instructions on pages 116-117.

(Shown on page 91.)
Skill Level: Intermediate
Size: 9¼"w x 21¼"h
Supplies: Worsted weight yarn (refer to color key), one 10½" x 13½" sheet of clear 7 mesh plastic canvas, #16 tapestry needle, three 11" lengths of ⅞"w lt pink grosgrain ribbon, three 38mm gold liberty bells, hand-sewing needle and thread, sawtooth hanger, and craft glue.
Stitches Used: Backstitch, French Knot, Gobelin Stitch, Lace Stitch, Overcast Stitch, and Tent Stitch.
Instructions: Follow charts to cut and stitch Door Hanger pieces, working backstitches and French knots last. Tack Small Flowers, Flowers, and Small Hearts to Heart. Using sewing needle and thread, sew ribbons to back of Heart near bottom edge. Fold each ribbon end to form a point; glue in place. Sew a liberty bell to point of each ribbon. Securely tack hanger to back of Heart.

COLOR	
	yellow
	orange
	lt pink
	pink
	lavender
	blue
	green
	tan
	brown
	orange Fr. knot
	lavender Fr. knot
	*black Fr. knot

*Use two plies of yarn.

Heart (52 x 52 threads)

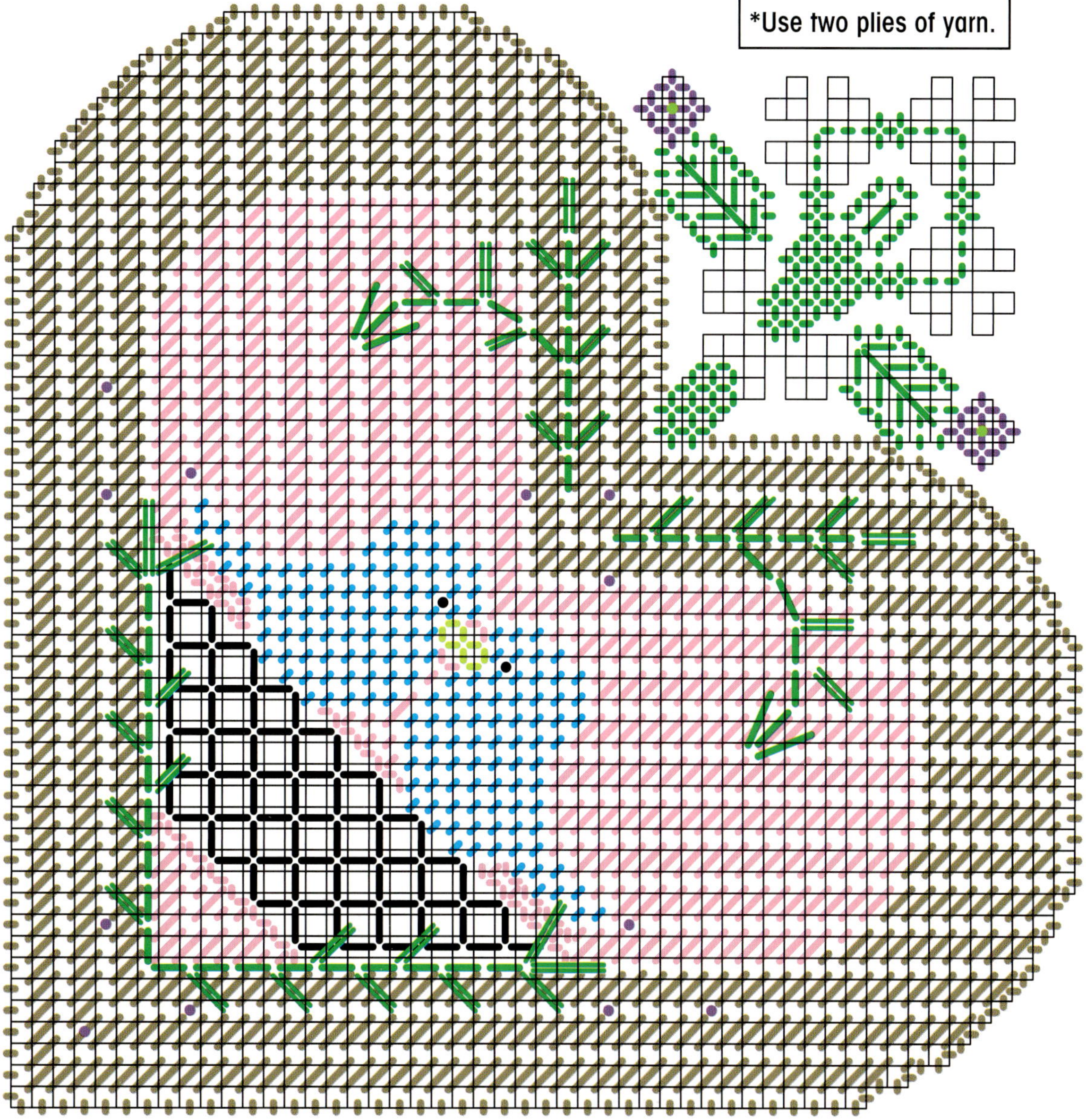

Small Flower
(4 x 4 threads)
(stitch 4)

Flower
(6 x 6 threads)
(stitch 3)

Small Heart
(9 x 9 threads)
(stitch 3)

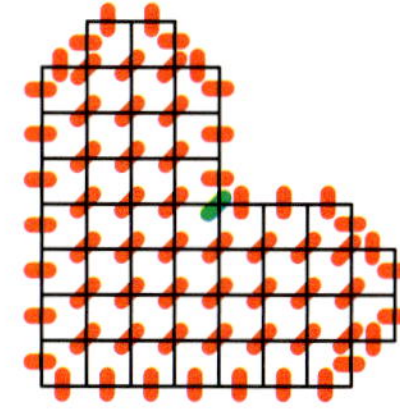

PENCIL CUP

(Shown on page 89.)
Skill Level: Beginner
Size: 4¼"h x 3" dia.
Supplies: Worsted weight yarn (refer to color key), one 10½" x 13½" sheet of clear 7 mesh plastic canvas, and #16 tapestry needle.
Stitches Used: Gobelin Stitch, Mosaic Stitch, Overcast Stitch, and Tent Stitch.
Instructions: Follow charts to cut and stitch Pencil Cup pieces, leaving blue shaded area unworked. Matching ▲'s and ■'s, work stitches in blue shaded area to join short edges of Side, forming a cylinder. Using gold overcast stitches, join Bottom to Side.

NOTEPAD HOLDER

(Shown on page 89.)
Skill Level: Beginner
Size: 3½"w x 1"h x 5½"d
(Holds a 3"w x 5"h notepad.)
Supplies: Worsted weight yarn (refer to color key), one 10½" x 13½" sheet of clear 7 mesh plastic canvas, and #16 tapestry needle.
Stitches Used: Gobelin Stitch, Mosaic Stitch, Overcast Stitch, and Tent Stitch.
Instructions: Follow charts to cut and stitch Notepad Holder pieces, leaving pink shaded area unworked. Using gold overcast stitches, join Front and Back to Sides along short edges. Join Top to Back and Sides. Cover unworked edges of Sides. Work stitches in pink shaded area to join Bottom to Front, Back, and Sides.

CALENDAR CORNER

(Shown on page 88.)
Skill Level: Beginner
Size: 4½"w x 4½"h
Supplies: Worsted weight yarn (refer to color key), one 10½" x 13½" sheet of clear 7 mesh plastic canvas, and #16 tapestry needle.
Stitches Used: Gobelin Stitch, Mosaic Stitch, Overcast Stitch, and Tent Stitch.
Instructions: Follow chart to cut and stitch Calendar Corner pieces. Using gold overcast stitches, join one Front to one Back along unworked edges. Repeat for remaining Corner.

Pencil Cup Bottom
(20 x 20 threads)

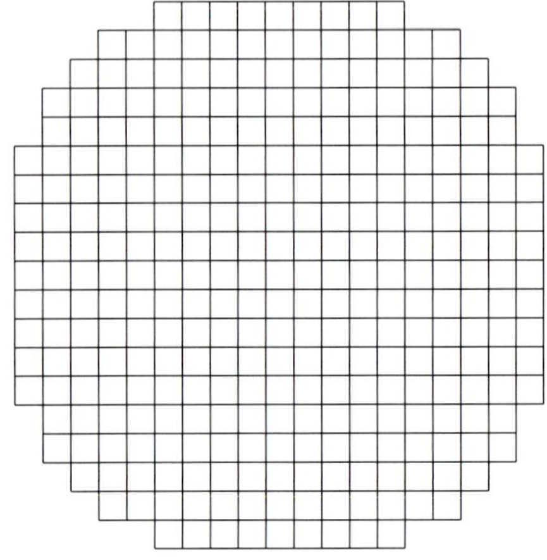

COLOR	
⁄	ecru
⁄	gold
⁄	rust
⁄	black

Pencil Cup Side (66 x 28 threads)

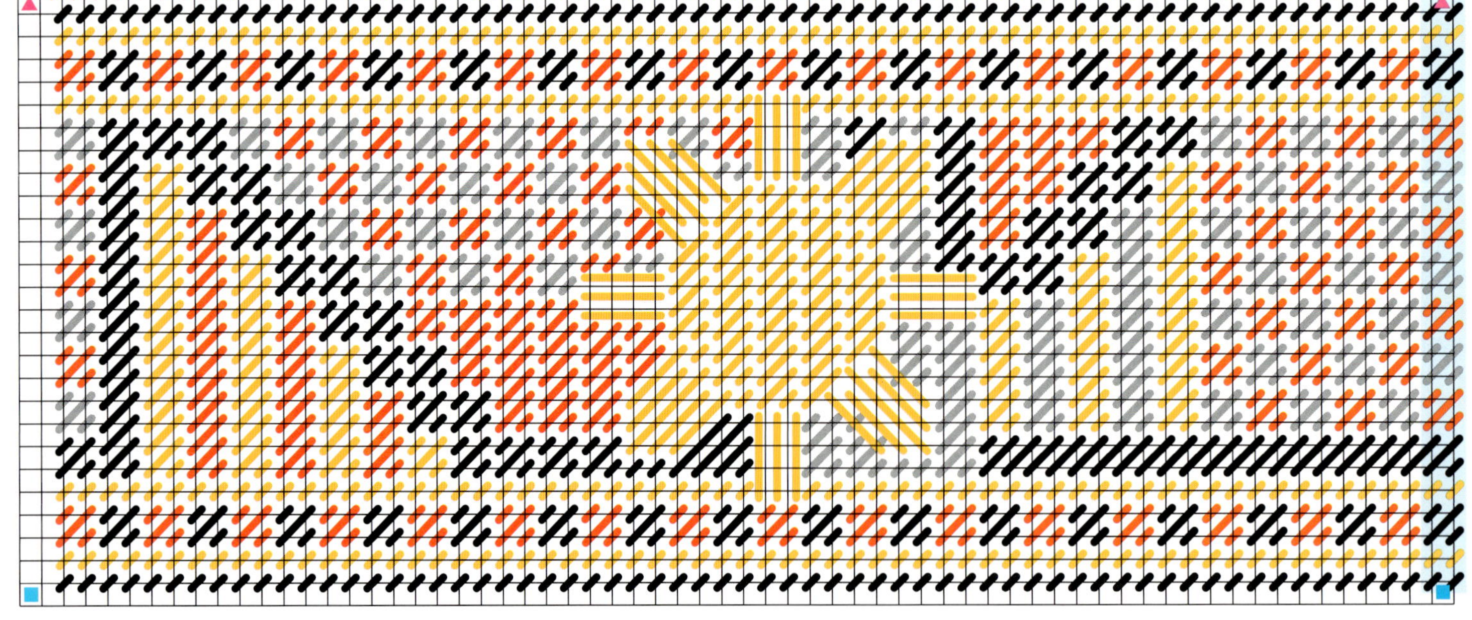

Notepad Holder Bottom
(24 x 38 threads)

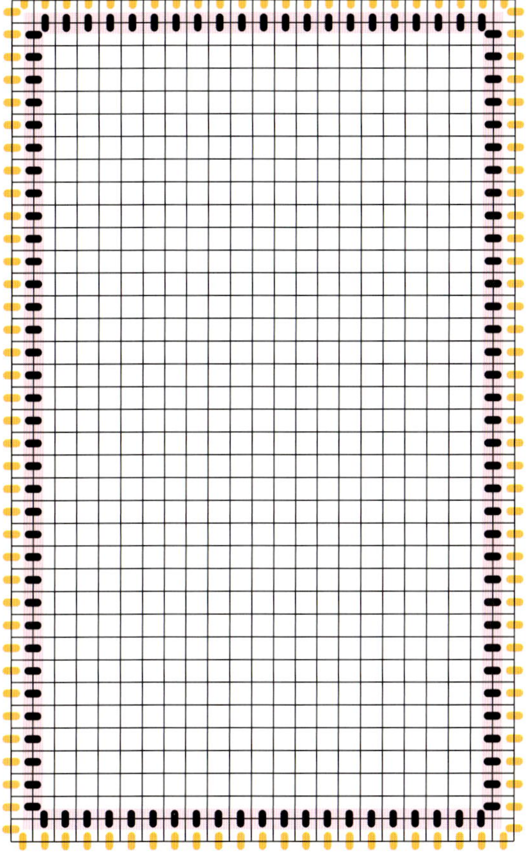

Calendar Corner Front/Back
(30 x 30 threads) (cut 4) (stitch 2)

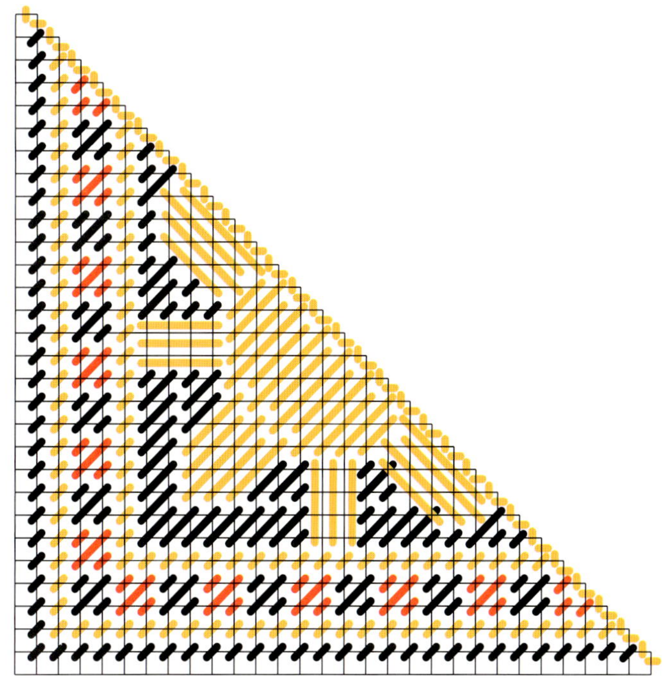

Notepad Holder Front
(22 x 7 threads)

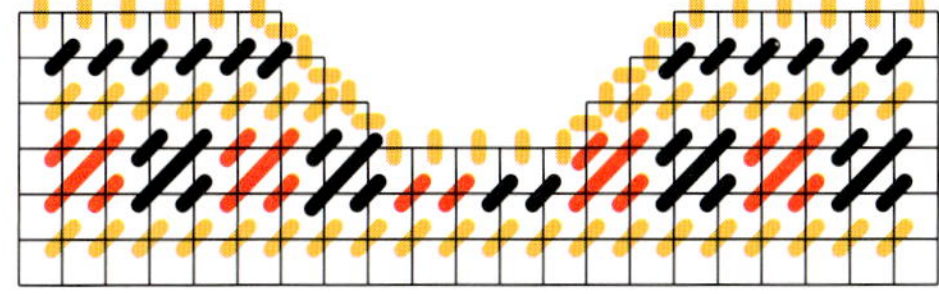

Notepad Holder Back
(22 x 7 threads)

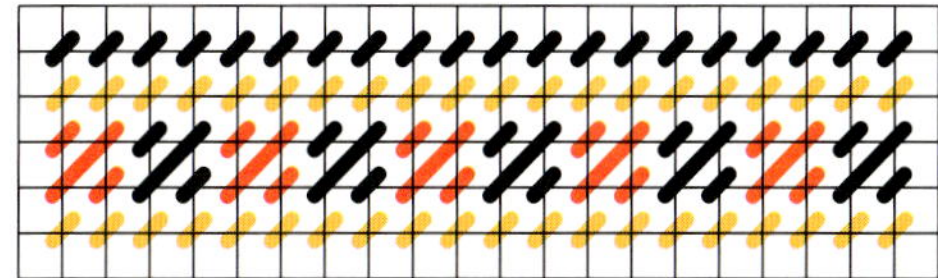

Notepad Holder Top
(22 x 12 threads)

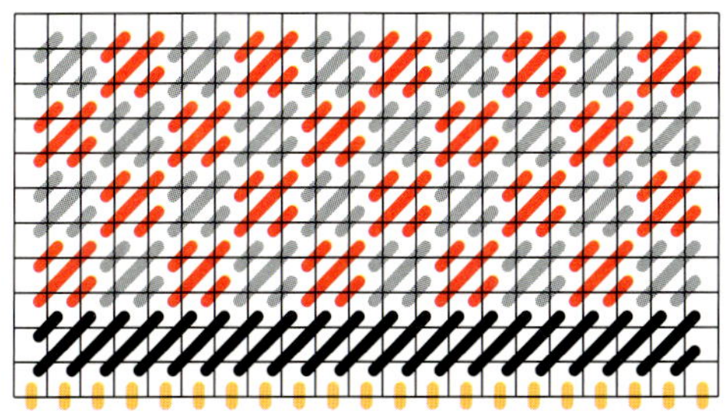

Notepad Holder Side
(36 x 7 threads) (stitch 2)

BOX

(Shown on page 89.)

Skill Level: Beginner

Size: 7¹/₄"w x 2"h x 4¹/₂"d

Supplies: Worsted weight yarn (refer to color key), two 10¹/₂" x 13¹/₂" sheets of clear 7 mesh plastic canvas, and #16 tapestry needle.

Stitches Used: Gobelin Stitch, Mosaic Stitch, Overcast Stitch, and Tent Stitch.

Instructions: Follow charts to cut and stitch Box pieces, leaving shaded areas unworked. Using black overcast stitches, join Box Top Side pieces along short edges, alternating Side #1 and Side #2 pieces to form a rectangle. Work stitches in pink shaded area to join Top Side pieces to Top. Join Box Bottom Side pieces together along short edges, alternating Side #1 and Side #2 pieces to form a rectangle. Work stitches in blue shaded area to join Bottom Side pieces to Bottom.

BOOKEND COVERS

(Shown on page 88.)

Skill Level: Beginner

Size: 5"w x 7¹/₂"h x 2¹/₂"d

Supplies: Worsted weight yarn (refer to color key), two 10¹/₂" x 13¹/₂" sheets of clear 7 mesh plastic canvas, #16 tapestry needle, and two 4³/₄"w x 5"h x 5¹/₄"d metal bookends.

Stitches Used: Gobelin Stitch, Mosaic Stitch, Overcast Stitch, and Tent Stitch.

Instructions: Follow charts to cut and stitch Bookend Cover pieces. Using gold overcast stitches, join one Bookend Cover Front to one Base between ▲'s. Matching ■'s, place Base on top of one Base Bottom. Join Base Bottom to Base along unworked edges of Base. Join remaining unworked edges of Front to Back. Repeat for remaining pieces.

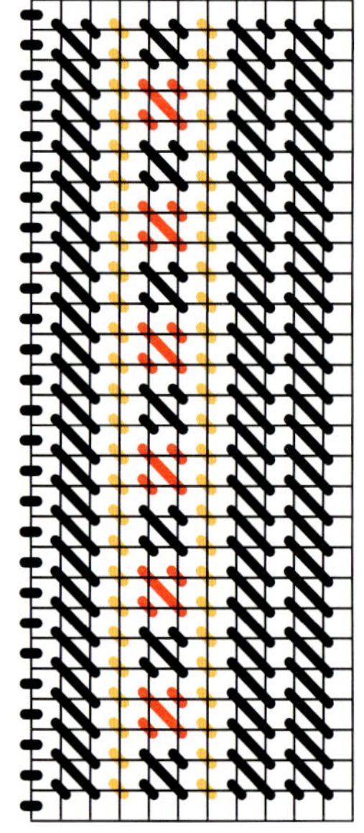

Box Bottom Side #1
(12 x 28 threads) (stitch 2)

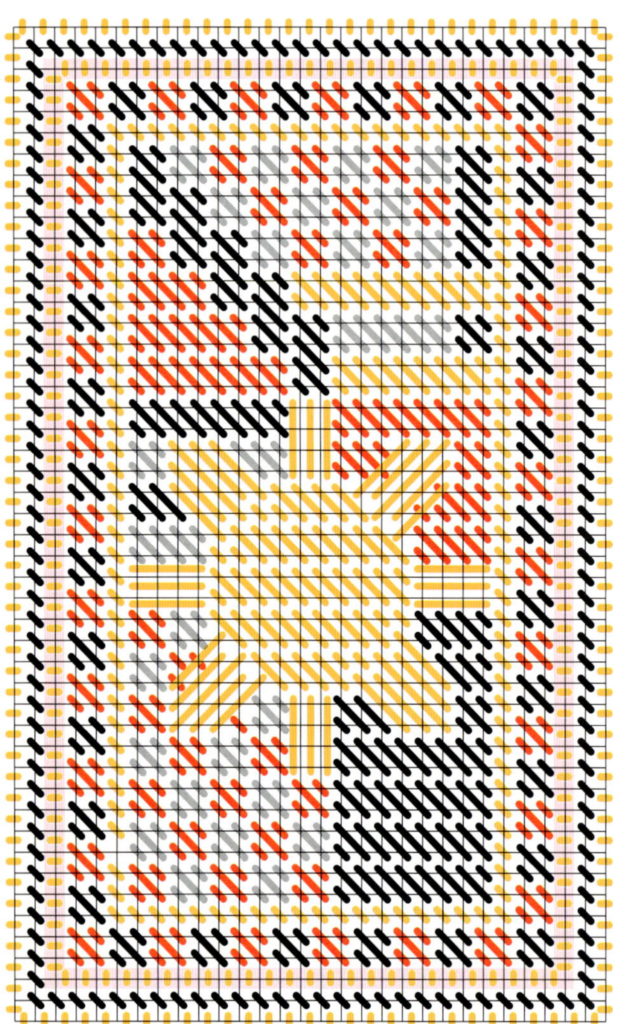

Box Top (30 x 48 threads)

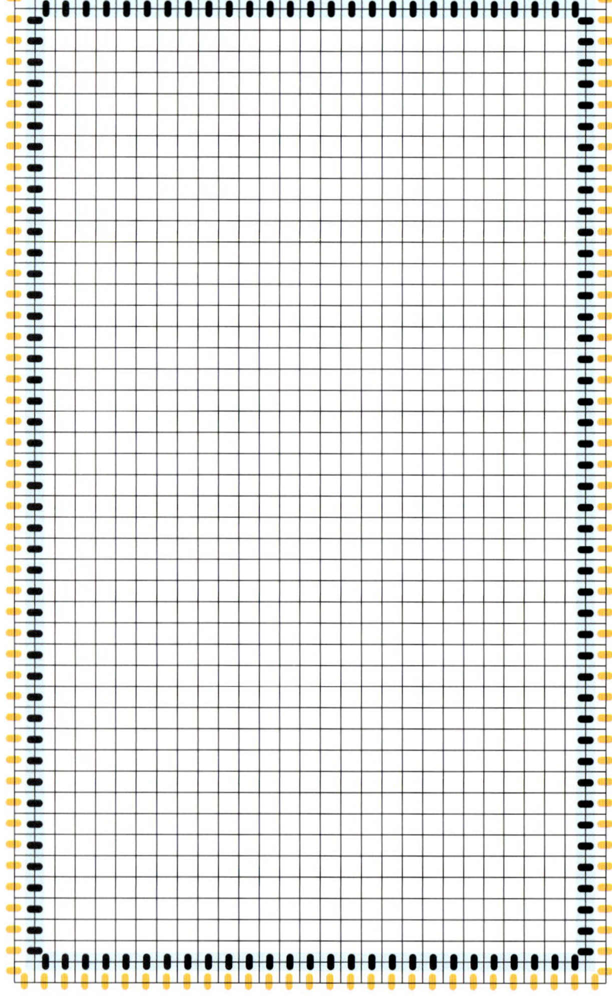

Box Bottom (30 x 48 threads)

COLOR

⁄	ecru
⁄	gold
⁄	rust
⁄	black

Bookend Cover Base Bottom (34 x 8 threads) (cut 2)

Bookend Cover Base (34 x 16 threads) (stitch 2)

Box Bottom Side #2 (12 x 46 threads) (stitch 2)

Box Top Side #1 (4 x 26 threads) (stitch 2)

Box Top Side #2 (4 x 44 threads) (stitch 2)

Bookend Cover Front/Back (34 x 47 threads) (cut 4) (stitch 2)

WEDDING KEEPSAKE

(Shown on page 84.)

Skill Level: Intermediate

Frame Size: 8"w x 9¾"h

Supplies: DMC #3 pearl cotton (refer to color key), two 10½" x 13½" sheets of clear 7 mesh plastic canvas, #16 tapestry needle, 1 yd of ⅝"w ecru ribbon, forty-two 4mm pearl beads, sawtooth hanger, sewing needle and thread, and craft glue.

Stitches Used: Backstitch, Gobelin Stitch, Overcast Stitch, Reversed Tent Stitch, and Tent Stitch.

Instructions: Follow charts to cut and stitch Frame pieces, using one strand of pearl cotton and working backstitches last and leaving green shaded areas unworked. Cut two 5" lengths and two 7" lengths from ribbon. Referring to photo, thread ribbons through Front. Glue ends in place on wrong side of Front. With right sides up, match ♥'s and work stitches in green shaded areas to join Front to Back. Matching ■'s, tack Leaves to Front. Matching ▲'s, tack Large Heart to Front. Matching ♦'s, tack Heart to Front. Sew one Flower and one pearl bead to Front and Hearts at each ✖. Sew one pearl bead to Front and Back at each ★. Tie bow with remaining ribbon; trim ends. Glue bow to Large Heart. Securely tack hanger to wrong side of Back. Insert invitation through opening in Back.

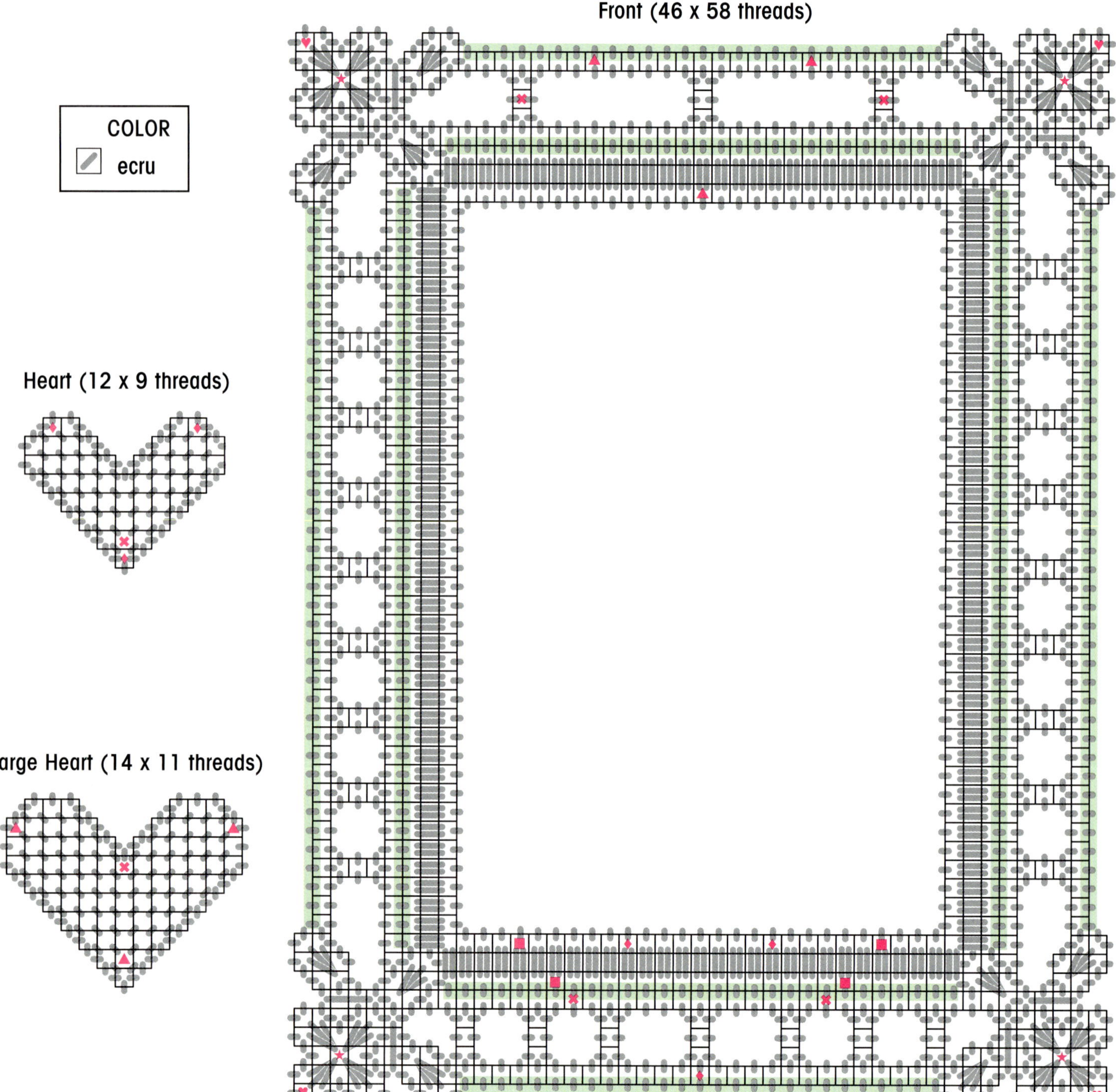

Flower (4 x 4 threads)
(stitch 6)

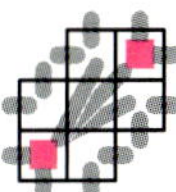

Leaf (4 x 4 threads)
(stitch 2)

Back (54 x 66 threads)

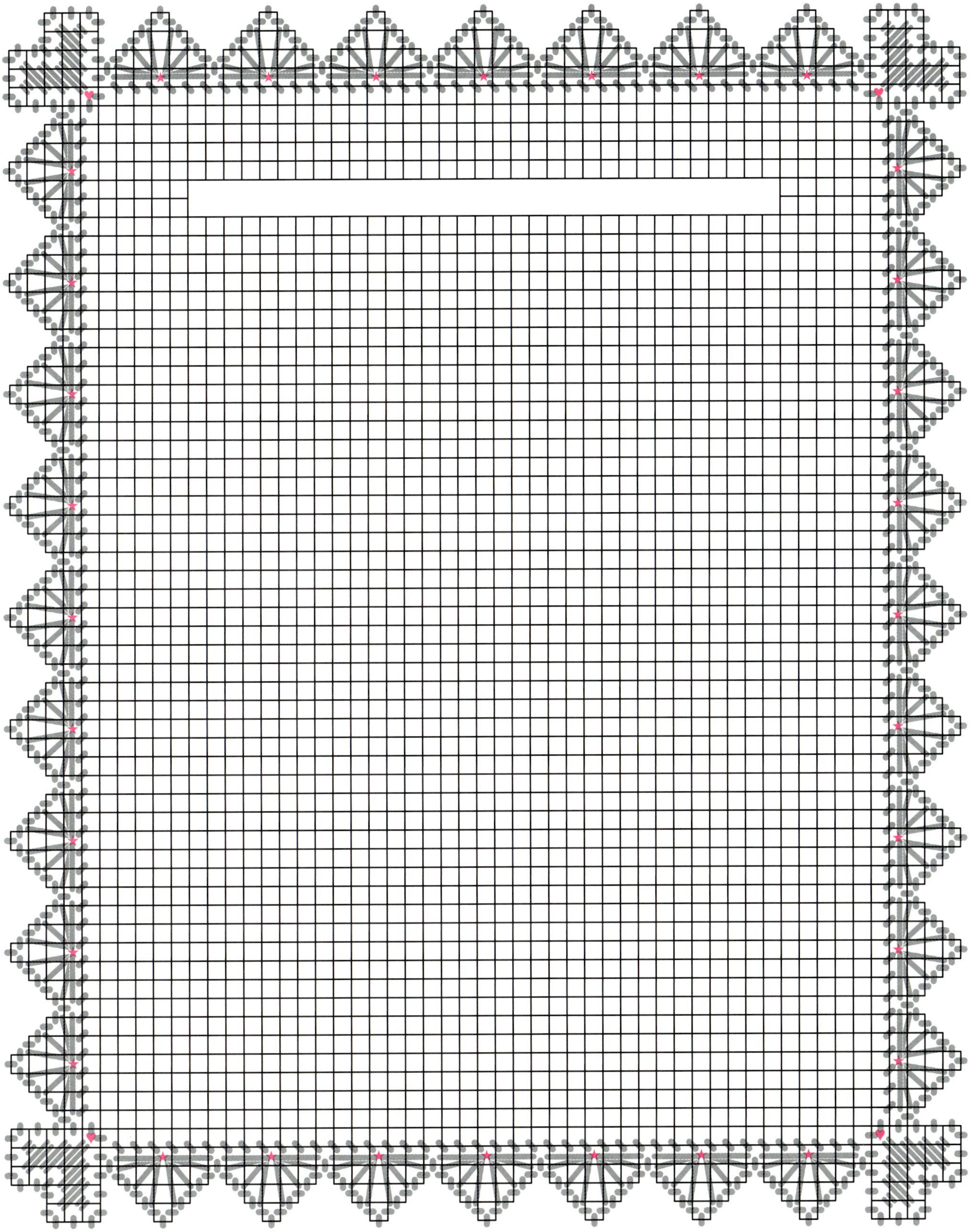

(Shown on page 85.)
Skill Level: Intermediate
Approx. Size: 1½"w x 7"h each
Supplies for one Bookmark: DMC #3 pearl cotton (refer to color key), one 10½" x 13½" sheet of 10 mesh plastic canvas (refer to photo for color), and #20 tapestry needle.
For Girl Bookmark only: One 8" length of pink (776) #3 pearl cotton and craft glue.
Stitches Used: Backstitch, French Knot, Gobelin Stitch, Overcast Stitch, Reversed Tent Stitch, and Tent Stitch.
Instructions: Follow chart to cut and stitch desired Bookmark, using one strand of pearl cotton and working backstitches and French knots last.
For Girl Bookmark only: Tie bow with pink pearl cotton. Glue bow to Bookmark; trim ends

GIRL

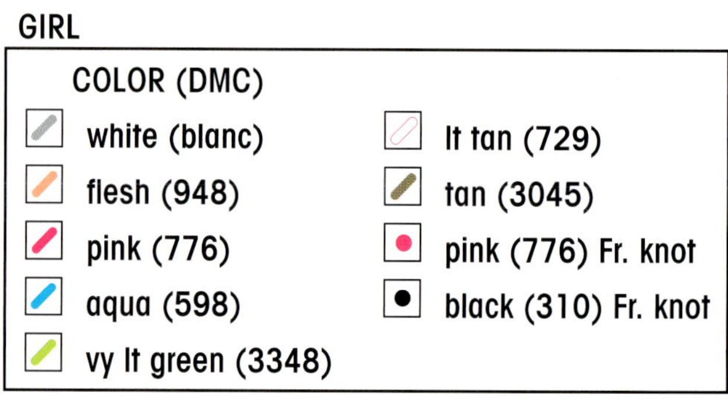

DUCK

Duck (59 x 59 threads)

Girl (56 x 56 threads)

BUTTERFLY

COLOR (DMC)
- lt yellow (727)
- dk yellow (444)
- peach (402)
- blue (3325)
- green (989)
- black (310)

TULIP

COLOR (DMC)
- pink (776)
- green (989)
- lt brown (436)

PANSY

COLOR (DMC)
- vy lt yellow (745)
- lt yellow (727)
- vy dk yellow (972)
- lt lavender (211)
- lt green (368)

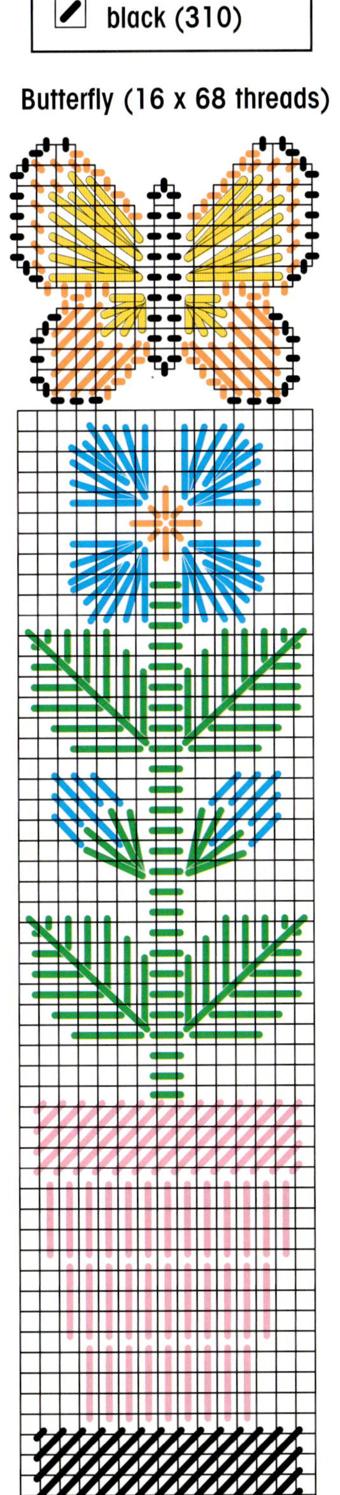

Butterfly (16 x 68 threads)

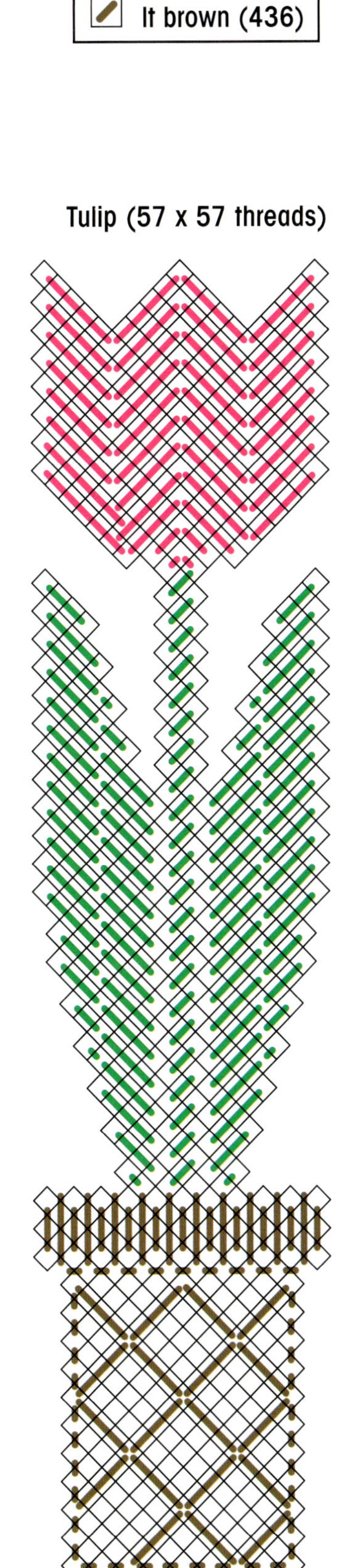

Tulip (57 x 57 threads)

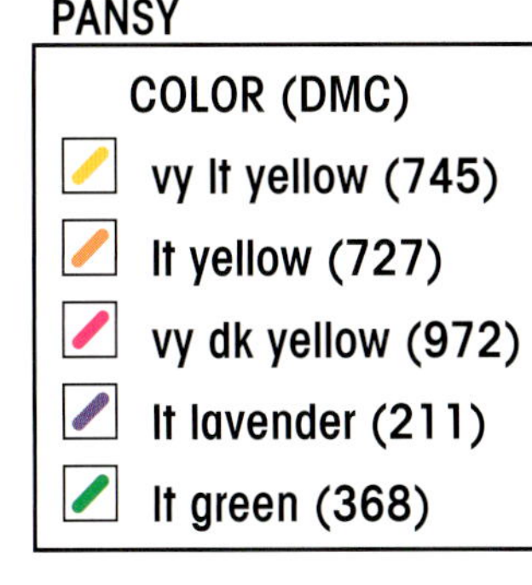

Pansy (53 x 53 threads)

(Shown on page 86.)
Skill Level: Intermediate
Size: 10"w x 8"h
Supplies: Worsted weight yarn and embroidery floss (refer to color key), one 10½" x 13½" sheet of clear 7 mesh plastic canvas, one 8" x 11" sheet of ivory 14 mesh plastic canvas, #16 and #24 tapestry needles, 10" x 8" frame, and craft glue.
Stitches Used: Backstitch, Cross Stitch, French Knot, Overcast Stitch, Reversed Tent Stitch, and Tent Stitch.
Instructions: Follow charts to cut and stitch pieces, working backstitches and French knots last. Glue Ducks to Background. Insert Background into frame.

YARN		YARN		FLOSS	
▨	white	▨	lt grey	▨	lt aqua
▨	gold	▨	grey	▨	aqua
▨	blue	▨	dk grey	▨	lt green
▨	dk green	▨	black	▨	green
▨	rust	●	dk brown	▨	dk green
▨	dk brown		Fr. knot	▨	brown
				▨	black

Duck (26 x 13 threads)
Cut from clear 7 mesh canvas
and stitch with worsted weight yarn.

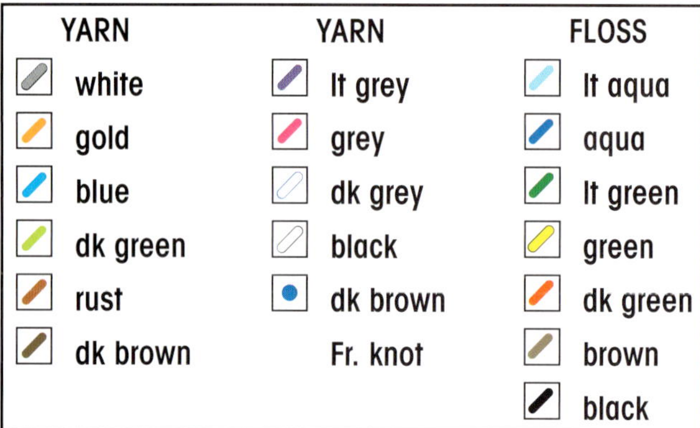

Duck (28 x 24 threads)
Cut from clear 7 mesh canvas
and stitch with worsted weight yarn.

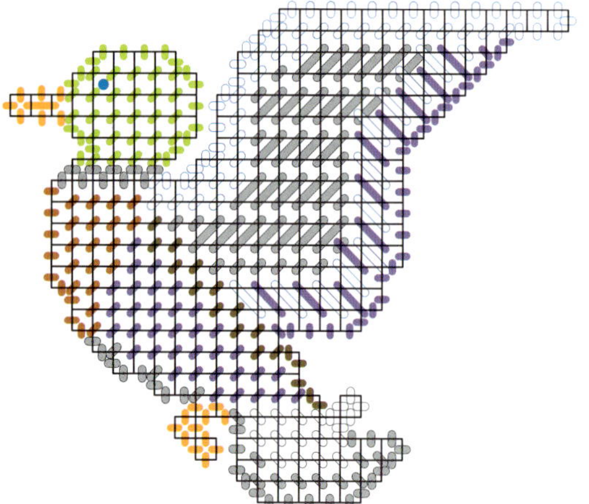

Background (140 x 112 threads)
Cut from ivory 14 mesh canvas
and stitch with 6 strands of floss.

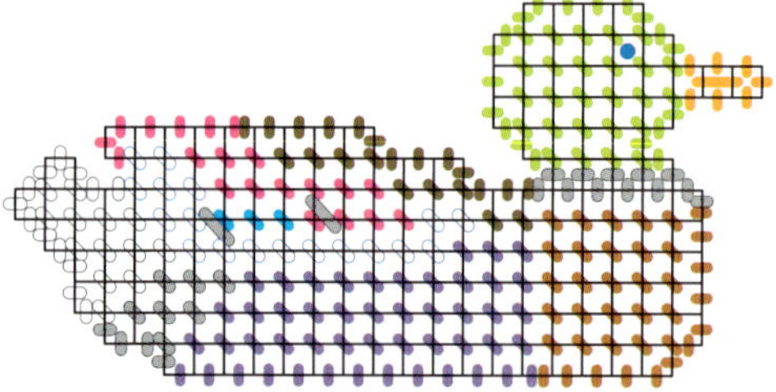

This chart of the Background represents one 140 x 112 thread canvas piece.
It is spread across two pages to make it large enough to be followed easily.
No threads or stitches are repeated from one page to the next.

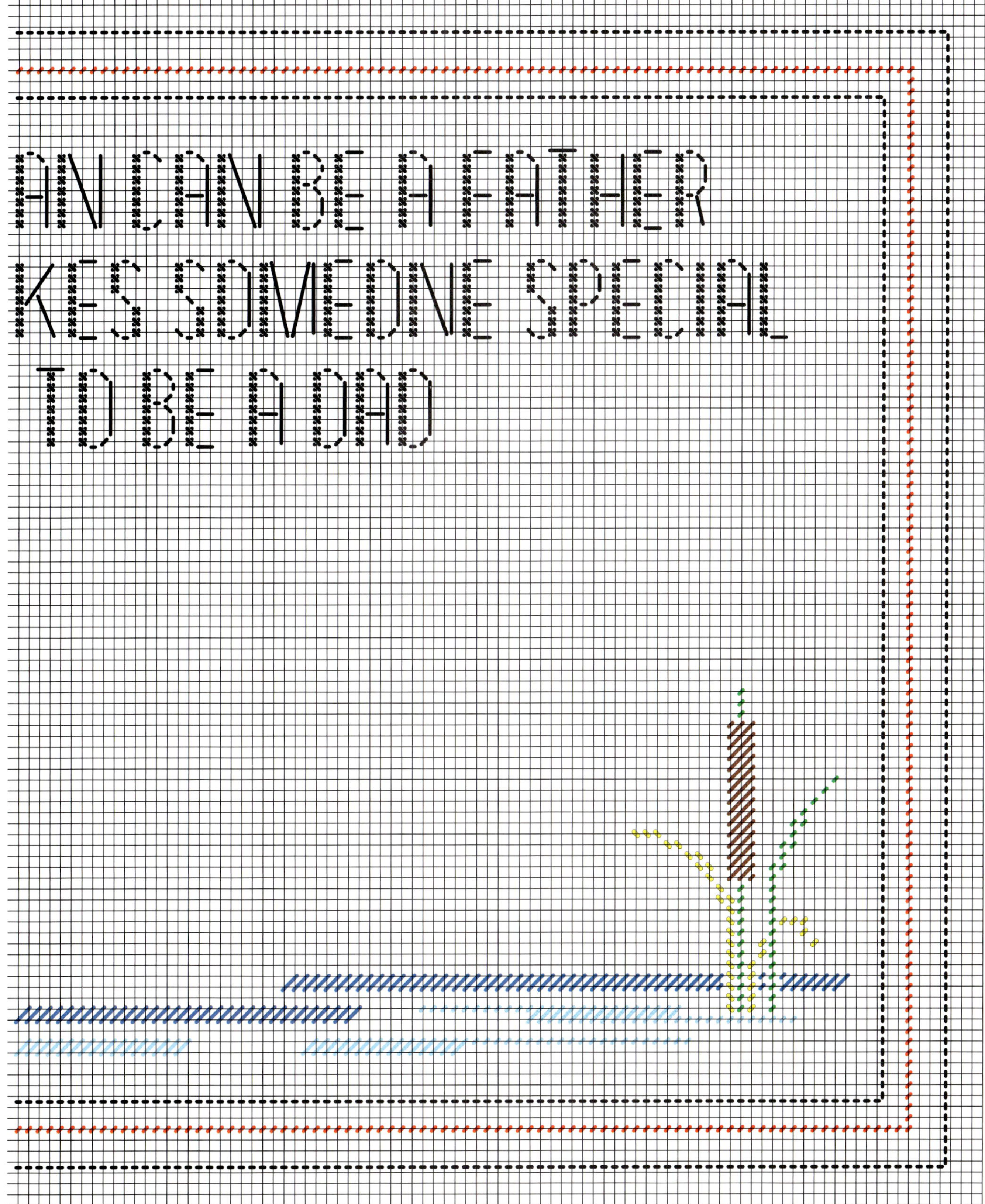

(Shown on page 87.)
Skill Level: Intermediate
Size: 14"w x 8¹/₂"h x 3¹/₂"d
(Fits an 8"w x 3¹/₄"h x 2¹/₄"d brick.)
Supplies: Worsted weight yarn (refer to color key), three 10¹/₂" x 13¹/₂" sheets of clear 7 mesh plastic canvas, #16 tapestry needle, three 10" wooden skewers, five 6mm brown chenille stems, brick, plastic wrap, and craft glue.
Stitches Used: Backstitch, Gobelin Stitch, Overcast Stitch, Reversed Tent Stitch, and Tent Stitch.
Instructions: Follow charts to cut and stitch Doorstop pieces, working backstitches last. For Front and Back, cut two pieces of plastic canvas 57 x 27 threads each. For Top and Bottom, cut two pieces of plastic canvas 57 x 17 threads each. For Sides, cut two pieces of plastic canvas 17 x 27 threads each. Cover Front, Back, Top, Bottom, and Sides with green Gobelin stitches over two threads. Using green overcast stitches, join Top and Bottom to Sides along short edges. Join Front to Top, Bottom, and Sides. Tack Leaves to Duck. Tack Duck to Front. Wrap brick with plastic wrap. Place brick inside Doorstop. Join Back to Top, Bottom, and Sides. For cattails, cut skewers into three 4" sections, one 4¹/₂" section, and one 5¹/₂" section. Wrap one chenille stem around the end of each skewer section and secure with glue. Glue skewers to Duck.

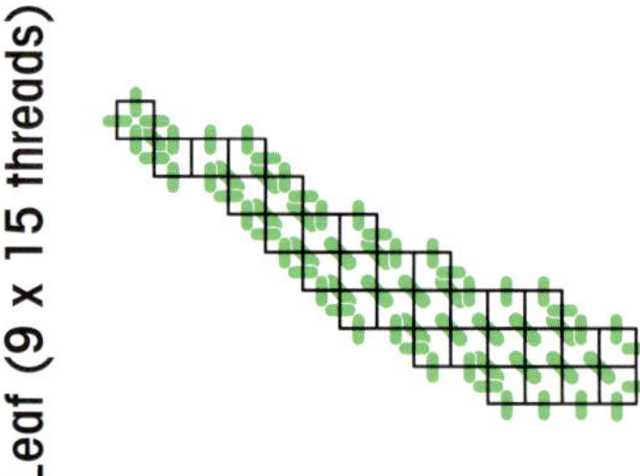

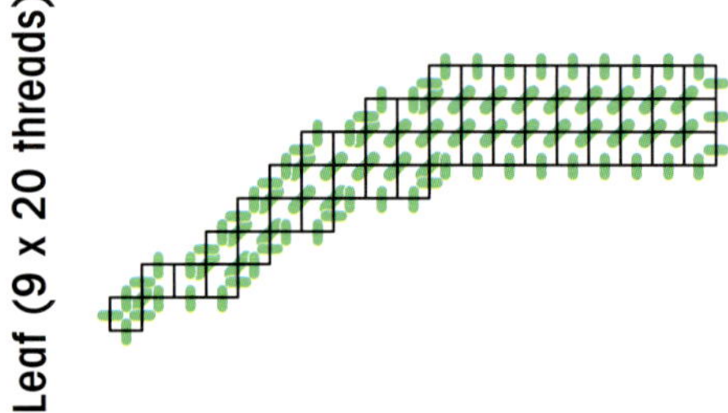

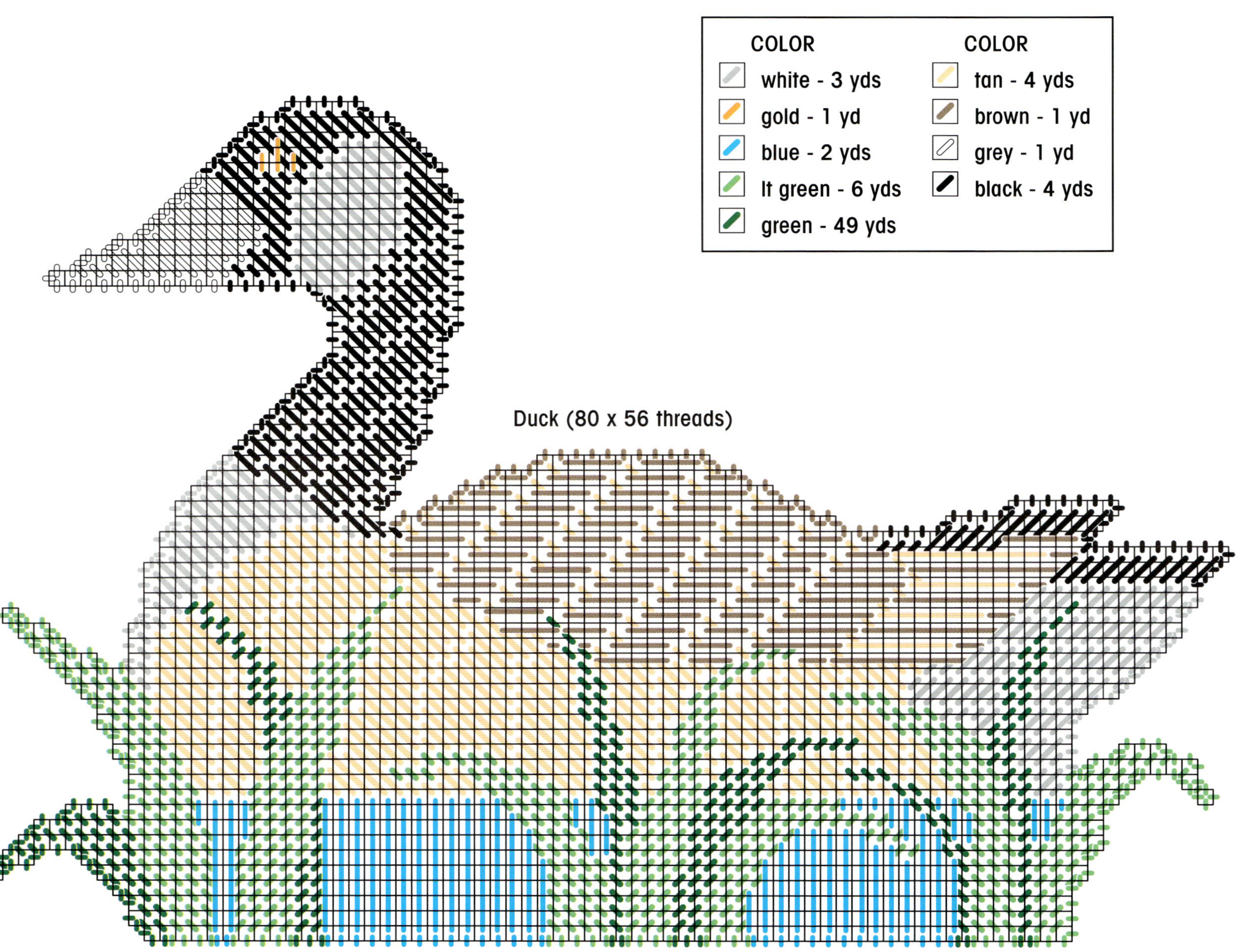

COLOR
white - 3 yds
gold - 1 yd
blue - 2 yds
lt green - 6 yds
green - 49 yds
COLOR
tan - 4 yds
brown - 1 yd
grey - 1 yd
black - 4 yds
Duck (80 x 56 threads)

FLOWER-OF-THE-MONTH BOXES

(Shown on pages 82-83.)
Skill Level: Advanced
Size: 3¹/₄"w x 1¹/₂"h x 3¹/₄"d each
Supplies For One Box: Worsted weight yarn (refer to color keys), one 10¹/₂" x 13¹/₂" sheet of clear 7 mesh plastic canvas, and #16 tapestry needle.
Stitches Used: Backstitch, Cross Stitch, French Knot, Gobelin Stitch, Overcast Stitch, Reversed Tent Stitch, Scotch Stitch Variation, and Tent Stitch.

BOX

Instructions: Follow the charts to cut and stitch flower and box pieces, working backstitches and French knots last and leaving shaded areas unworked. Using ecru overcast stitches, join Bottom Sides along short edges. Work stitches in pink shaded area to join Bottom Sides to wrong side of Bottom. Join Top Sides along short edges. Work stitches in pink shaded area to join Top Sides to wrong side of Top. Follow individual flower instructions to assemble flowers. Tack flowers, leaves, and stems to Top.

JANUARY CARNATION

Instructions: Tack Petal B in center of Petal C. Tack Petal A pieces in center of Petal B.

FEBRUARY VIOLET

Instructions: For each flower, match ✖'s and use purple overcast stitches to join Petal B on top of Petal A. Work a yellow French Knot at ✖.

MARCH DAFFODIL

Instructions: Using yellow overcast stitches, join ends of Center, forming a cylinder. Matching ✖'s, join Petal B on top of Petal A. Tack Center to Petals. Tack Petals to Stem A.

APRIL SWEET PEA

Instructions: Insert Petal A into slit of Petal B. Tack Petal A to Petal B.

MAY LILY OF THE VALLEY

Instructions: Tack three Petals to each Leaf.

JUNE ROSE

Instructions: Matching ▲'s, tack Small Center to wrong side of Center. Fold Center and tack together at ✖'s. Tack Petals to Center.

JULY LARKSPUR

Instructions: For each flower, tack sections of Petals together, forming a cup shape.

AUGUST GLADIOLA

Instructions: For each flower, match ✖'s and tack three Petal B pieces together, forming a flower. Tack Petal A in center of flower at ♥.

SEPTEMBER ASTER

Instructions: Tack Petal A, Petal B, Petal C, and Petal D pieces together.

OCTOBER CALENDULA

Instructions: Matching ✖'s and ★'s, work stitches in blue shaded area to join Petal B on top of Petal C. Matching ▲'s and ■'s, work stitches in blue shaded area to join Petal A to Petal B and Petal C through three thicknesses of canvas.

NOVEMBER MUM

Instructions: Tack Petals together. Use orange overcast stitches to join Center B pieces through three thicknesses of canvas. Tack Center A to Center B pieces. Tack Center to Petals.

DECEMBER POINSETTIA

Instructions: Tack Petal A on top of Petal B.

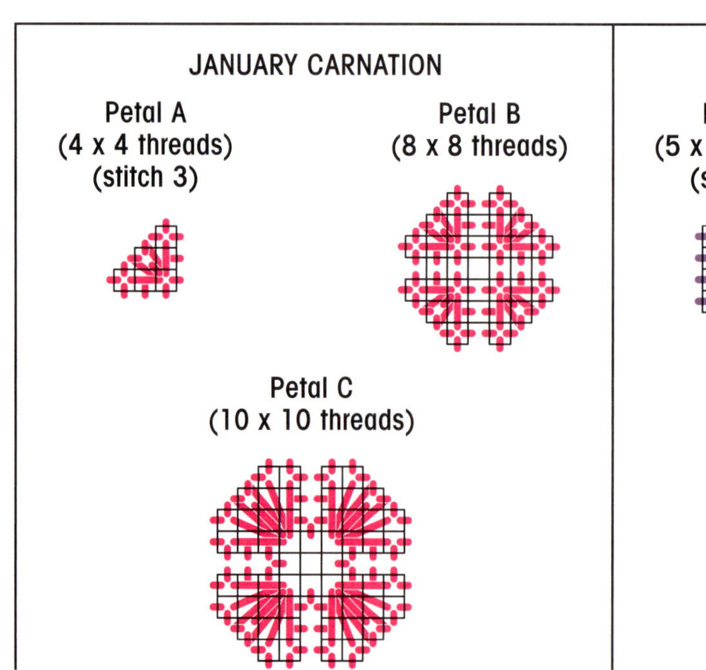

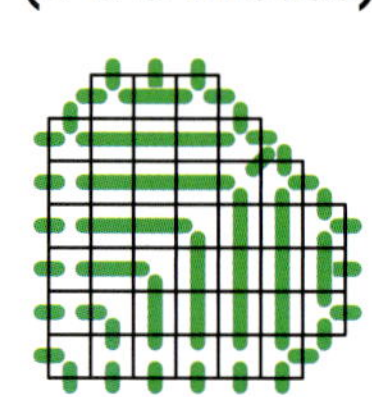

MARCH DAFFODIL

Petal A
(8 x 6 threads)

Petal B
(8 x 8 threads)

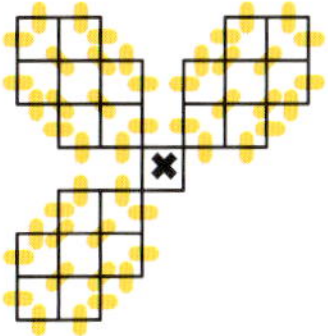

Center
(10 x 10 threads)

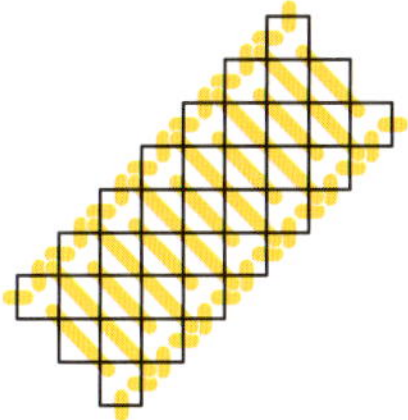

Leaf (15 x 15 threads)

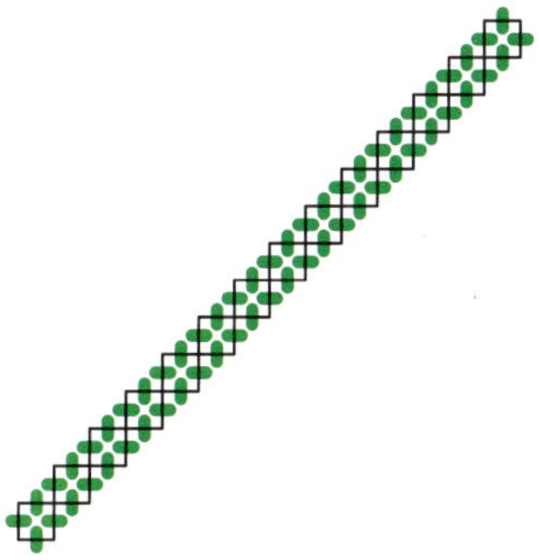

Stem A (16 x 13 threads)

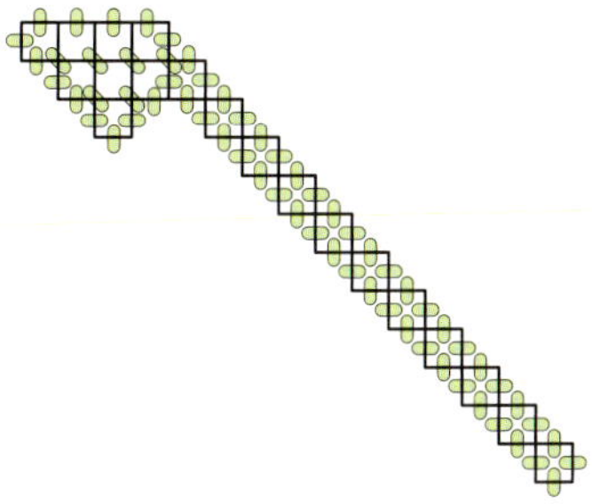

Stem B (15 x 11 threads)

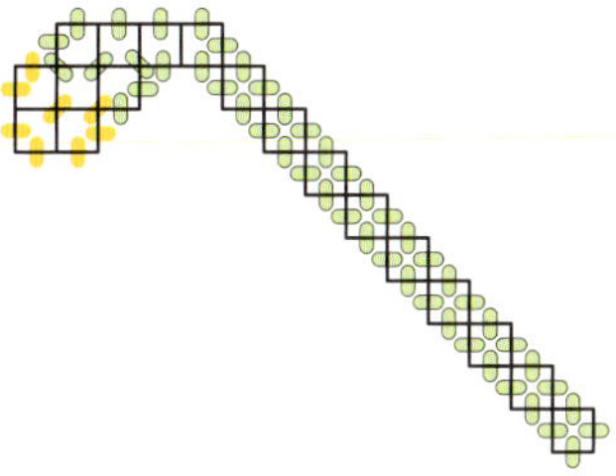

Stem C (15 x 11 threads)

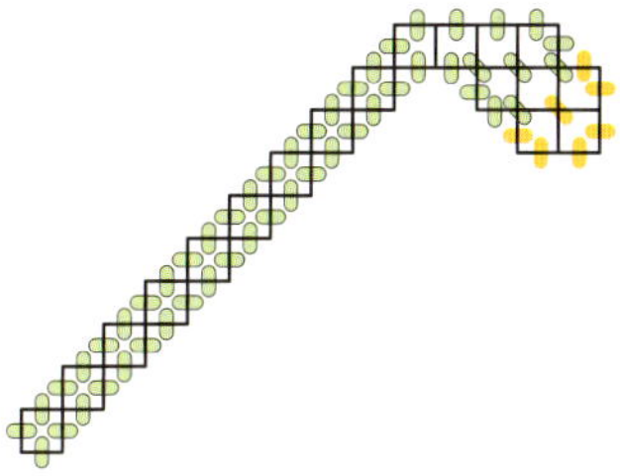

APRIL SWEET PEA

Petal A
(6 x 4 threads)

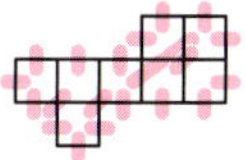

Petal B
(8 x 8 threads)

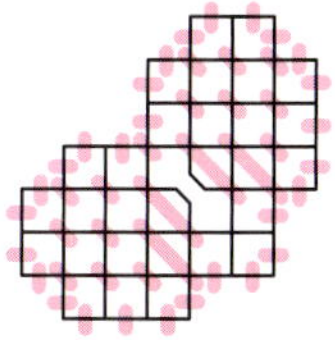

JULY LARKSPUR

Petal
(6 x 6 threads)
(stitch 6)

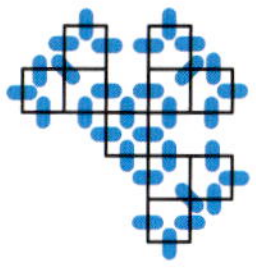

MAY LILY OF THE VALLEY

Leaf A
(13 x 13 threads)

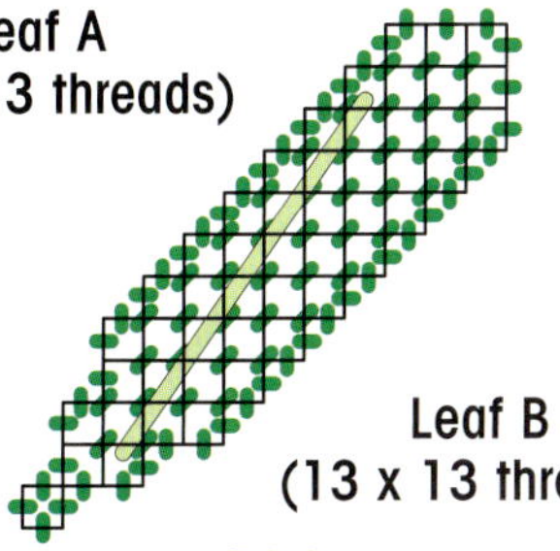

Leaf B
(13 x 13 threads)

Petal
(3 x 3 threads)
(stitch 8)

JUNE ROSE

Center
(8 x 10 threads)

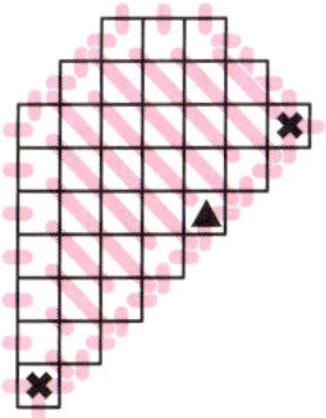

Small Center
(5 x 5 threads)

Petal
(6 x 6 threads)
(stitch 8)

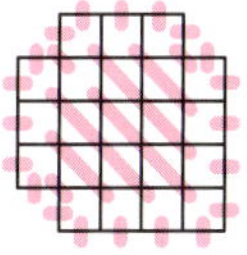

Leaf A
(6 x 6 threads)

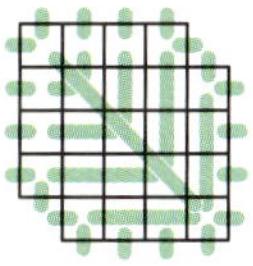

Leaf B
(8 x 8 threads)

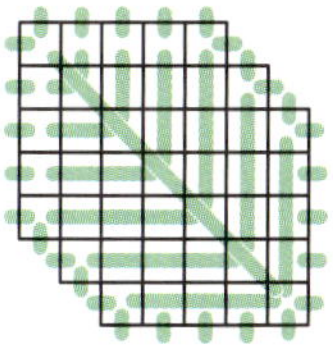

AUGUST GLADIOLA

Petal A
(4 x 4 threads)
(stitch 3)

Petal B
(4 x 5 threads)
(stitch 9)

SEPTEMBER ASTER

Leaf A
(8 x 8 threads)

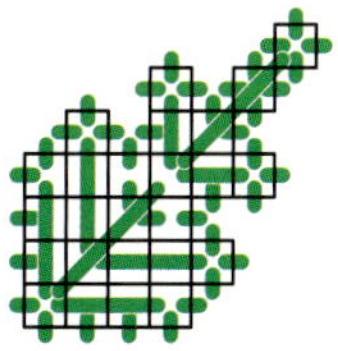

Leaf B
(8 x 8 threads)

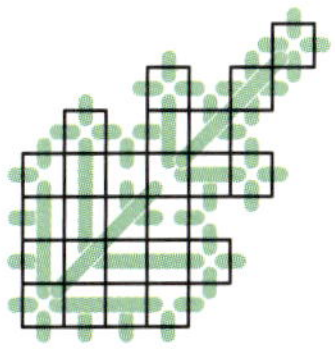

Petal A
(4 x 4 threads)

Petal B
(8 x 8 threads)

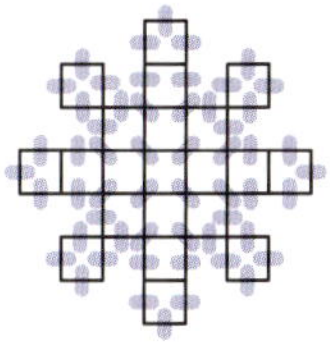

Petal C
(10 x 10 threads)

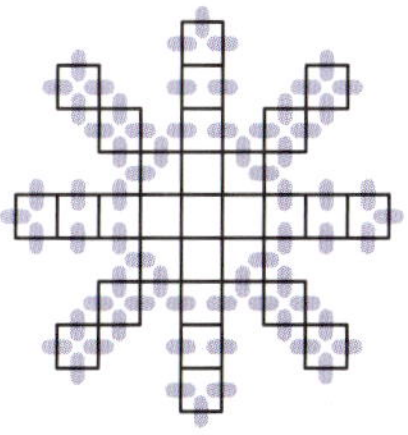

Petal D
(12 x 12 threads)

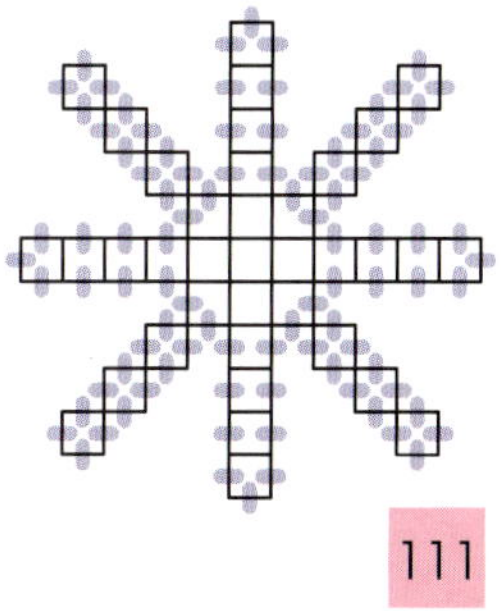

OCTOBER CALENDULA

Petal A
(8 x 8 threads)

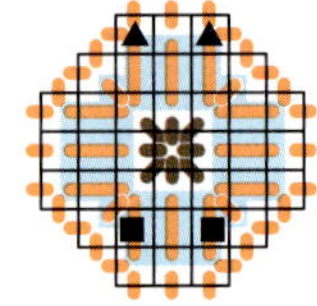

Petal B
(10 x 10 threads)

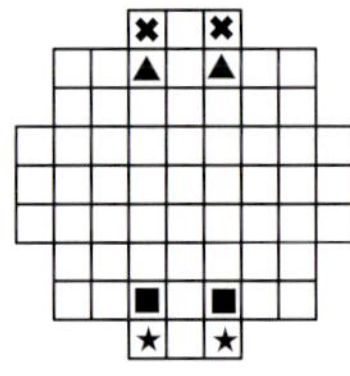

Petal C
(12 x 12 threads)

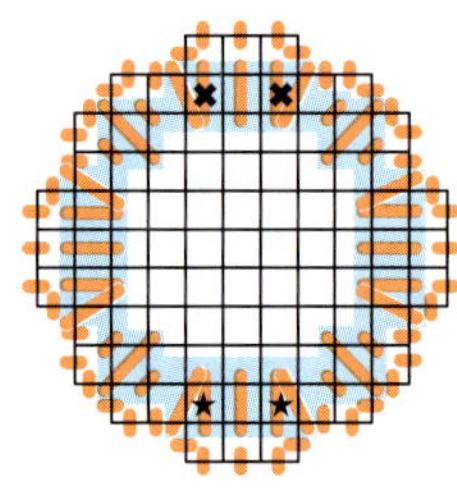

NOVEMBER MUM

Petal
(12 x 12 threads)
(stitch 2)

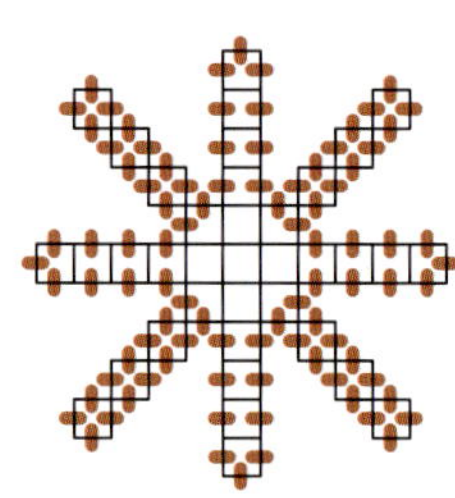

Leaf
(5 x 5 threads)

Center A
(4 x 4 threads)

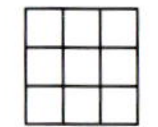

Center B
(4 x 4 threads)
(cut 3)

DECEMBER POINSETTIA

Petal A
(8 x 8 threads)

Petal B
(14 x 14 threads)

Leaf
(7 x 7 threads)
(stitch 3)

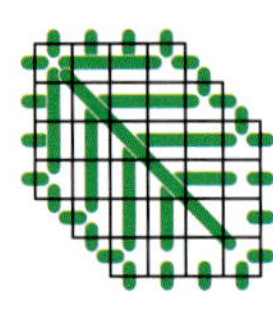

BOX

Top Side (18 x 4 threads) (stitch 4)

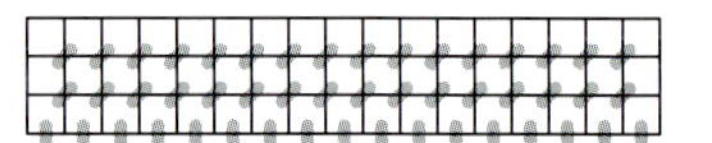

Bottom (22 x 22 threads)

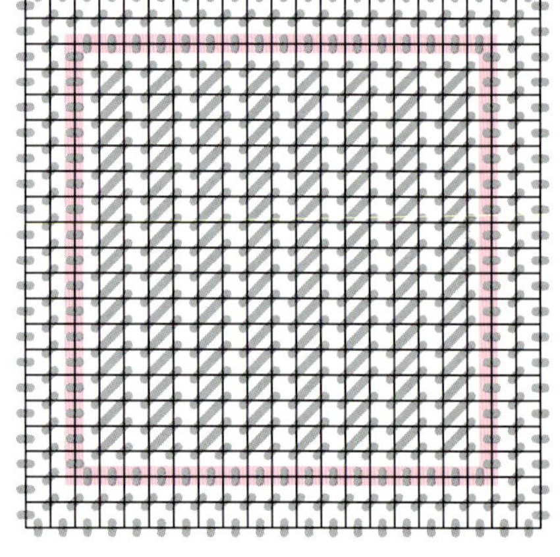

Bottom Side
(20 x 12 threads) (stitch 4)

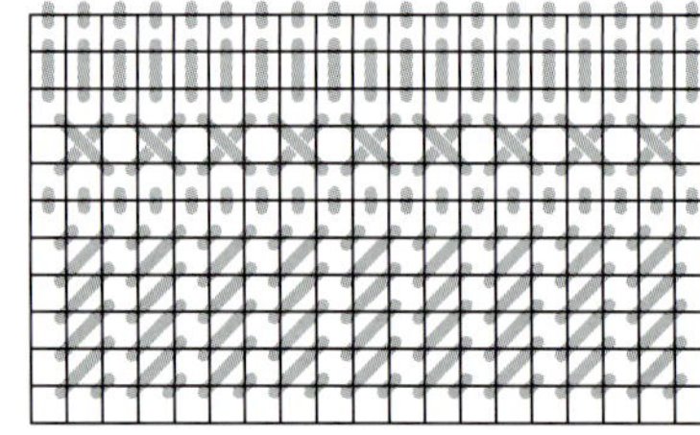

January Top (22 x 22 threads)

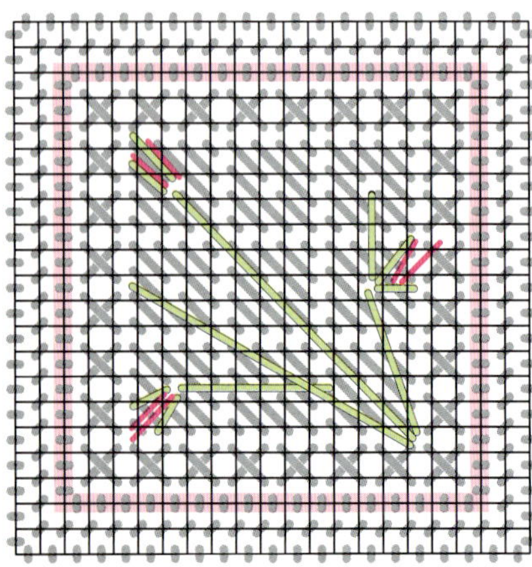

February Top (22 x 22 threads)

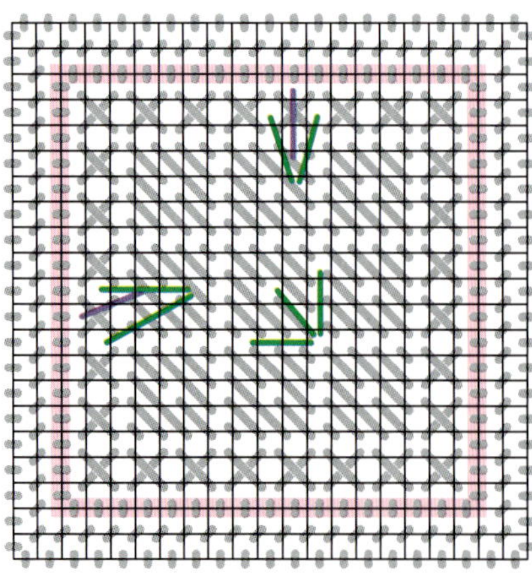

March Top (22 x 22 threads)

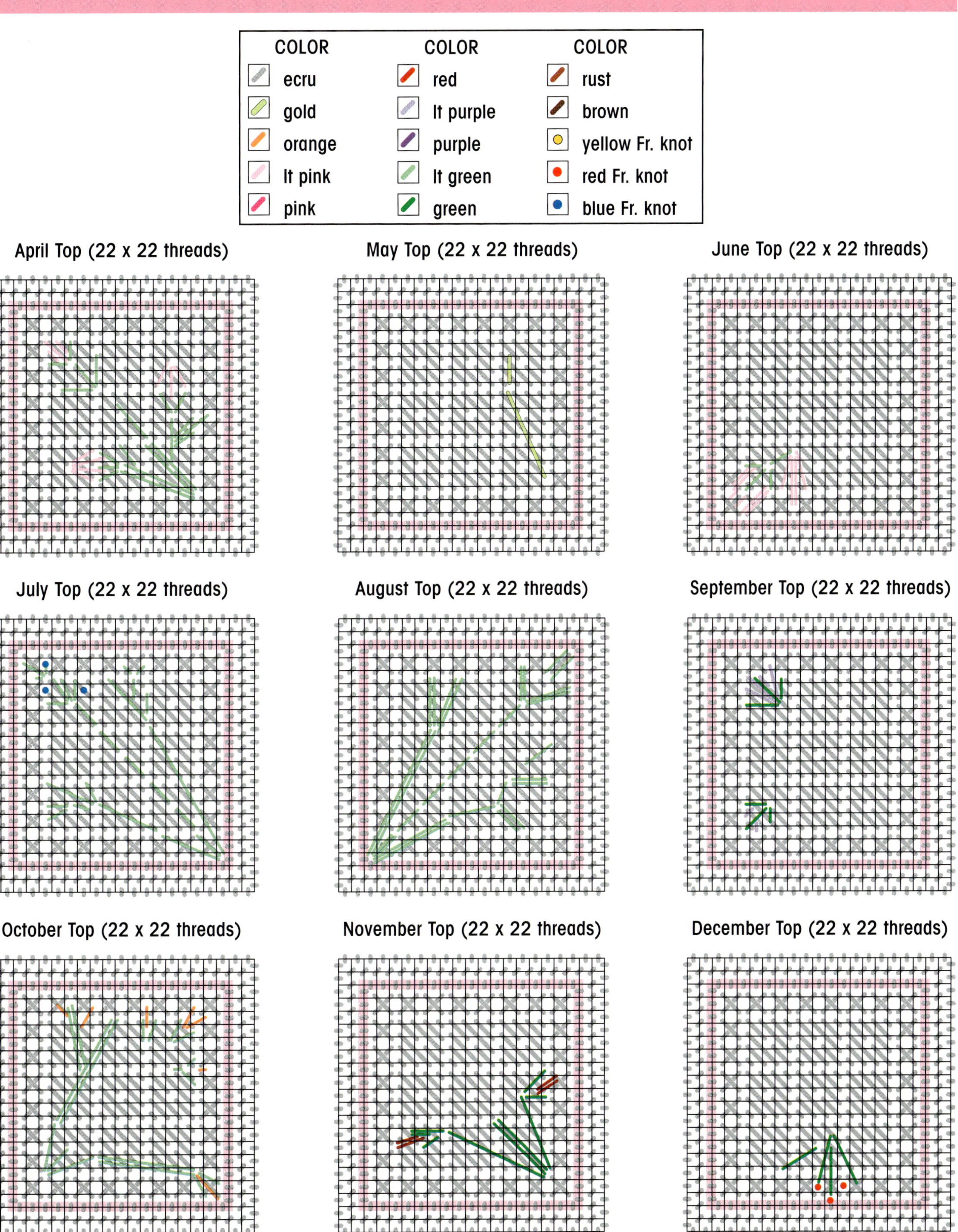

April Top (22 x 22 threads) **May Top (22 x 22 threads)** **June Top (22 x 22 threads)**

July Top (22 x 22 threads) **August Top (22 x 22 threads)** **September Top (22 x 22 threads)**

October Top (22 x 22 threads) **November Top (22 x 22 threads)** **December Top (22 x 22 threads)**

THRU THE SEASONS

(Shown on page 93.)
Skill Level: Intermediate
Size: 10¼"w x 12"h x 2¾"d
(Fits a 9¾"w x 11½"h x 2"d photo album.)
Supplies: Worsted weight yarn (refer to color key), three 10½" x 13½" sheets of clear 7 mesh plastic canvas, #16 tapestry needle, and photo album.
Stitches Used: Backstitch, French Knot, Gobelin Stitch, Mosaic Stitch, Overcast Stitch, Reversed Tent Stitch, and Tent Stitch.
Instructions: Follow charts to cut and stitch Photo Album Cover pieces, working backstitches and French knots last. For Back, cut a piece of canvas 68 x 80 threads. Cover Back using white Gobelin stitches over three threads. Using white overcast stitches, join Front and Back to Spine along long edges. For Sleeves, cut two pieces of canvas 15 x 80 threads each. Sleeves are not worked. Join one Sleeve to wrong side of Front along unworked edges of Front. Repeat to join remaining Sleeve to Back. Cover unworked edges of Back.

COLOR	
/	white
/	yellow
/	gold
/	red
/	lt blue
/	blue
/	dk blue
/	green
/	black
/	*black
●	*white Fr. knot
Use two plies of yarn.	

Spine (18 x 80 threads)

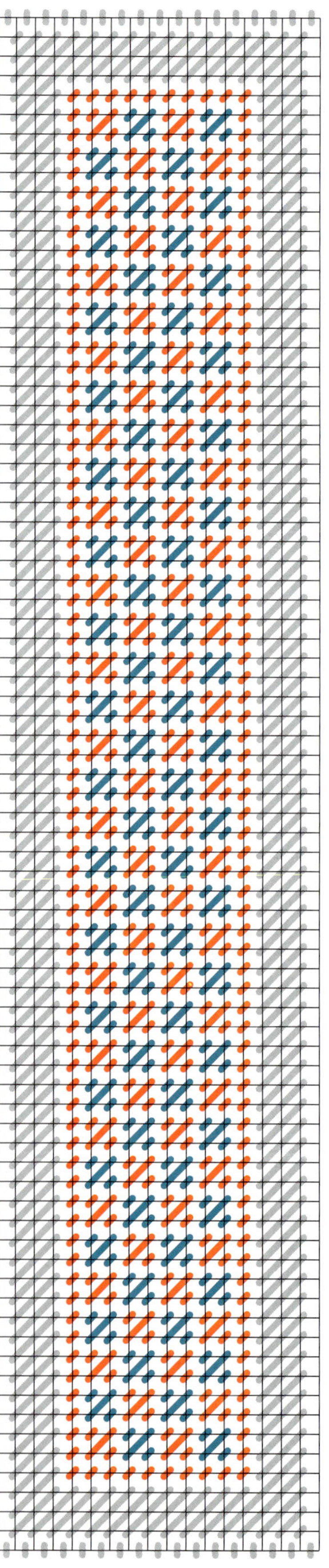

Front (68 x 80 threads)

DOOR SIGN

(Shown on page 96.)
Skill Level: Beginner
Size: 5"w x 10³/₄"h
Supplies: Worsted weight yarn (refer to color key), one 10¹/₂" x 13¹/₂" sheet of clear 7 mesh plastic canvas, and #16 tapestry needle.
Stitches Used: Cross Stitch, Gobelin Stitch, Overcast Stitch, Reversed Tent Stitch, and Tent Stitch.
Instructions: Follow chart to cut and stitch Door Sign piece.

COLOR	
⁄	white
⁄	yellow
⁄	red
⁄	green
⁄	rust

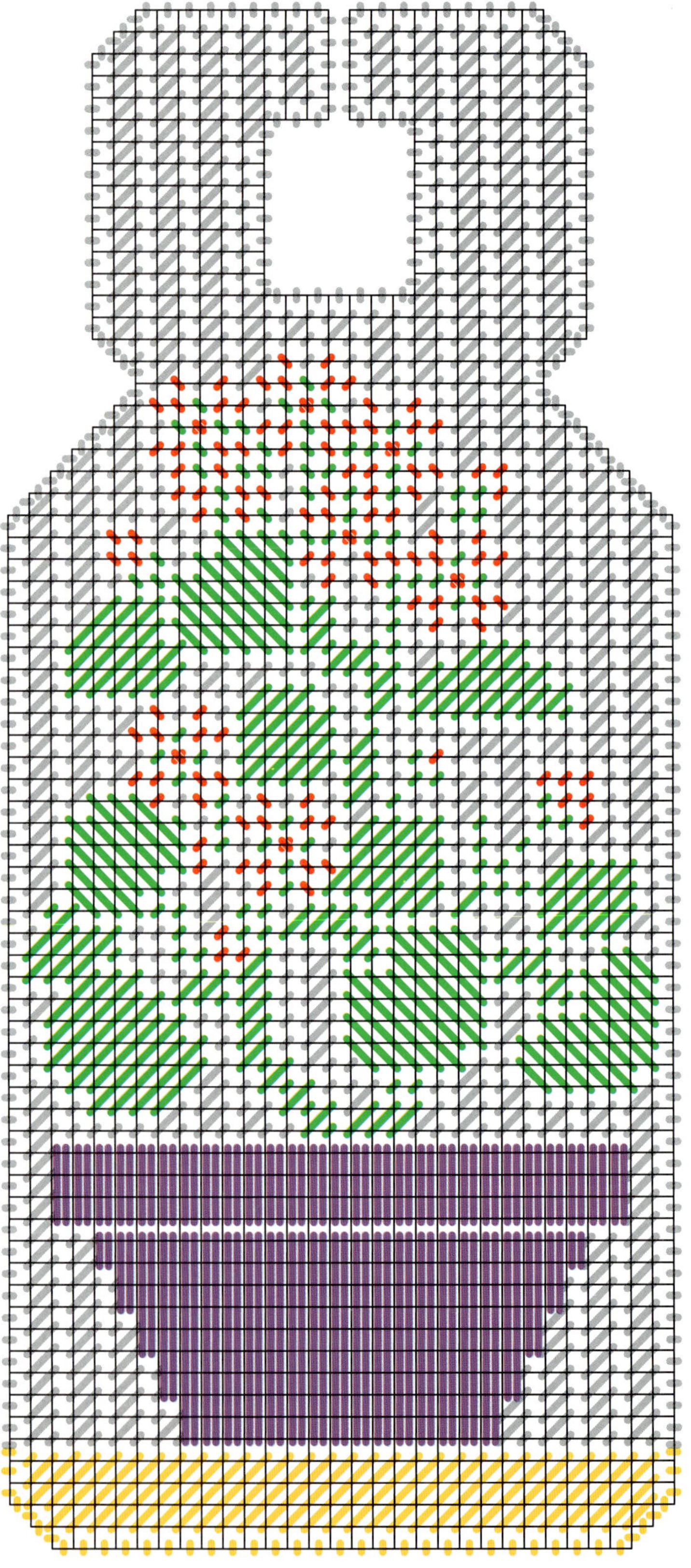

MAGNET

(Shown on page 96.)
Skill Level: Beginner
Size: 3"w x 3¼"h
Supplies: Worsted weight yarn (refer to color key), one 10½" x 13½" sheet of clear 7 mesh plastic canvas, #16 tapestry needle, magnetic strip, and craft glue.
Stitches Used: Backstitch, Gobelin Stitch, Overcast Stitch, Reversed Tent Stitch, and Tent Stitch.
Instructions: Follow chart to cut and stitch Magnet piece, working backstitches last. Glue magnetic strip to back of Magnet.

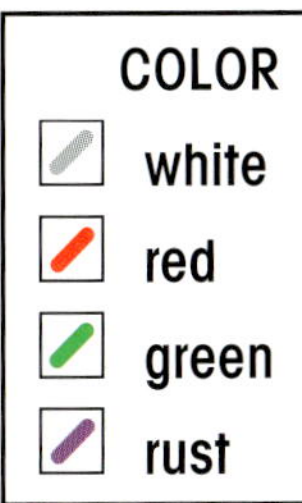

COLOR	
	white
	red
	green
	rust

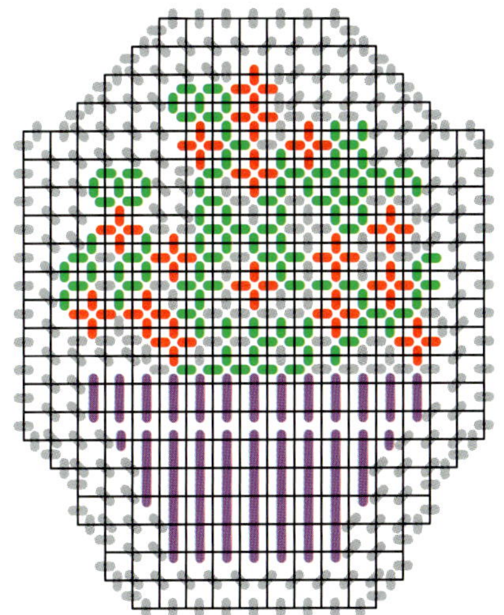

Magnet
(18 x 22 threads)

SWITCH PLATE COVER

(Shown on page 96.)
Skill Level: Beginner
Size: 3¾"w x 5½"h
Supplies: Worsted weight yarn (refer to color key), one 10½" x 13½" sheet of clear 7 mesh plastic canvas, and #16 tapestry needle.
Stitches Used: Backstitch, Gobelin Stitch, Overcast Stitch, and Tent Stitch.
Instructions: Follow chart to cut and stitch Switch Plate Cover piece, working backstitches last.

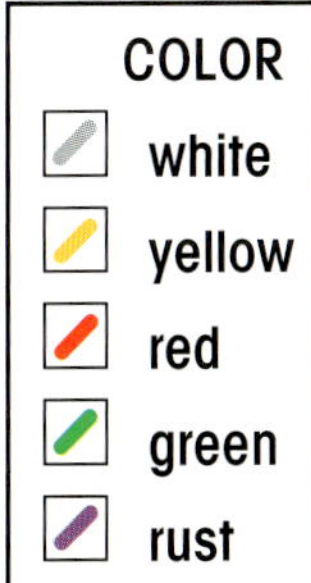

COLOR	
	white
	yellow
	red
	green
	rust

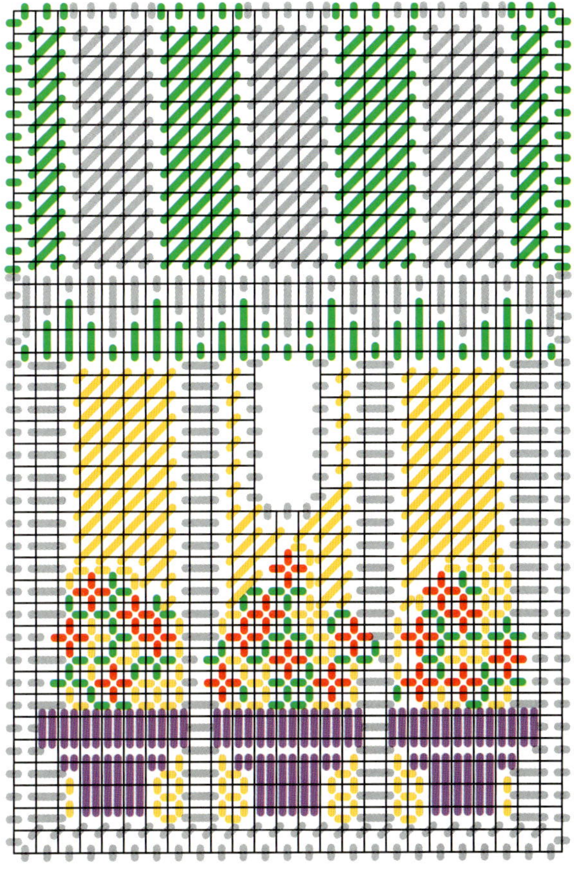

Switch Plate Cover (26 x 38 threads)

(Shown on page 95.)
Skill Level: Beginner
Size: 2"w x 4"h x ⅝"d
Supplies: Worsted weight yarn (refer to color key), one 10½" x 13½" sheet of clear 7 mesh plastic canvas, #16 tapestry needle, magnetic strip, and craft glue.
Stitches Used: Backstitch, Overcast Stitch, and Tent Stitch.

Instructions: Follow charts to cut and stitch Magnet pieces, working backstitch last and leaving blue shaded area unworked. Matching ◆'s, work stitches in blue shaded area to join Petal to Front. Matching ✖'s, use brown overcast stitches to join Flowerpot Edge to Front between ✖'s. Tack Leaf to Front. Using matching color overcast stitches, join Back to Front along unworked edges. Glue magnetic strip to Back.

COLOR	
✓	green
✓	dk green
✓	brown
✓	Tulip color

Flowerpot Edge
(11 x 11 threads)

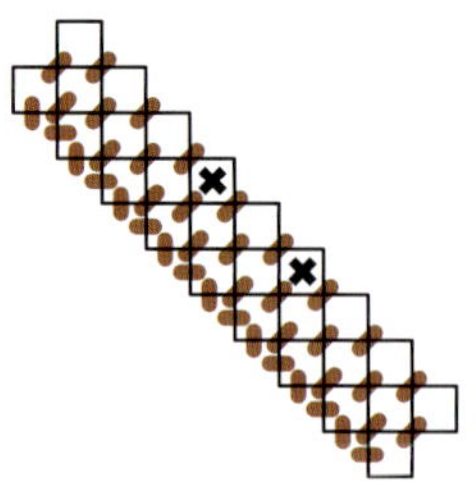

Petal (11 x 11 threads)

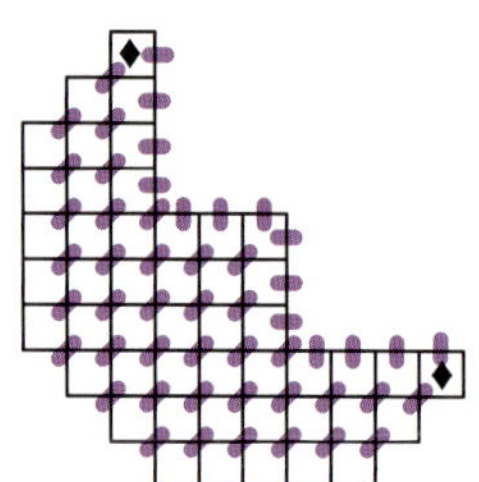

Front/Back
(24 x 24 threads) (cut 2) (stitch 1)

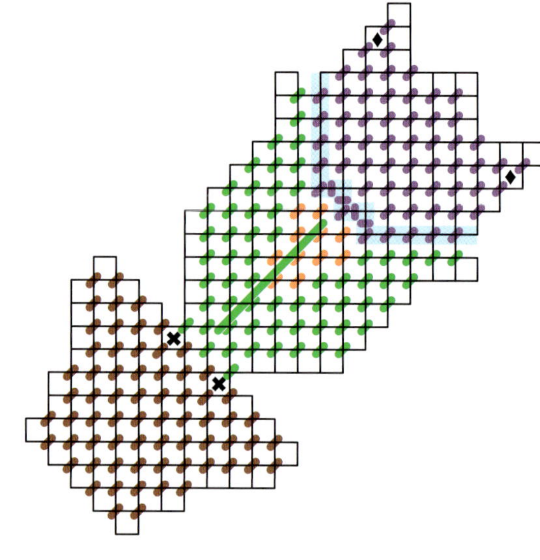

Leaf (8 x 8 threads)

(Shown on page 95.)
Skill Level: Beginner
Size: 4¼"w x 4"h
Supplies: Worsted weight yarn (refer to color key), one 10½" x 13½" sheet of clear 7 mesh plastic canvas, #16 tapestry needle, cork or felt (optional), and craft glue (optional).
Stitches Used: Backstitch, French Knot, Gobelin Stitch, Overcast Stitch, and Tent Stitch.

Instructions: Follow chart to cut and stitch Fish Coaster, working backstitches and French knot last. If backing is desired, cut cork or felt slightly smaller than Coaster; glue to back of Coaster.

COLOR	
✓	white
✓	lt yellow
✓	yellow
✓	black
●	black Fr. knot

Fish Coaster (25 x 26 threads)

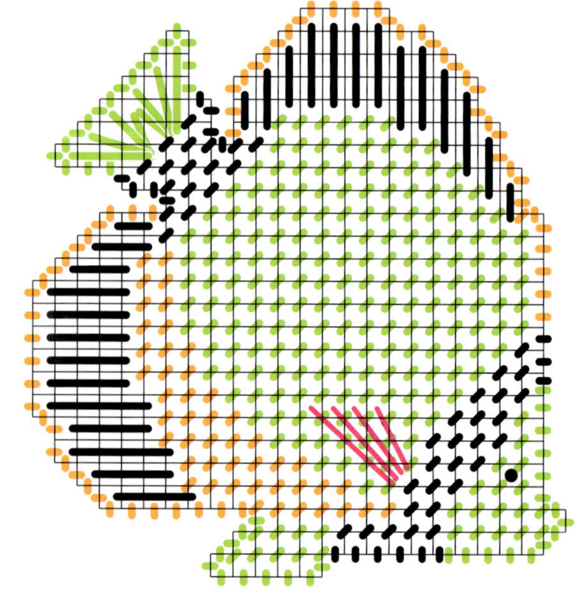

HOMEGROWN GOODNESS

(Shown on page 94.)
Skill Level: Advanced
Size: 8"w x 6¾"h x 7"d
(Fits a 4¼"w x 5¼"h x 4¼"d boutique tissue box.)

Supplies: Worsted weight yarn or Needloft® Plastic Canvas Yarn (refer to color keys), three 10½" x 13½" sheets of clear 7 mesh plastic canvas, and #16 tapestry needle.

Stitches Used: Backstitch, Cross Stitch, French Knot, Gobelin Stitch, Mosaic Stitch, Overcast Stitch, Reversed Tent Stitch, Smyrna Cross Stitch, and Tent Stitch.

Instructions: Follow charts to cut and stitch Tissue Box Cover pieces, working backstitches and French knots last and leaving shaded areas unworked. Matching ■'s and ▲'s, use tan overcast stitches to join Front Vegetable Display to pink shaded thread on Front. Matching ♠'s and ✖'s, join Front Vegetable Display to Front Stand along unworked long edges. Matching ♠'s, use white overcast stitches to join Front Stand to one Right Stand End along short edges. Matching ✖'s, join remaining short edge of Front Stand to short edge of one Left Stand End. Matching ■'s and ♠'s, use tan overcast stitches to join Front Vegetable Display to Right Stand End. Matching ✖'s and ▲'s, join Front Vegetable Display to Left Stand End. Repeat for Back pieces.

Matching ■'s and ▲'s, use tan overcast stitches to join one Side Vegetable Display piece to yellow shaded thread on Side #1. Matching ♠'s and ✖'s, join Side Vegetable Display to Side Stand piece along unworked long edges. Matching ♠'s, use white overcast stitches to join Side Stand to one Right Stand End along short edges. Matching ✖'s, join remaining short edge of Front Stand to short edge of one Left Stand End. Matching ■'s and ♠'s, use tan overcast stitches to join Side Vegetable Display to Right Stand End. Matching ✖'s and ▲'s, join Side Vegetable Display to Left Stand End. Repeat for Side #2 pieces.

From ▼'s and ★'s, use white overcast stitches to join Front to Side #1. Matching ◆'s and ✚'s, join Front to Side #2. Join Back to Sides. From ★'s to ♣'s, join Front to Side #1 and Stand End pieces through four thicknesses of canvas. From ✚'s to ♣'s, join Front to Side #2 and Stand End pieces. Join Back to Sides and Stand Ends. Using green overcast stitches, join Awning Top to Awning Front along long edges. Join remaining long edge of Awning Top to Awning Back. Referring to photo for yarn colors, use overcast stitches to join Awning to Front, Back, and Sides.

Matching ♥'s, tack Signs to Awning Front and Awning Back.

Sign (34 x 10 threads) (stitch 2)

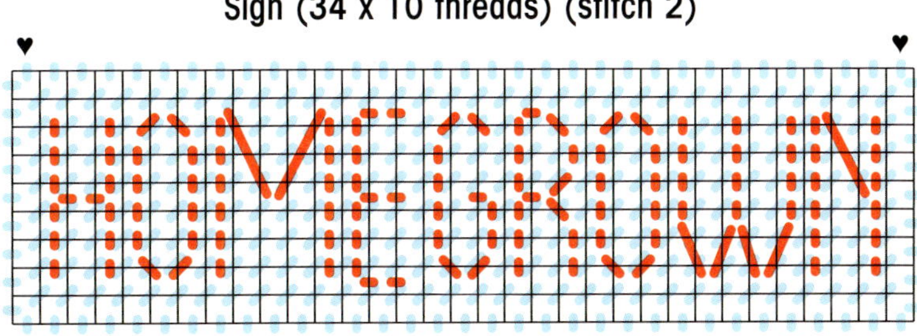

Front/Back Stand
(38 x 11 threads) (stitch 2)

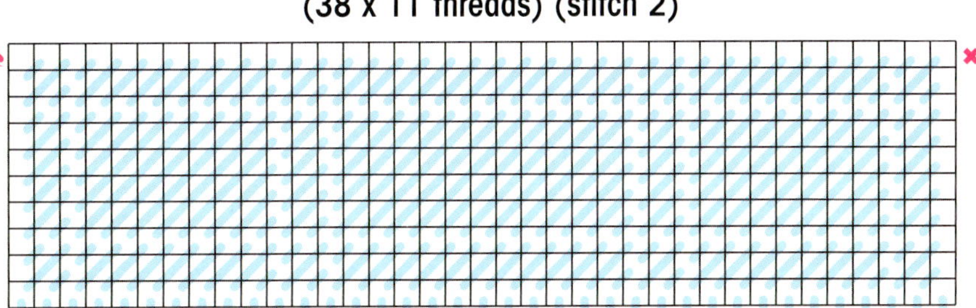

Awning Top (38 x 8 threads)

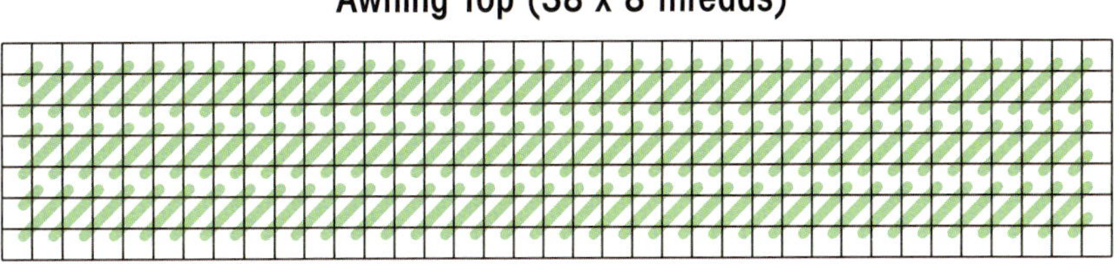

Awning Front/Back
(38 x 22 threads) (stitch 2)

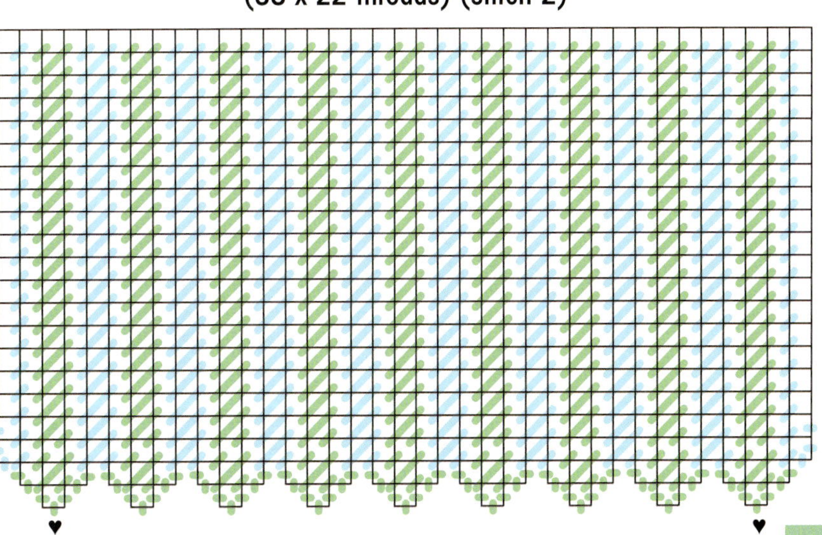

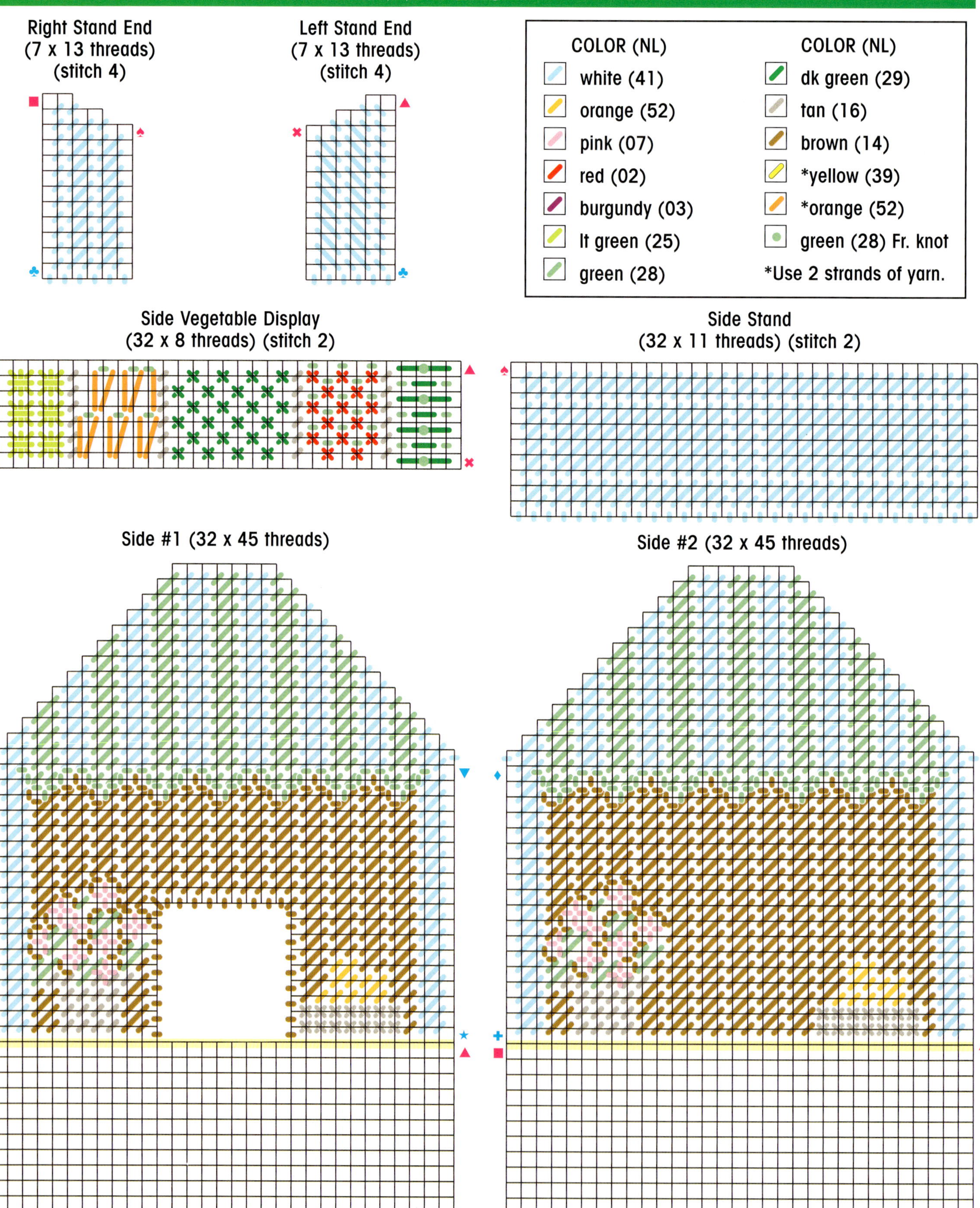

Right Stand End
(7 x 13 threads)
(stitch 4)

Left Stand End
(7 x 13 threads)
(stitch 4)

COLOR (NL)
white (41)
orange (52)
pink (07)
red (02)
burgundy (03)
lt green (25)
green (28)

COLOR (NL)
dk green (29)
tan (16)
brown (14)
*yellow (39)
*orange (52)
green (28) Fr. knot
*Use 2 strands of yarn.

Side Vegetable Display
(32 x 8 threads) (stitch 2)

Side Stand
(32 x 11 threads) (stitch 2)

Side #1 (32 x 45 threads)

Side #2 (32 x 45 threads)

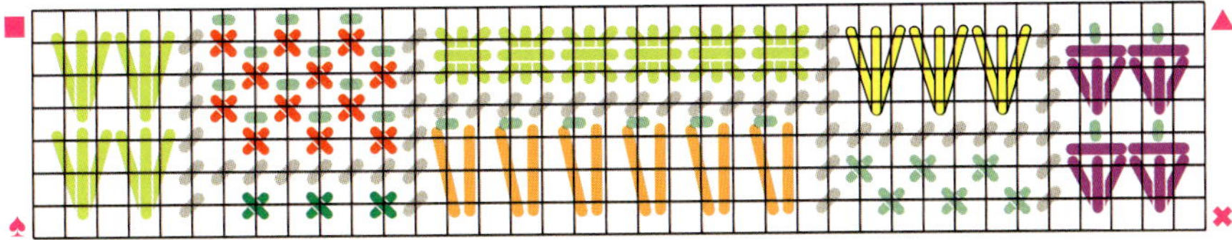

Front/Back Vegetable Display
(38 x 8 threads) (stitch 2)

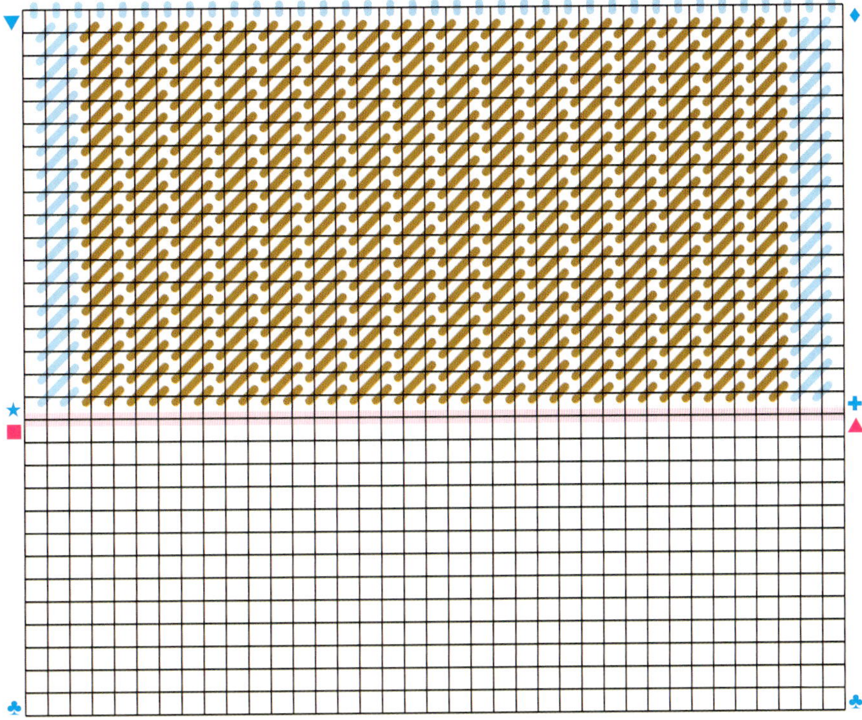

Front/Back
(38 x 32 threads) (stitch 2)

LI'L LADYBUG

(Shown on page 92.)
Skill Level: Beginner
Size: 3"w x 4³/₄"h
Supplies: Worsted weight yarn (refer to color key), one 10¹/₂" x 13¹/₂" sheet of clear 7 mesh plastic canvas, #16 tapestry needle, wooden skewer, 3" length of 3mm black chenille stem, and craft glue.
Stitches Used: Backstitch, Overcast Stitch, and Tent Stitch.
Instructions: Follow chart to cut and stitch Plant Poke piece, working backstitches last. Fold chenille stem in half and glue to back of Ladybug. Glue skewer to back of Ladybug.

Ladybug (20 x 20 threads)

COLOR	
✏	red - 4 yds
✏	black - 2 yds

PENCIL HOLDER

(Shown on page 92.)
Skill Level: Beginner
Size: 4¼"w x 3½"h x 4¼"d
Supplies: Worsted weight yarn (refer to color key), one 10½" x 13½" sheet of clear 7 mesh plastic canvas, and #16 tapestry needle.
Stitches Used: Gobelin Stitch and Overcast Stitch.
Instructions: Follow charts to cut and stitch Pencil Holder pieces, leaving blue shaded areas unworked. Matching ★'s, work stitches in blue shaded areas to join ends of Side, forming a cylinder. To form apple shape, fold down sections of Side, matching A's to B's. Using red overcast stitches, join sections as indicated by heavy black lines. Using tan overcast stitches, join unworked edges of Side to Base along placement line. Tack Leaves to Side.

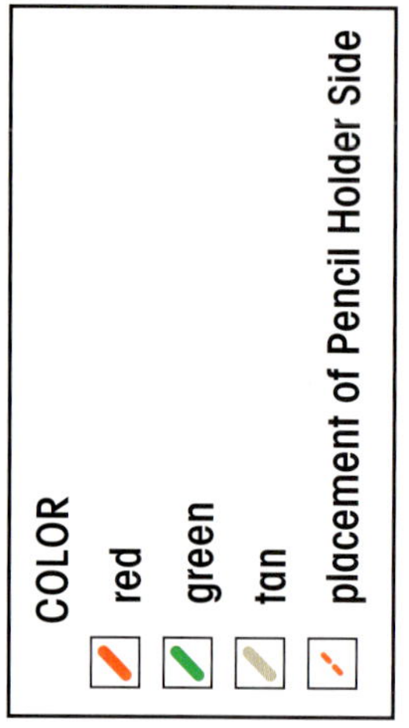

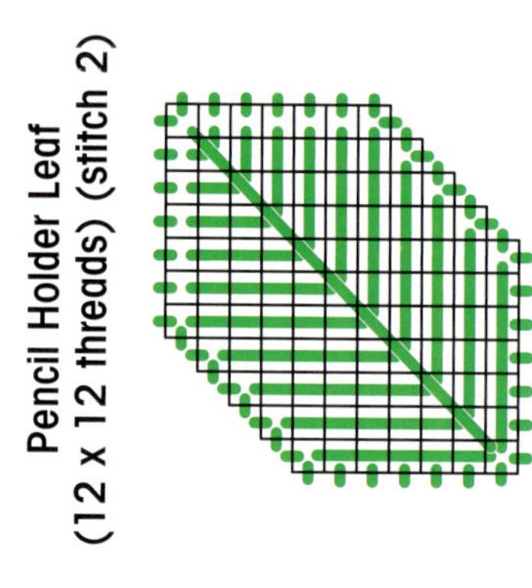

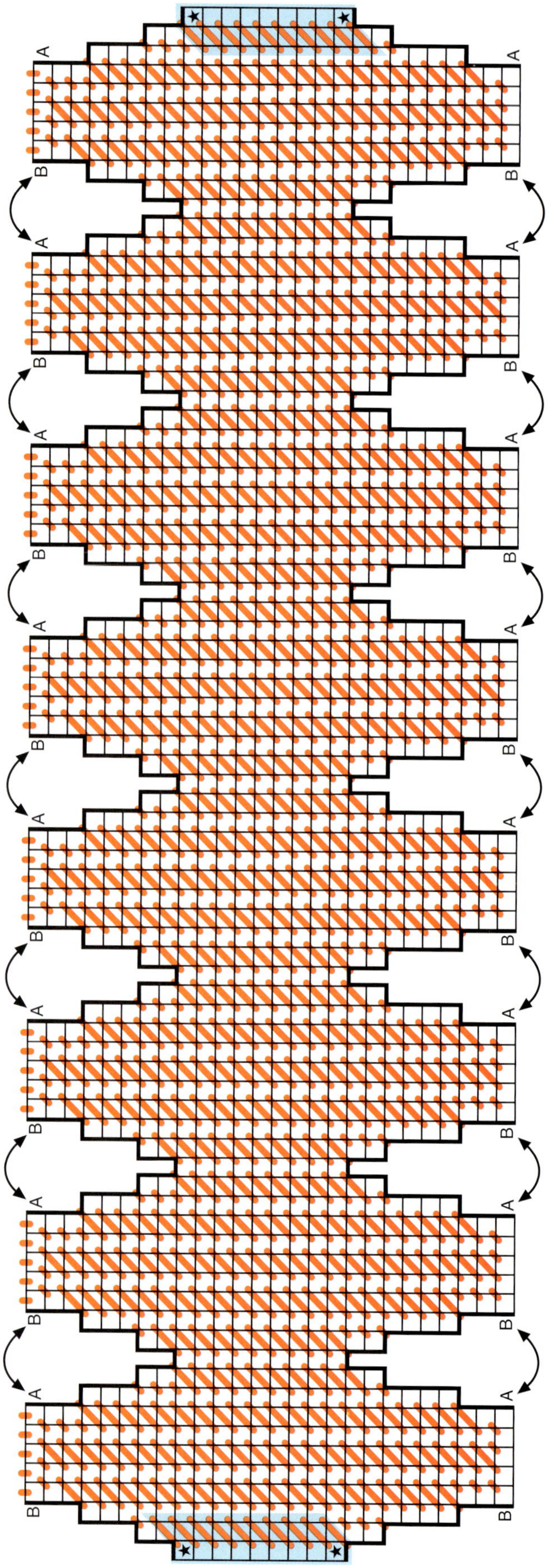

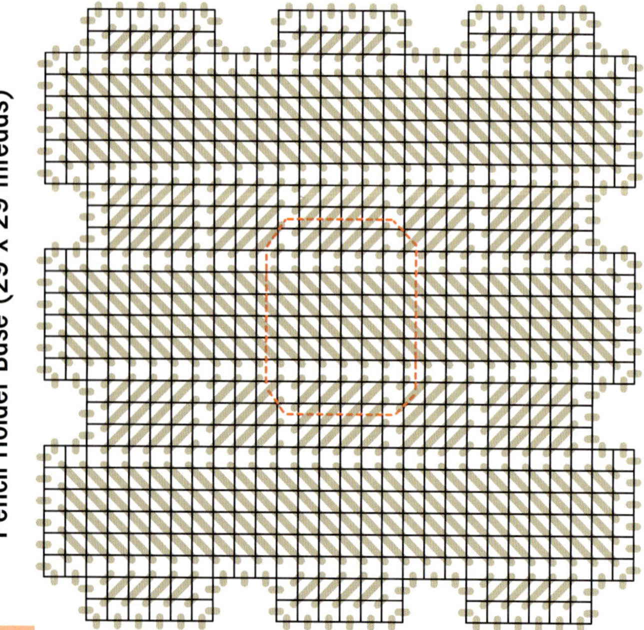

STORAGE BOX

(Shown on page 92.)
Skill Level: Beginner
Size: 5"w x 1³/₄"h x 5"d
Supplies: Worsted weight yarn (refer to color key), two 10¹/₂" x 13¹/₂" sheets of clear 7 mesh plastic canvas, #16 tapestry needle, and 2 yds yellow worsted weight yarn.
Stitches Used: Backstitch, French Knot, Gobelin Stitch, Overcast Stitch, Tent Stitch, and Turkey Loop Stitch.
Instructions: Follow charts to cut and stitch Box pieces, working backstitches and Turkey Loops last. Using tan overcast stitches, join Top Sides along short edges. Join Top to Top Sides. Join Bottom Sides along short edges. Join Bottom Sides to Bottom. Matching ▲'s, use red overcast stitches to join Divider #2 pieces to both sides of Divider #1, working through three layers of canvas. Join Dividers to Bottom along unworked threads. Using tan overcast stitches, join short edges of Dividers to Bottom Sides along unworked threads. Using yellow Fr. knots, join Box Flowers to Box Top at ★'s.

COLOR		COLOR	
⟋	white	⟋	black
⟋	red	○	green Turkey loop
⟋	tan		

Box Flower
(4 x 4 threads)
(stitch 8)

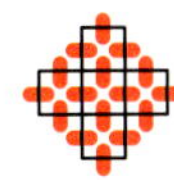

Box Divider #2
(15 x 9 threads) (stitch 2)

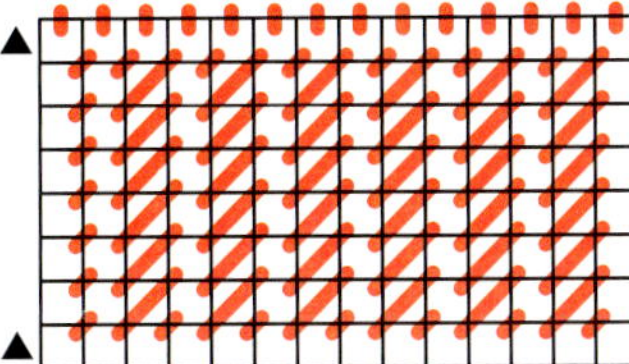

Box Divider #1 (31 x 9 threads)

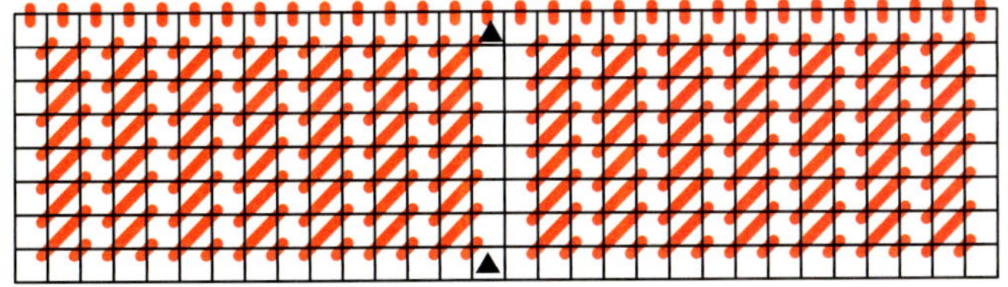

Box Bottom Side (31 x 10 threads) (stitch 4)

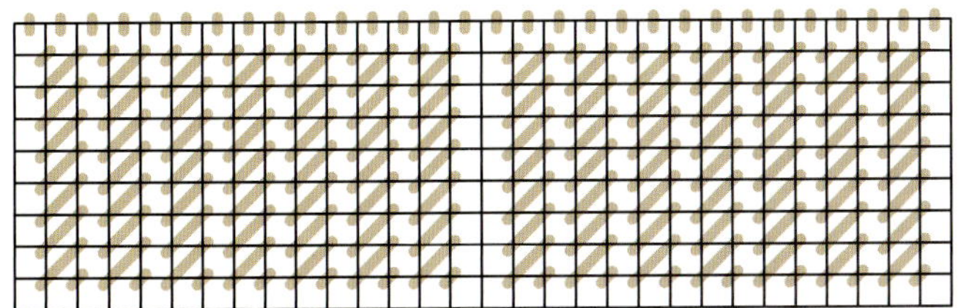

Box Top Sides (33 x 5 threads) (stitch 4)

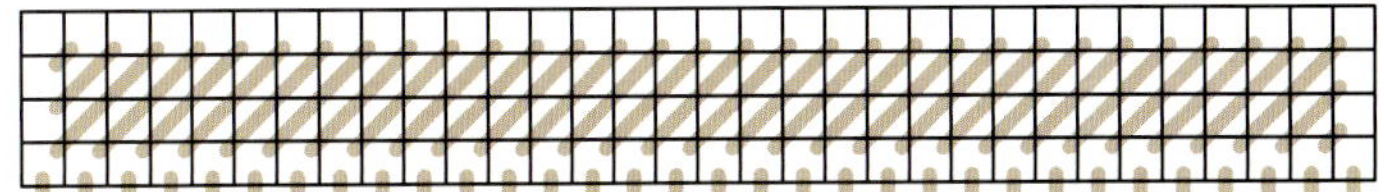

Box Top (33 x 33 threads)
Complete background with black tent stitches as indicated on the chart.

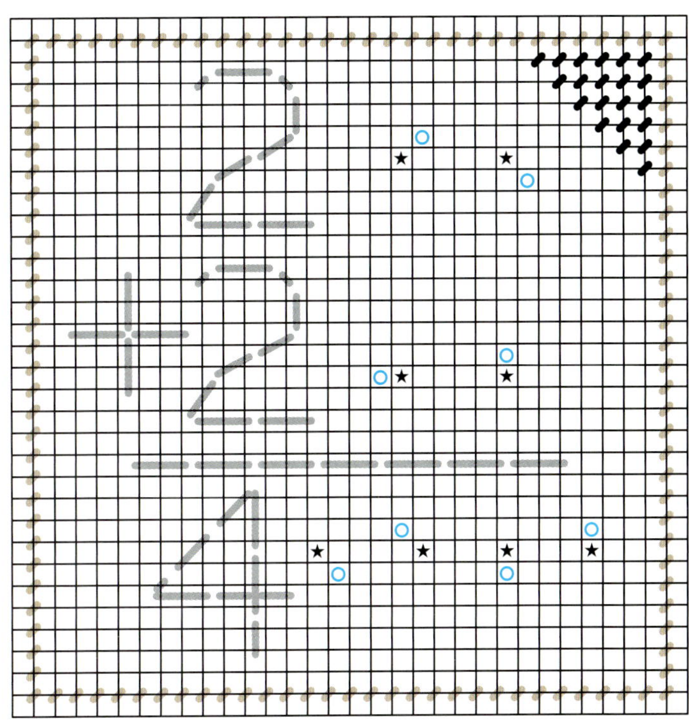

Box Bottom (31 x 31 threads)

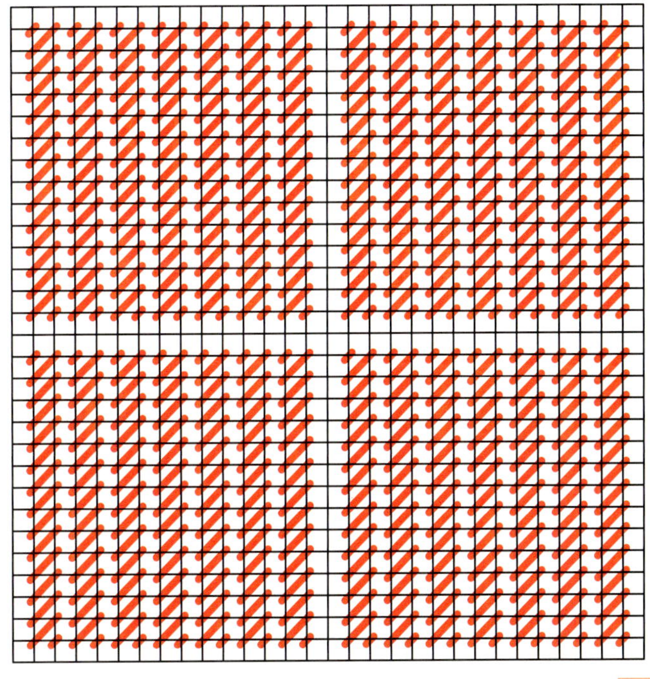

"GET WELL" WISHES

(Shown on page 90.)
Skill Level: Beginner
Size: 5"w x 11½"h
Supplies: Worsted weight yarn (refer to color key), one 10½" x 13½" sheet of clear 7 mesh plastic canvas, and #16 tapestry needle.
Stitches Used: Backstitch, Gobelin Stitch, Mosaic Stitch, Overcast Stitch, Reversed Tent Stitch, and Tent Stitch.
Instructions: Follow charts to cut and stitch Sign pieces, working backstitches last. Tack Flower to Sign.

COLOR
- yellow - 2 yds
- orange - 2 yds
- pink - 10 yds
- lt green - 4 yds
- green - 10 yds

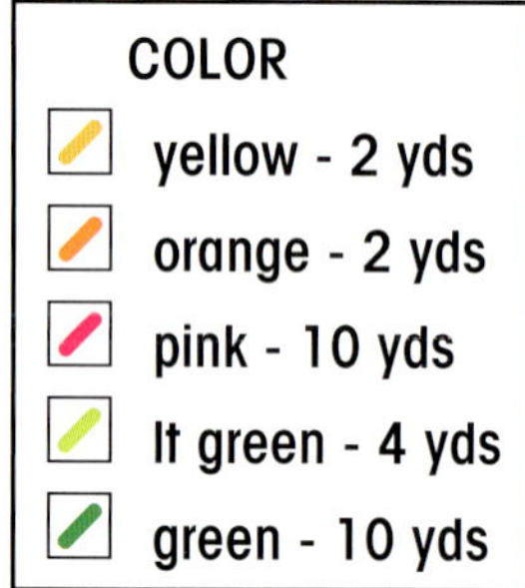

Flower (12 x 12 threads)

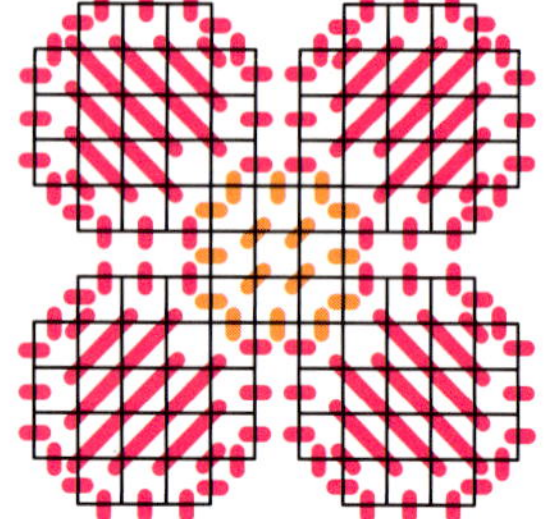

Sign (34 x 79 threads)

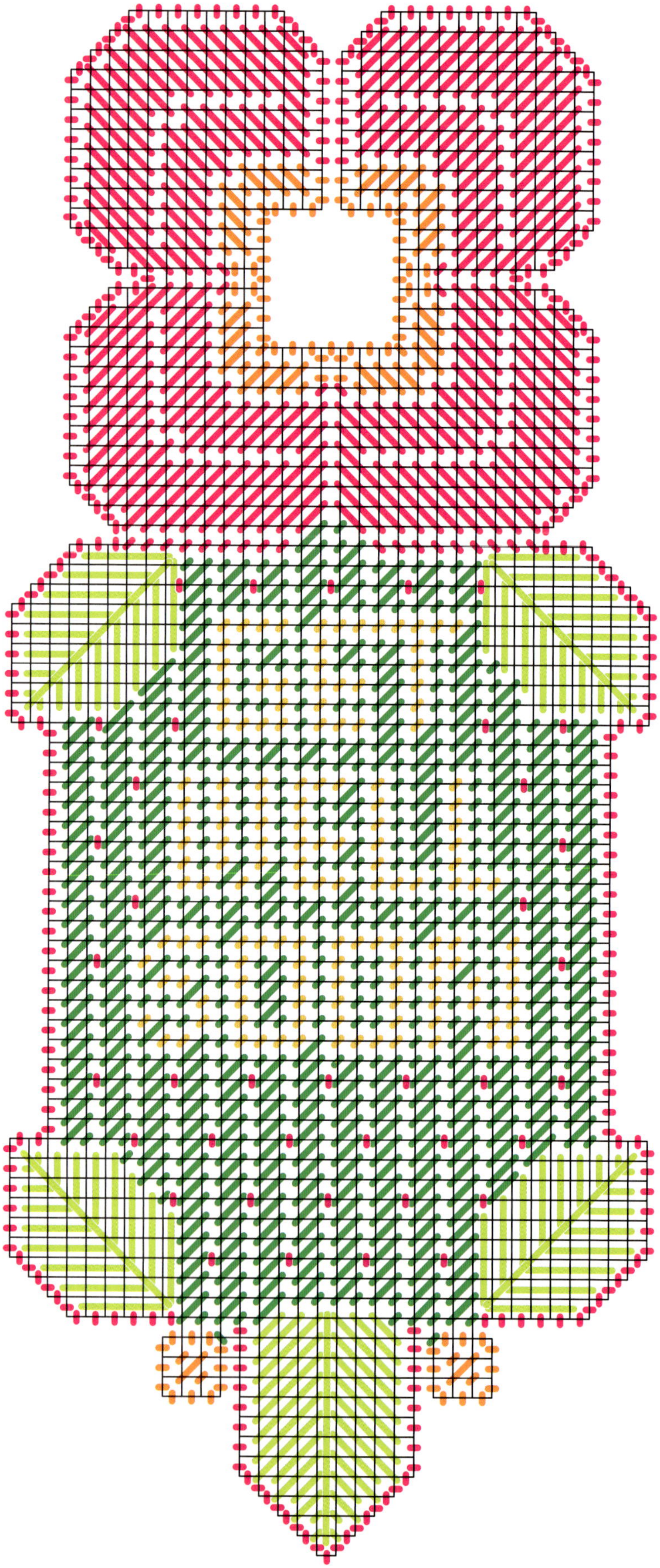

GENERAL INSTRUCTIONS

SELECTING PLASTIC CANVAS

Plastic canvas is a molded material that consists of "threads" and "holes," but the threads aren't actually "threads" since the canvas is not woven. Project instructions often refer to the threads, especially when cutting out plastic canvas pieces. The holes are the spaces between the threads. The Stitch Diagrams, pages 127-128, will refer to holes when explaining where to place your needle to make a stitch.

TYPES OF CANVAS

The main difference between types of plastic canvas is the mesh size. Mesh size refers to the number of holes in one inch of canvas. The projects in this book were stitched using 7 mesh, 10 mesh, or 14 mesh canvas. Seven mesh canvas is the most popular size.

7 mesh = 7 holes per inch
10 mesh = 10 holes per inch
14 mesh = 14 holes per inch

Your project supply list will tell you the size mesh needed for your project. If your project calls for 7 mesh canvas and you use 10 mesh, your finished project will be much smaller than expected.

Most plastic canvas is clear, but colored plastic canvas is also available. Colored canvas is ideal when you don't want to stitch the entire background.

AMOUNT OF CANVAS

The project supply list will tell you how much canvas will be needed to complete the project. As a general rule, it is better to buy too much canvas and have leftovers than to run out of canvas before you finish your project.

SELECTING NEEDLES

TYPES OF NEEDLES

A blunt needle called a tapestry needle is used for stitching on plastic canvas. Tapestry needles are sized by numbers; the higher the number, the smaller the needle. The correct size needle to use depends on the canvas mesh size and the yarn thickness. The needle should be small enough to allow the threaded needle to pass through the canvas holes easily. The eye of the needle should be large enough to allow yarn to be threaded easily. If the eye is too small, the yarn will wear thin and may break. You will find the recommended needle size listed in the supply section of each project. The chart below will be helpful if you need to select the correct needle for your project.

Mesh	Needle
7	#16 tapestry
10	#20 tapestry
14	#24 tapestry

SELECTING YARN

We have a few hints to help you choose the perfect yarns for your project.

COLORS

Your project will tell you what yarn colors you will need. Brand names and color numbers listed in some color keys are included only as a guide when choosing colors for your project. Choose colors and brands to suit your needs and your taste.

TYPES OF YARN

The types of yarns available are endless, and each grouping of yarn has its own characteristics and uses. The following is a brief description of the yarns used in this book.

Worsted Weight Yarn - This yarn may be found in acrylic, wool, wool blends, and a variety of other fiber contents. Worsted weight yarn is the most popular yarn used for 7 mesh plastic canvas because one strand covers the canvas very well. This yarn is inexpensive and comes in a wide range of colors. Worsted weight yarn has four plies that are twisted together to form one strand. When the instructions call for two plies of yarn, simply remove two plies of the yarn and stitch with the remaining two plies.

Needloft® Plastic Canvas Yarn - This yarn is a 100% nylon worsted weight yarn and is suitable only for 7 mesh canvas. It will not easily separate. When stitching with Needloft and the instructions indicate two plies of yarn, substitute six strands of embroidery floss.

FLOSS AND PEARL COTTON

Embroidery Floss - Embroidery floss is made up of six strands. For smooth coverage when using embroidery floss, separate and realign the strands of floss before threading your needle. Twelve strands of floss may be used for covering 10 mesh canvas. Use six strands to cover 14 mesh canvas. Embroidery floss can also be used to add details on 7 mesh canvas by using six strands of floss.

Pearl Cotton - Sometimes #3 pearl cotton is used on plastic canvas to give it a dressy, lacy look. It is not meant to cover 7 mesh canvas completely but to enhance it. Pearl cotton works well on 10 mesh canvas when you want your needlework to have a satiny sheen. If you can't locate #3 pearl cotton, you can substitute twelve strands of embroidery floss.

WORKING WITH PLASTIC CANVAS

Throughout this book, the lines of the canvas will be referred to as threads. To cut plastic canvas pieces accurately, count **threads** (not **holes**) as shown in **Fig. 1**.

Fig. 1

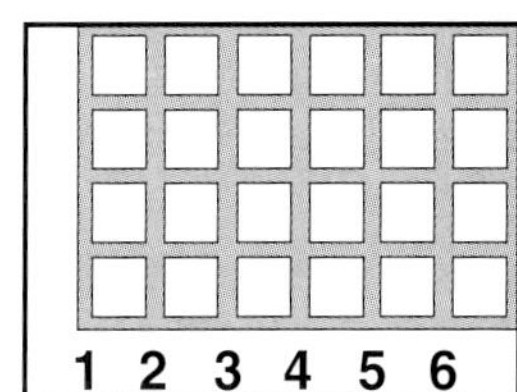

PREPARING AND CUTTING CANVAS

Before cutting out your pieces, note the thread count located above the chart for each piece. The thread count tells you the number of threads in the width and the height of the canvas piece. It can be helpful to follow the thread count to cut out a rectangle the specified size before cutting out your shape. Then, remembering to count threads, not holes, follow the chart to trim the rectangle into the desired shape.

You may want to use an overhead projector pen to outline the piece on the canvas before cutting it out. Before you begin stitching, be sure to remove all markings with a damp towel. Any markings could rub off on the yarn as you stitch.

A good pair of household scissors is recommended for cutting plastic canvas. However, a craft knife is helpful when cutting out small areas. When using a craft knife, protect the table below your canvas with a layer of cardboard or a magazine.

When cutting canvas, cut as close to the thread as possible without cutting into the thread. If you don't cut close enough, "nubs" or "pickets" will be left on the edge of your canvas. Make sure to cut all nubs from the canvas before you begin to stitch because nubs will snag the yarn and are difficult to cover.

When cutting plastic canvas along a diagonal, cut through the center of each intersection. This will leave enough plastic canvas on both sides of the cut so that both pieces of canvas may be used. Diagonal corners will also snag yarn less and be easier to cover.

The charts may show slits in the plastic canvas **(Fig. 2)**. To make slits, use a craft knife to cut exactly through the center of an intersection of plastic canvas threads. Repeat for number of intersections needed. When working piece, be careful not to carry yarn across slits.

Fig. 2

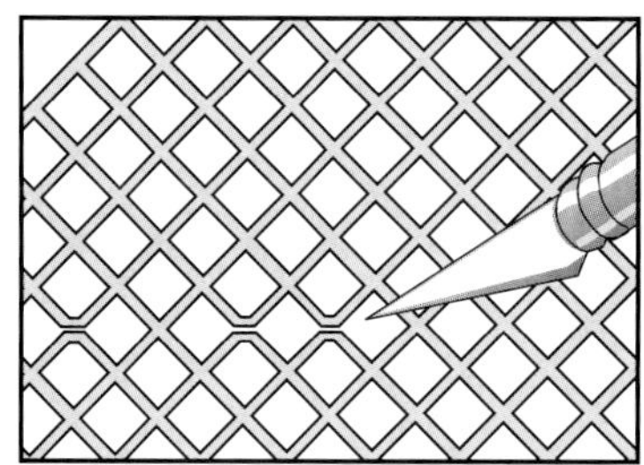

THREADING YOUR NEEDLE

Several brands of yarn-size needle threaders are available at your local craft store. Here are a couple of methods that will make threading your needle easier without a purchased threader.

FOLD METHOD

First, sharply fold the end of yarn over your needle; then remove needle. Keeping the fold sharp, push the needle onto the yarn **(Fig. 3)**.

Fig. 3

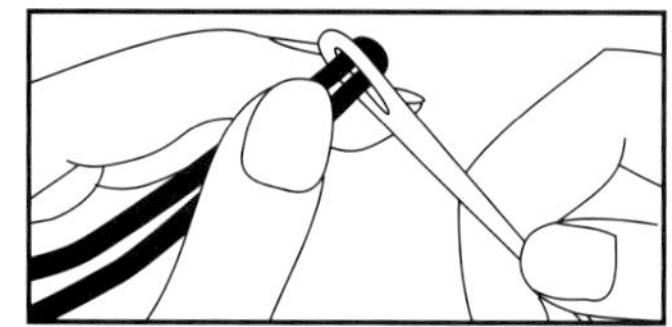

THREAD METHOD

Fold a 5" piece of sewing thread in half, forming a loop. Insert loop of thread through the eye of your needle **(Fig. 4)**. Insert yarn through the loop and pull the thread back through your needle, pulling yarn through at the same time.

Fig. 4

READING THE CHART

Whenever possible the drawing on the chart looks like the completed stitch. For example, a tent stitch on the chart is drawn diagonally across one intersection of threads just like a tent stitch looks when stitched on your canvas. A symbol will be used on the chart when a stitch, such as a French knot, cannot be clearly drawn. If you have difficulty determining how a particular stitch should be worked, refer to the list of stitches in the project information and the Stitch Diagrams on pages 127-128.

READING THE COLOR KEY

A color key is given with each group of projects. The key indicates the color used for each stitch on the chart. For example, when white yarn is represented by a grey line in the color key, all grey stitches on the chart should be stitched using white yarn.

To help you select colors for your projects, we have included color numbers for Needloft Plastic Canvas Yarn **(NL)**, DMC Embroidery Floss **(DMC)**, and DMC Pearl Cotton **(DMC)** in some of our color keys. Many other different brands are available and may be used to stitch your project.

Additional information may also be included in the color key, such as the number of strands or plies to use when working a particular stitch.

STITCHING THE DESIGN

Securing the First Stitch - Don't knot the end of your yarn before you begin stitching. Instead, begin each length of yarn by coming up from the wrong side of the canvas and leaving a 1" - 2" tail on the wrong side. Hold this tail against the canvas and work the first few stitches over the tail. When secure, clip the tail close to your stitched piece. Clipping the tail closely is important because long tails can become tangled in future stitches or show through to the right side of the canvas.

Using Even Tension - Keep your stitching tension consistent, with each stitch lying flat and even on the canvas. Pulling or yanking the yarn causes the tension to be too tight, and you will be able to see through your project. Loose tension is caused by not pulling the yarn firmly enough; consequently, the yarn will not lie flat on the canvas.

Ending Your Stitches - After you've completed all of the stitches of one color in an area, end your stitching by running your needle under several stitches on the back of the stitched piece. To keep the tails of the yarn from showing through or becoming tangled in future stitches, trim the end of the yarn close to the stitched piece.

JOINING PIECES

Straight Edges - The most common method of assembling stitched pieces is joining two or more pieces of canvas along a straight edge using overcast stitches. Place one piece on top of the other with right or wrong sides together. Make sure the edges being joined are even, then stitch the pieces together through all layers.

Tacking - To tack pieces, run your needle under the backs of some stitches on one stitched piece to secure the yarn. Then run your needle through the canvas or under the stitches on the piece to be tacked in place. The idea is to securely attach your pieces without your tacking stitches showing.

Shaded Areas - The shaded area is part of a chart that has colored shading on top of it. Shaded areas usually mean that all the stitches in that area are used to join pieces of canvas. Do not work the stitches in a shaded area until your project instructions say you should.

Uneven Edges - Sometimes you'll have to join a diagonal edge to a straight edge. The holes of the two pieces will not line up exactly. Just keep the pieces even and work overcast stitches through holes as many times as necessary to completely cover the canvas.

STITCH DIAGRAMS

> Unless otherwise indicated, bring threaded needle up at 1 and all odd numbers and down at 2 and all even numbers.

BACKSTITCH

This stitch is worked over completed stitches to outline or define **(Fig. 5)**. It is sometimes worked over more than one thread. Backstitch may also be used to cover canvas as shown in **Fig. 6**.

Fig. 5

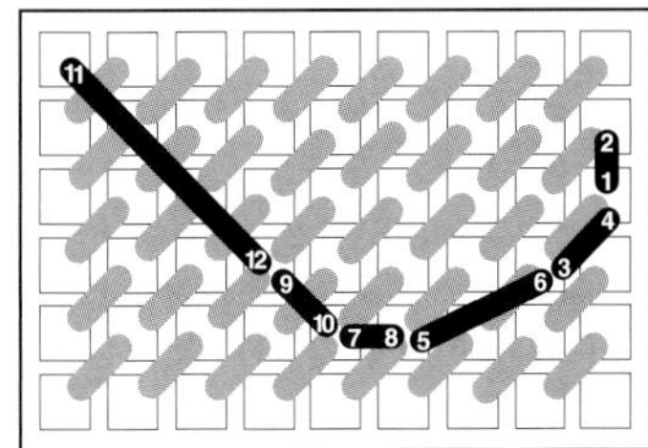

Fig. 6

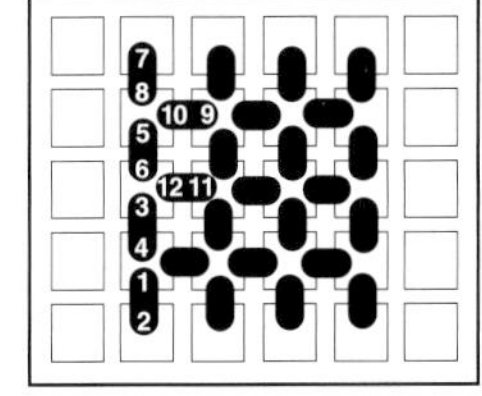

CROSS STITCH

This stitch is composed of two stitches **(Fig. 7)**. The top stitch of each cross must always be made in the same direction. The number of intersections may vary according to the chart.

Fig. 7

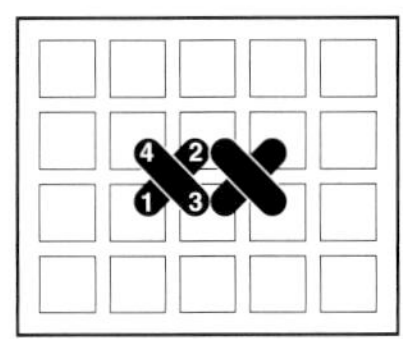

DIAGONAL MOSAIC STITCH

A variation of the mosaic stitch, this stitch is worked in diagonal rows **(Fig. 8)**.

Fig. 8

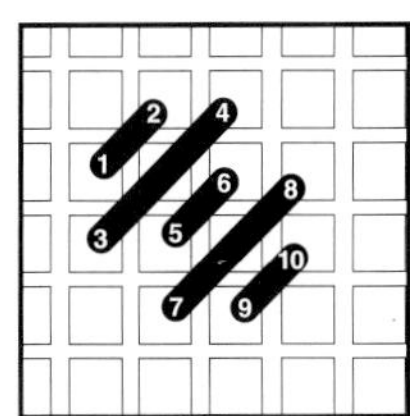

EYELET STITCH

This stitch forms a square over four threads of canvas **(Fig. 9)**. It consists of 16 stitches worked in a clockwise fashion. Each stitch is worked from the outer edge into the same central hole.

Fig. 9

FRENCH KNOT

Bring needle up through hole. Wrap yarn around needle once and insert needle in same hole **(Fig. 10)**. Tighten knot as close to the canvas as possible as you pull the needle and yarn back through canvas.

Fig. 10

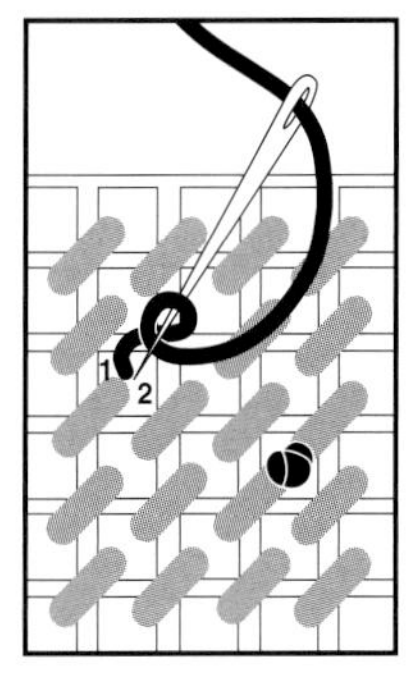

FRINGE STITCH

Fold a length of yarn in half. Thread needle with loose ends of yarn. Bring needle up at 1, leaving a 1" loop on the back of the canvas. Bring needle around the edge of canvas and through loop **(Fig. 11)**. Pull to tighten loop **(Fig. 12)**. Trim fringe to desired length. A dot of glue on back of fringe will help keep stitch in place.

Fig. 11

Fig. 12

GOBELIN STITCH

This basic straight stitch is worked over two or more threads or intersections. The number of threads or intersections may vary according to the chart (**Fig. 13**).

Fig. 13

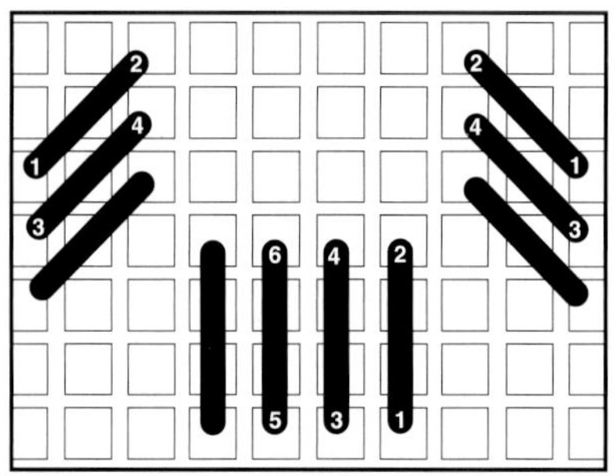

LACE STITCH

This stitch pattern forms small, open squares (**Fig. 14**).

Fig. 14

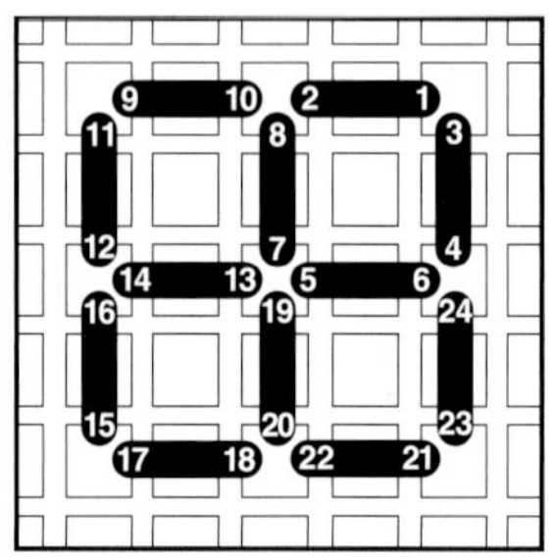

MOSAIC STITCH

This three-stitch pattern forms small squares (**Fig. 15**).

Fig. 15

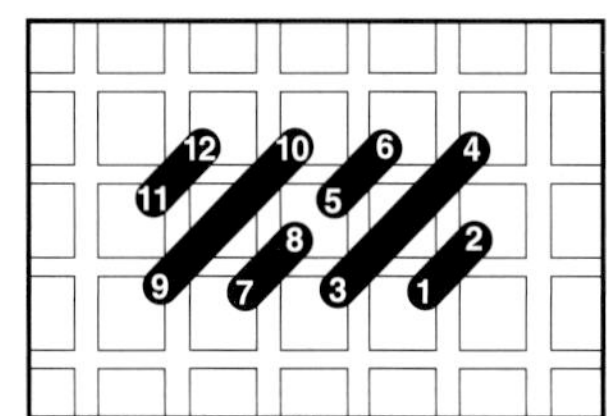

OVERCAST STITCH

This stitch covers the edge of the canvas and joins pieces of canvas (**Fig. 16**). It may be necessary to go through the same hole more than once to get even coverage on the edge, especially at the corners.

Fig. 16

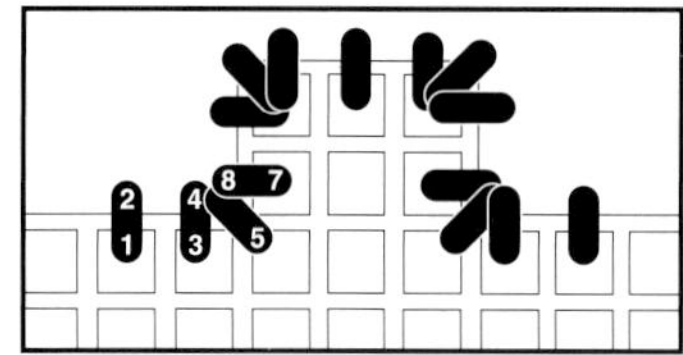

SCOTCH STITCH

This stitch may be worked over three or more threads and forms a square. **Fig. 17** shows the Scotch stitch worked over three threads.

Fig. 17

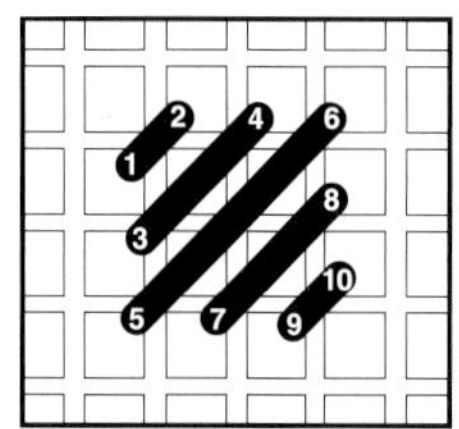

SCOTCH STITCH VARIATION

This stitch is a Scotch stitch with a dimple in the center (**Fig. 18**). The stitches that make up this pattern may slant in the opposite direction.

Fig. 18

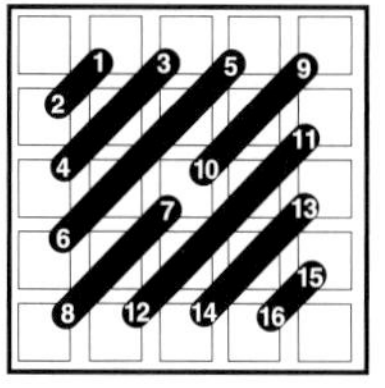

SMYRNA CROSS STITCH

This stitch is worked over two threads as a decorative stitch. Each stitch is worked completely before going on to the next stitch (**Fig. 19**).

Fig. 19

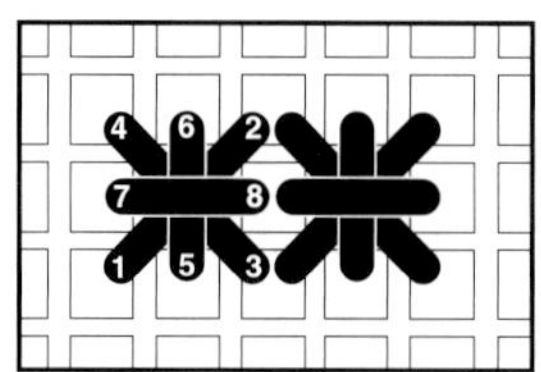

TENT STITCH

This stitch is worked in horizontal or vertical rows over one intersection as shown in **Fig. 20**. Refer to **Fig. 21** to work the reversed tent stitch.

Fig. 20

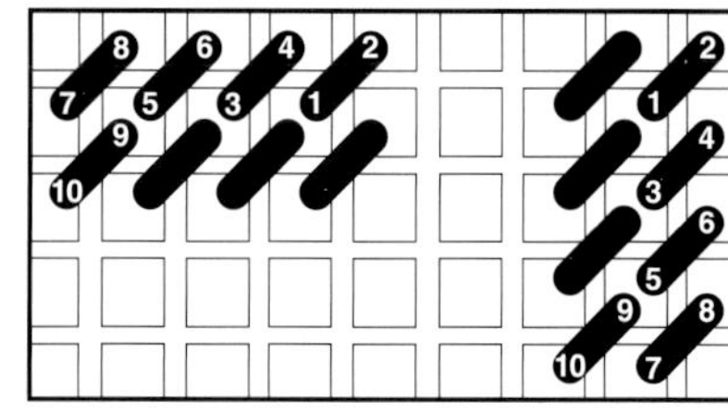

Fig. 21

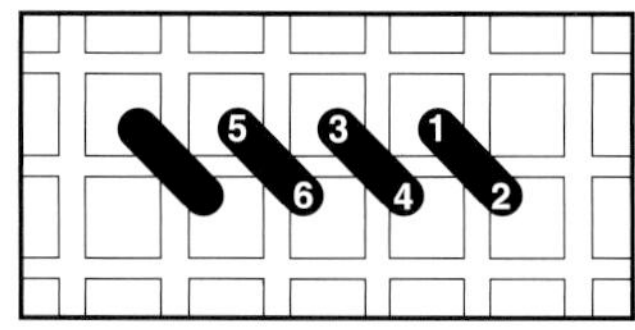

TURKEY LOOP STITCH

This stitch is composed of locked loops. Bring needle up through hole and back down through same hole, forming a loop on top of the canvas. A locking stitch is then made across the thread directly below or to either side of the loop as shown in **Fig. 22**.

Fig. 22

UPRIGHT CROSS STITCH

This stitch is worked over two threads as shown in **Fig. 23**. The top stitch of each cross must always be made in the same direction.

Fig. 23

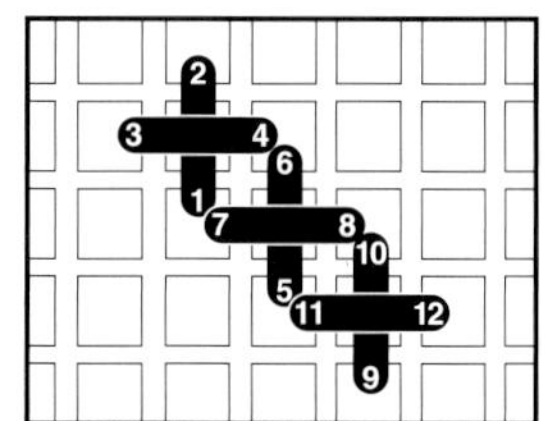

Some photography models made by Juanita Criswell, Carlene Hodge, Mary Kennemur, and Linda Rogers-Peters.